CW00482259

The Films of
RIDLEY SCOTT

Richard A. Schwartz

PRAEGER

Westport, Connecticut
London

Library of Congress Cataloging-in-Publication Data

Schwartz, Richard Alan, 1951–
    The films of Ridley Scott
        p.   cm.
    Includes bibliographical references and index.
    ISBN 0–275–96976–2 (alk. paper)
    1. Scott, Ridley.
    PN1998.3.S393S394   2001
    791.43′0233′092—dc21   00–052425

British Library Cataloguing in Publication Data is available.

Library of Congress Catalog Card Number: 00–052425
ISBN: 0–275–96976–2

First published in 2001

Praeger Publishers, 88 Post Road West, Westport, CT 06881
An imprint of Greenwood Publishing Group, Inc.
www.praeger.com

Printed in the United States of America

The paper used in this book complies with the
Permanent Paper Standard issued by the National
Information Standards Organization (Z39.48–1984).

10 9 8 7 6 5 4 3 2 1

Copyright Acknowledgments

The author and publisher gratefully acknowledge permission to use the following material:

Excerpts from the book *Ridley Scott Close Up* by Paul M. Sammon. Copyright © 1999 by Paul M.
Sammon. Appears by permission of the publisher, Thunder's Mouth Press, and Orion Media.

Excerpts from Charles Elkins, ed., "Symposium on *Alien*." *Science Fiction Studies* 7 (1980):
278–304. Reprinted by permission.

Excerpts from Richard A. Schwartz, "The Tragic Vision of *Thelma & Louise*." *Journal of Evolutionary Psychology* 17.1 (March 1996):101–107. Reprinted by permission.

Contents

Contents

Photo essay follows page 78.

Introduction

In the twenty-four years since Ridley Scott's first feature film, *The Duellists*, received the Special Jury Prize at the 1977 Cannes Film Festival, he has emerged as a major director of entertainment movies. Scott has had critically acclaimed hits in at least four different popular genres: *Alien* (1979) is now regarded as a classic horror film; *Blade Runner* (1982), which projects the *film noir* detective tradition into the twenty-first century, has emerged as one of the premier science fiction films of the 1980s; *Thelma & Louise* (1991), whose roots extend to earlier road, buddy, and outlaw movies, became one of the most popular and provocative feminist stories in twentieth-century cinema; and *Gladiator* (2000) was recognized upon its release for reinvigorating the long dormant "sword and sandal" epic that uses "a cast of thousands" to recreate the personal passions and political turbulence of ancient times.

Much of Scott's success in these and other films is attributable to his strong visual sense. From the eerie, ever-changing images of the murderous creature in *Alien*, to the industrial processing plants that erupt with fire and the dark city streets that teem with people at all hours in *Blade Runner*'s futuristic Los Angeles and in *Black Rain*'s contemporary Japan (1989), to the tastefully decorated interiors in *Someone to Watch over Me* (1987), to the idyllic European countryside in *The Duellists* (1977), to the lush tropical forests in *1492: Conquest of Paradise* (1992) and the tranquil ocean views and deadly storms in *White Squall* (1996), to the celebration of the Grand Canyon and western desert in *Thelma & Louise*, the enchanted world of sprites and princesses in *Legend* (1985), the harsh training grounds in *G.I. Jane* (1997), the gorgeous views of Florence bathed in golden light in *Hannibal* (2001), and the brutal hand-to-hand combat in *Gladiator*, Scott routinely produces images that linger far after the final credits roll.

Beautiful and striking in their own right, Scott's visual effects often carry much of the weight in his films by creating atmosphere and mood and shaping the audience's desires and expectations. He manifests horror in *Alien*, for instance, by offering only incomplete views of the creature and showing reaction shots as people and the cat experience or view the terrifying events. The sets and costumes in *Legend* make us feel that the action occurs in some mythological place and time; the liberation of Thelma and Louise's spirits coincides with their entry into the wide-open spaces of the American West; the exquisitely photographed ocean almost emerges as a separate character in *White Squall*; and the large scale of everything from the cast to the Colosseum imposes epic scope onto *Gladiator*.

But even though he received his college degree from the West Hartlepool College of Art (1958), where he studied painting, still photography, and graphic design, and completed postgraduate work in graphic design at the Royal College of Art, Scott brings more than just strong visuals to his work. His films project a set of values that at once reflect left-wing liberalism and an essentially neoclassical conservatism that insists on tempering passion with reason, choosing wise and intelligent courses of action, and acting with honor, virtue, and concern for the good of society at large, as well as for the individual. For instance, *Thelma & Louise* raises feminist issues typically associated with the political Left, but it expresses these concerns in conjunction with traditionally conservative notions about proper action, personal responsibility, and the tension between passion and reason. *The Films of Ridley Scott* will therefore endeavor to explore how Scott integrates liberal and neoclassical values in visually striking settings and to consider the range and depth of his achievement in this regard.

Although the chapters on the individual films stand alone, taken collectively they reveal several recurring themes in Scott's work. Notably, throughout his movies we observe the need to temper passion with reason without eviscerating our emotions, the need for personal honor and responsibility, the tendency of self-important individuals in positions of authority to subvert the sincere and altruistic work of their underlings, the importance of creativity and imagination, and the value of teamwork. In addition, Scott often celebrates the working classes over the privileged classes, and he consistently presents strong women in his movies. His view of gender equality rests on the notion not only that women can perform most tasks equally as well as men, but that to succeed, become truly fulfilled, and be socially responsible, women must live up to the same high standards of proper conduct and personal integrity that male heroes typically possess.

The problem of striking a viable balance between passion and reason has appeared in Western literature since the ancient Greeks and Romans; it permeates the works of Chaucer and Shakespeare, and resurfaces in the work of

Sigmund Freud, as well as in twentieth-century film and fiction. *The Duellists* presents Scott's most direct exploration of the conflict, as it shows the quandary of an honorable man who seeks to live his life rationally but must repeatedly confront the antagonism of a professional equal who is completely imbued with bitterness and hatred. As the story depicts the battle between the forces of order and chaos (superego and id in Freudian terms), Scott seems to ask whether sane, rational people can honorably and successfully deal with the untempered, irrational, even monomaniacal forces of evil that sometimes assault them. This question resurfaces in different shapes and forms in *Blade Runner*, *Legend*, *Someone to Watch over Me*, *1492*, *Gladiator*, *Thelma & Louise*, and *Alien*. In these last two films, rape becomes the dominant metaphor for the action of evil, literally in *Thelma & Louise* and figuratively in *Alien*. Like the rapist, other perpetrators of evil are also greedy, relentless, entirely self-centered, insensitive to the pain and suffering of others, and driven by a powerful desire to dominate and assert control. *Alien* further shows how evil can take either a completely visceral, irrational shape or a totally rational, dispassionate one. The more pernicious manifestation is the indifferent, dispassionate, excessively rational side of evil, embodied by the Company in *Alien*, Tyrell in *Blade Runner*, and the Spanish Inquisition in *1492*. Commodus in *Gladiator* is similarly cold and calculating. By contrast, Harlan in *Thelma & Louise* and the space creature in *Alien* are driven by visceral impulses. But like their more cerebral counterparts, they care only about their own dominance and gratification.

Despite his deep appreciation for nature, which his photography repeatedly reveals, and his concern for the free play of the imagination, Scott's sensibility remains more neoclassic than romantic. Scott frequently shows that, both as individuals and as societies, we must retain control over the passionate, irrational forces within and around us, but we must never fully stifle them altogether, as do the Company in *Alien* and the Spanish inquisitors. In *Hannibal* Dr. Lecter identifies the essence of Clarice Starling's personal strength when he observes that her bosses at the FBI resent her because, "You serve the idea of order, they don't. They are weak and unruly and believe in nothing." Moreover, by changing the ending of Thomas Harris's novel, from which *Hannibal* was adapted, Scott rejects Harris's rejection of corrupted authority and instead has Starling remain faithful to her belief in social order, even though the institutions for maintaining it are flawed and sometimes work against her. In *White Squall*, Captain Sheldon, also apparently speaking for Scott, strives to impress on the boys and his wife that "if we don't have order, we have nothing." And though never depicted as evil—and often beautiful and awe inspiring—nature in that film and in *1492* appears as a powerful irrational force that becomes destructive when it shatters the order the protagonists have created and causes them to lose control. Like his neoclassical predecessors and the medieval writers before them who invoked the image of the horse (passion) guided by the rider (reason), Scott endorses a golden mean in which passion can be given full rein, but remains under the control of our rational faculties.

In *The Duellists* the protagonist is improperly obsessed with conventional notions of honor, but acting honorably is a frequent concern in Scott's films. Honor is the core issue in *Black Rain*; it also plays a major role in *Blade Runner, Legend, 1492, White Squall, G.I. Jane,Gladiator*, and *Hannibal*. In *Blade Runner* Deckard learns about honor from his replicant foe, Roy Batty; in *Black Rain*, Nick Conklin learns it from his Japanese partner, Masahiro; in *1492* Columbus tries to treat the natives honorably and is punished for his efforts; in *White Squall* Captain Sheldon leads by example as he instills integrity in the boys on his ship, and in *Hannibal* Clarice Starling fascinates Hannibal Lecter with her unassailable personal integrity and eventually wins his admiration and perhaps his love because of it. In every case, honor involves accepting personal responsibility and recognizing and adopting the proper course of action, regardless of the personal cost.

In contrast to the working-class heroes who honorably struggle to do the right thing, privileged individuals and corporate leaders in Scott's films frequently appear more concerned with their own personal ambition and gratification. Often, they undermine their well-intended employees to serve their private interests. In *Alien* the Company tries to subvert the best efforts of the *Nostromo*'s crew; in *Blade Runner* the industrialist Tyrell and police chief Bryant are willing to use both Deckard and the replicants for their own purposes; bureaucrats ("suits") from both New York and Japan inhibit the work of the detectives on the street who must actually fight the criminals in *Black Rain*; Sanchez cynically uses Columbus for his own purposes in *1492*; motivated by envy and spite, the wealthy Francis Beaumont in *White Squall* tries to ruin Sheldon's career; both the navy brass and Senator DeHaven seek to undermine Jordan O'Neil in *G.I. Jane*; Emperor Commodus, who is filled with jealousy and insecurity, ruins the personal and professional life of Maximus, his best and most virtuous general; in *Hannibal* Starling's life and her mission to protect the public by apprehending Lecter, a mass murderer on the loose, are most threatened by Mason Verger, a wealthy, vengeful child molester who callously employs his immense power and influence to destroy her career so he can use her as bait to catch Lecter, and by Paul Krendler, Starling's vindictive, chauvinistic superior at the FBI who sells her out to Verger for money and to humiliate her for rejecting his sexual advances years before.

Along with depicting perverted authority figures from the privileged ranks, Scott reveals a predilection in such films as *Alien, Blade Runner, Someone to Watch over Me, White Squall, Gladiator,* and *Hannibal* for showing working-class individuals as more honorable and virtuous than their upper-class counterparts. For instance, Columbus, a commoner, emerges as a more attractive personality than the nobles Noxica and Sanchez; Deckard is more admirable than Tyrell; and the crew members of the Nostromo in *Alien* are more honest and loyal than the corporate executives who have decided they are expendable. In *Gladiator* we learn that Maximus was dismissed as an unacceptable mate for Lucilla because he was of an inferior social rank; yet he is a far better person in every respect than the children of Marcus Aurelius or most of the other nobles in Rome. In *Hannibal* both Lecter and Krendler attempt to humiliate Starling by trying to make her feel like "white trash," due to her poor, rural background; but she consistently responds with more class than either, and she emerges as the most admirable character in the story. *Thelma & Louise* does not contrast the social classes, but it does make working-class figures the focus of our desires and concerns.

The film *1492* offers Scott's strongest endorsement of the power of creative imagination, especially when it is coupled with dedication and determination. Of all his attributes, Columbus's imagination is his strongest virtue, and the film concludes with the written quotation, "Life has more imagination than we carry in our dreams." But imagination is also celebrated in *Legend* and *Gladiator*, where Maximus repeatedly reminds his men that they can manifest victory if they can imagine it. Imagination is also one of the tools with which Sheldon invests the wayward youth under his charge. Sheldon is even more explicit about the value of teamwork, as are Master Chief Urgayle in *G.I. Jane* and Maximus in *Gladiator*.

Thelma & Louise is Scott's best known and most compelling presentation of strong, self-reliant women, although *G.I. Jane* also makes a forceful case for women's equality. But even in his other films Scott consistently presents women as intelligent, capable, and resourceful. Certainly, Ripley in *Alien* is such a character, as are Queen Isabel in *1492* (also played by Sigourney Weaver); Ellie Keegan in *Someone to Watch over Me* (another working-class hero who prevails over an upper-class rival); Lucilla in *Gladiator*; and Starling in *Hannibal*. In *Alien*, *Thelma & Louise*, *G.I. Jane*, and *Hannibal*, Scott makes his case for women by utilizing the plot structures of popular genres (horror films, road/buddy films, war films, and thrillers, respectively) and filling the roles traditionally given to the male protagonists with females. Although women occupy relatively minor roles in *Blade Runner*, Deckard's personal growth and ability to experience happiness and a sense of regeneration result from his becoming re-attuned to his anima, or "female side."

Scott's success in integrating his thematic concerns within a dramatically compelling story has been mixed. Several of his films have been criticized for relying too much on visuals and neglecting plot and character development. But when he is at his best, as in *Alien* and *Thelma & Louise*, Scott places convincing characters of multiple dimensions in exciting situations in which they are tasked with behaving honorably, forcefully, imaginatively, and in ways that do justice to both the individual and society. In interviews, Scott has taken the position that he is primarily an entertainer, not a social critic. But like Proximus in *Gladiator*, who also claims to be just an entertainer, Scott knows that entertainment is a form of power. He uses his power to liberate us from preconceived restrictions, whether they be restrictions on opportunity due to gender or limitations that inhibit the imagination—visually or cognitively. However, once the imagination is liberated, Scott shows that it is best employed when it enhances the greater good and brings forth virtue in individuals and societies.

The Duellists

(1977)

CAST

D'Hubert	Keith Carradine
Feraud	Harvey Keitel
Laura	Diana Quick
Adèle	Cristina Raines
Treillard	Robert Stephens
Commander	John McEnery
Fouche	Albert Finney
Reynard	Edward Fox

PRODUCTION

Director/Camera operator	Ridley Scott
Producer	David Puttnam (a CIC release of an Enigma/Paramount production)
Screenplay	Gerald Vaughan-Hughes (based on *The Duel* by Joseph Conrad)
Director of photography	Frank Tidy
Art director	Bryan Graves

Costumer	Tom Rand
Production designer	Peter Hampton
Editor	Pamela Power
Music director	Howard Blake

SYNOPSIS

The Duellists presents a series of duels fought between two of Napoleon's army officers throughout their careers. The feud begins when D'Hubert, an earnest, upright lieutenant on a general's staff, is ordered to arrest Lieutenant Feraud for dueling with the mayor's son. In contrast to D'Hubert's rational restraint, Feraud is passionate and obsessive. A fanatical supporter of Napoleon, he distorts an innocent comment of D'Hubert's into an insult and provokes a duel in which D'Hubert reluctantly finds himself honor bound to participate. D'Hubert's remark had alluded both to Napoleon and Madame de Lionne, a prominent woman of the town. But Feraud's reply is ambiguous, so neither D'Hubert nor the audience is certain on whose behalf Feraud has taken offense. D'Hubert assumes Feraud intended Madame de Lionne, but fifteen years and four duels later, we learn he meant Napoleon.

Set against the rise and fall of Napoleon's fortunes, the film shows how, over the years, D'Hubert jeopardizes his military career and loses a woman he cares for in order to protect his honor. To keep his reputation unsullied, he continues to accept Feraud's challenges, even after he comes to believe Feraud is a lunatic. Having lost the affection of Laura because of his dueling, D'Hubert eventually falls in love with and marries Adèle, the daughter of an aristocrat. Even though his young wife is pregnant, D'Hubert agrees to fight Feraud one last time, to the death. Feraud unsuccessfully fires both of his pistols, but D'Hubert, at point-blank range, retains a loaded one. He declares that under the rules of single combat Feraud's life now belongs to him and insists that in all future dealings with D'Hubert, Feraud must conduct himself "as a dead man." The film concludes as D'Hubert, having finally rid himself of his nemesis, returns happily to his loving wife. The final shot shows Feraud, dressed like Napoleon, standing alone, staring bitterly into the distance.

RECEPTION

The Duellists was a critical success but a disappointment at the box office. It won several awards, including Best Debut Film at the 1977 Cannes Film Festival, and it received praise for its carefully composed photography, accurate recreation of the period, and vigorous fight scenes. Vincent Canby of the *New York Times* called it a "dazzling" visual experience, adding that it leaves "a memory of almost indescribable beauty." The reviewer for *Variety*, who described *The Duellists* as an "arty swashbuckler," also praised the beautiful imagery but criticized the movie's failure to explore character (Sammon, *Ridley Scott*, 134–135). However, despite the warm reviews *The Duellists* did not enjoy a long run in movie houses, is rarely shown on television, and has fallen into relative obscurity since its premiere. It is the least viewed of all of Scott's films.

DISCUSSION

The Duellists asks if it is possible for a person to respond rationally to a spiteful, envious, passionate adversary bent on inflicting harm, regardless of the price. Even more, is it possible to maintain honor and dignity if such a madman is regarded by law and convention as a social and professional equal? Based on Joseph Conrad's novella, *The Duel* (1908), which in turn is based on a newspaper account of two French officers who fought eighteen duels throughout their careers, Ridley Scott's first film examines the impact of Gabriel Feraud's enduring, obsessive resentment of Armand D'Hubert, both officers in Napoleon's army at the beginning of the nineteenth century. While Conrad uses the story to explore regional and class differences and how lack of self-confidence can impede an otherwise successful person, Scott delves more fully into the fundamental absurdity of the situation. He also implicitly critiques Napoleon's appetite for war, examines the duel's impact on the women in the officers' lives, and projects the human conflict against stunning natural backdrops that accentuate the insignificance of human concerns. Both Conrad and Scott use the fifteen-year conflict to depict the interplay between reason and passion, or in Freudian terms, between forces of the superego and the id.

Both renditions of the story relate the conflict from the point of view of D'Hubert, a highly professional, courageous, and well-connected staff officer who conducts himself rationally and conforms to codes of honor. However, Conrad's third-person narrator has access to D'Hubert's thoughts and feelings, while Scott, with the exception of one brief voice-over at the end, restricts his storytelling primarily to what the camera shows. Moreover, Scott's D'Hubert is especially laconic and reveals little of his interior world through dialogue. Consequently, Conrad is more successful than Scott at showing D'Hubert's emotional responses to the developing feud. And Conrad's ending shows the dueling ironically to be an inadvertent vehicle for facilitating D'Hubert's self-knowledge and removing the final obstacle to his greatest happiness. On the other hand, although Scott's D'Hubert also prevails, his feelings of anger, hurt, disappointment, and stoical acceptance are less evident. Apart from his sense that the whole episode is absurd and he is glad when it concludes, he reveals little about how the dueling, its attendant dangers, and the professional and personal consequences of his forbidden fighting have affected him. Thus Conrad's story accentuates character more, while Scott's highlights the fundamental absurdity of the situation.

In Conrad's *The Duel* D'Hubert dreads "discredit and ridicule above everything" (Conrad, *The Duel*, 23). This excessive fear ultimately distorts his otherwise sane existence by compelling him to accept all challenges to his honor. In fact, the feud can be described as the clash between two obsessions: D'Hubert's obsession with protecting his reputation and Feraud's compulsion for feeding his spite and envy. Even though the dramatic action concludes when D'Hubert wins the final duel, the plot is not truly resolved until D'Hubert rids himself of his inordinate fear of dishonor and the insecurity that spawns it. Ironically, Feraud's insane passion for picking fights with D'Hubert proves to be the vehicle that finally forces D'Hubert to recognize how unnecessarily insecure he has been. " 'I owe it all to this stupid brute,' he thought. 'He has made plain in a morning what might have taken me years to find out—for I am a timid fool. No self-confidence whatever. Perfect coward' " (Conrad, *The Duel*, 116).

Despite its innate barbarism, dueling did serve a social purpose by providing a mechanism for resolving disputes, so they would not devolve further into ongoing feuds. Its purpose was to give "satisfaction" that would put an end to the matter in question. Should they survive, both duelists retained honor by showing their willingness to risk their lives for their cause; yet the single combat either produced a clear-cut winner or enabled the adversaries to conclude the dispute amicably and still save face. But Conrad shows how a hateful, obsessive fanatic can use the dueling ritual to provoke and prolong disputes instead of ending them. When D'Hubert crosses paths with Feraud, he encounters a man motivated not by reason but by envy, spite, and fanatical devotion to Napoleon. Feraud hails from a working-class family in the south of France, while D'Hubert comes from a family of higher station in the north. Conrad emphasizes the regional differences, suggesting they account for the men's dispositions. He describes Feraud as a "little Gascon, who . . . was as though born intoxicated with the sunshine of his vine-ripening country" and D'Hubert as a "Northman, who . . . was born sober under the watery skies of Picardy" (Conrad, *The Duel*, 14). But class differences also fuel Feraud's bitterness. The only son of a blacksmith, he envies privilege, and D'Hubert embodies everything he resents. In particular, D'Hubert's staff position and his higher birth enrage him.

D'Hubert's inability to find a way to deal rationally with Feraud's acute resentment compels him to engage in the increasingly absurd succession of duels. D'Hubert has no inkling of what fuels Feraud's anger, and he comes to regard Feraud as a lunatic. Nonetheless, because he dare not risk harm to his reputation, he allows his life to be shaped by the senseless conflict: "This affair had hopelessly and unreasonably complicated his existence for him. One absurdity more or less in the development did not matter—all absurdity was distasteful to him" (Conrad, *The Duel*, 49). The story thus shows how D'Hubert's antiquated code of honor—a code praised in literature as far back as the *Iliad*—ultimately undermines his attempt to conduct his life in a rational, morally upright fashion. Instead, his preoccupation with avoiding dishonor renders his existence unstable, uncertain, and absurd.

Conrad, a contemporary of Freud, reveals how D'Hubert's insistence on honor above everything actually hides his excessive dread of ridicule, which in turn results from his fundamental lack of self-confidence. Thus the real climax of Conrad's plot comes not when D'Hubert defeats Feraud for the last time, but when his fiancée's fear on his behalf demonstrates her deep love for him. Young Adèle's unexpected demonstration of passion removes D'Hubert's lingering doubts that she is settling to be a dutiful wife in an arranged marriage and has no true feelings for him. He is, after all, old enough to be her father. D'Hubert truly loves Adèle, and despite her apparent willingness to go along with the wedding plans, his fear that she is merely being obedient precludes him from enjoying his good fortune as fully as he might: "As far as he could make out . . . she felt no insurmountable dislike for [him] . . . and that this was quite sufficient for a well-brought-up young lady to begin married life upon. This view hurt and tormented the pride of General D'Hubert. And yet he asked himself, with a sort of sweet despair, what more could he expect?" (Conrad, *The Duel*, 83). In a society where convention forbids sincere expression of feelings between a betrothed couple, D'Hubert finally recognizes that Adèle reciprocates his love when, after discovering he is dueling and might be killed, she unself-consciously runs two miles in her peignoir from her house to his. In her haste to know D'Hubert's fate, she has even allowed the field workers to see her disheveled and distraught in her bedroom clothes.

Adèle's utter disregard for outward appearances when something more important is at stake underscores D'Hubert's failure to live by similarly appropriate priorities. After all, by accepting Feraud's absurd challenge, D'Hubert risks his life with Adèle in order to avoid the smallest possible question of dishonor. Adèle's love, by contrast, reveals itself to be stronger than D'Hubert's, for it supersedes any fear of discredit. At the conclusion D'Hubert acknowledges that he owes Feraud a debt for compelling him to see himself more clearly. "We must take care of [Feraud], secretly, to the end of his days. Don't I owe him the most ecstatic moment of my life? [when D'Hubert recognizes Adèle really does love him]. . . . It's extraordinary how in one way or another this man has managed to fasten himself on my deeper feelings" (Conrad, *The Duel*, 118).

If Conrad's plot culminates with D'Hubert's moment of self-discovery, Scott's climaxes when D'Hubert at last rids himself of his nemesis and can finally return to a sane, stable existence. His final words to Feraud are, "You have kept me at your beck and call for fifteen years. I shall never again do what you demand of me. . . . I have submitted to your notions of honor long enough. You will now submit to mine." Scott's story is thus less a tale of personal growth and more a study of how conflict between reason and passion results in absurdity (a topic Conrad also explored in *The Heart of Darkness*, 1899). If the actors depict characters who reveal little of their emotional state (Keitel's Feraud seems only to seethe inwardly and Carradine's D'Hubert maintains stoic reserve), Scott uses his cinematic tools to emphasize the depths of the absurdity, and he adds an additional subplot to demonstrate the personal sacrifice D'Hubert makes to protect his honor.

Like Conrad, Scott develops the story's absurdity in order to ask if human experience is essentially logical and sane, or irrational and insane. The same question has been repeatedly posed by storytellers throughout the century, including such diverse figures as Franz Kafka, Eugène Ionesco, Joseph Heller, Ishmael Reed, and Woody Allen. However, while Conrad embraces a Greek-like, paradoxical view of reality in which Feraud's bitter grudge can ironically occasion D'Hubert's greatest joy,[1] Scott concludes from a dualistic point of view consistent with more recent Western thought. Like such precursors as Cicero, Chaucer, and Shakespeare, Scott shows how only absurd chaos can result when powerful irrational passions go unchecked by temperance and reason. Thus chaos prevails until D'Hubert's unwavering reason, honor, and virtue finally subdue Feraud's bitter rage. At the same time, though, by setting the human drama against an expansive, dominating backdrop of nature, Scott suggests the ultimate insignificance of human affairs.

The story's central absurdity stems from D'Hubert's inability to handle an irrational problem in a rational fashion. In particular, Feraud's instinctive, visceral antipathy for him defies D'Hubert's attempts to reconcile their differences rationally and plunges both men into an insane, uncertain existence. Although D'Hubert's commander, General Treillard, calls him "an imbecile" for adhering so rigidly to his code of honor, D'Hubert refuses to disclose the cause of the duel until a hearing can be held where he and Feraud may present their cases. But when Napoleon initiates a new military campaign the court of inquiry fails to convene, and, in his mind, D'Hubert loses his opportunity to disclose the cause of their quarrel honorably. Because no other legal venue exists to conclude the dispute, dueling becomes their only viable alternative. Thus the legal system's failure to resolve the matter fairly and rationally opens the door for the absurd developments that follow.[2]

Scott develops the growing absurdity by showing how the feud takes on a life of its own, overshadowing the particulars of the dispute and becoming a piece of local popular culture. In both versions the conflict acquires an air of mystery, since no outsider knows its true cause. As a matter of honor, D'Hubert steadfastly refuses to explain the cause of their quarrel to any third party, even his commanding officer. Nor does Feraud speak of it until the end. As the mystery grows the duelists become celebrities. D'Hubert's friends tell him that, even though he does not identify with his growing reputation as a fighter, it has made him attractive to young women. His celebrity status rises to an even higher level when it becomes a source of gaming and entertainment, as the regiment assumes a proprietary interest in the personal combat. D'Hubert learns that his fellow soldiers not only have been placing bets on the outcome of his fourth duel, but they have also insisted that it be conducted on horseback "as a compliment to the cavalry." "The regiment expects it," his friend tells him. "You must think of yourself as fighting on parade." D'Hubert, struck by the absurdity of the demand, complies with sarcastic resignation: "I'm going to be killed, responsibly, on horseback, as a compliment to the cavalry."

Scott adds an additional element of absurdity not present in Conrad's story by showing how D'Hubert never even really knows the true cause of the feud that has so affected his life. When told that Feraud has accused him of not loving the emperor and that Feraud maintains that this has been the cause of their fifteen-year feud, D'Hubert denies it and intimates that the duels had been fought over Madame de Lionne. When the intermediary reports D'Hubert's response, Feraud becomes incensed. He vaguely recalls Madame de Lionne and asks if he would have called out D'Hubert half a dozen times over "such petty nonsense." Feraud goes on to maintain, "He said to me in a public street, 'For all that I care, they can spit upon Napoleon Bonaparte.' "

But the audience has witnessed the scene and knows that Feraud's account is incorrect. Scott thereby adds an additional layer of absurdity by showing how the feud is rooted in fantasy; it emanated entirely from an insult that Feraud has imagined. Prior to their first duel, as the officers are walking from Madame de Lionne's apartment to Feraud's quarters, Feraud maintains he fought the mayor's nephew to defend the reputation of his regiment. Then, in Scott's version but not Conrad's, he asks angrily, "Would you let me spit upon Napoleon Bonaparte?" D'Hubert replies that "Bonaparte has no more to do with this than Madame de Lionne." Feraud becomes incensed, asking if D'Hubert thinks "that name is common coin for the street." Disclaiming any intention to give insult, D'Hubert answers diplomatically, "Whichever name you choose to defend, I used it with the utmost respect and solely in the cause of logic." When Feraud replies, "What do you mean, whichever name? You know damn well which name," both D'Hubert and the audience infer he means Madame de Lionne, though D'Hubert later tells the doctor, "All in all, I'm far from certain, myself," about the cause of the fight.

Feraud, on the other hand, is passionately certain, but wrong. Either he has remembered his exchange with D'Hubert incorrectly, an exchange that the audience has seen directly and therefore incontrovertibly, or he misconstrued D'Hubert's words when they were first uttered. In either case, Feraud is disposed to think the worst of the staff officer who was simply executing an order. Feraud resists every attempt by D'Hubert to appease him in a dignified manner. He calls D'Hubert a "general's poodle" and finally provokes a duel from which D'Hubert cannot honorably back down, even though D'Hubert thinks Feraud is "a madman." Ultimately D'Hubert fights the entire series of duels without ever realizing that Feraud is defending Napoleon's name, not Madame de Lionne's.

The absurd feud actually emanates from Feraud's bitterness and personal dissatisfaction. Laura, D'Hubert's mistress, identifies this underlying cause when she accuses Feraud of fighting because he feeds his spite on D'Hubert "with no more sense than a nasty, blood-sucking louse." Like a mindless insect, Feraud is driven solely by instinct and visceral stimuli. He both feeds on and identifies with his inner rage. The sequence of duels thus shows the havoc that affects even innocent parties when raging emotions go unrestrained by reason.

When passion rules an entire nation, civilization itself breaks down; and by closely identifying Feraud with his emperor, Scott, an Englishman, implicitly condemns Napoleon for thrusting Europe into a state of absurd chaos analogous to D'Hubert's. Feraud dresses in black and wears the cape and hat in which Napoleon is typically shown. Like Napoleon, Feraud is a volatile figure from the south. As Feraud's appetite for dueling disrupted D'Hubert's existence for a decade and a half, Napoleon's passion for conquest required the rest of Europe to mobilize for a series of undesired campaigns. A revolutionary who, like Feraud, disdained the aristocracy that ruled Europe, Napoleon wrecked Europe's neoclassical hope that rational diplomacy might eliminate the need for warfare and produce political stability and peaceful relations among nations. At least according to the English point of view on which Scott was presumably raised, only by standing firm against Napoleon did Great Britain and the other European nations restore stability to the Continent and initiate almost a century of relative peace among nations. Like D'Hubert, Britain had been at Napoleon's beck and call for over fifteen years, but in exiling him to St. Helena, the British effectively relegated him, like Feraud, to the status of a dead man. Thus, by creating visual and spoken identification between Feraud and Napoleon, Scott suggests that on both the individual and national levels, when envy, spite, and similar irrational passions dictate behavior, destructive chaos ensues.

In Freudian terms, this tension between passion and reason is understood as the interplay between the id, or libido, which seeks immediate physical and emotional satisfaction regardless of consequences, and the superego, whose impulse is to create order and social harmony. The ego governs and is in turn shaped by the interplay between the id and superego. A healthy ego permits the expression of libidinal impulses, but only as regulated by the superego. When unbridled libidinal forces run free, the result is often short-term gratification but long-term destruction. In *The Duellists* Feraud's indulgence of his envy and spite goes unchecked because he does not appropriately subordinate his id to his superego. Nor does the military legal system impose external restraints to compel him to control his passions. As a result, not only is D'Hubert's life thrown out of joint, but Feraud becomes progressively enveloped and warped by his bitterness, so that by the end of the saga he is left alone with his hatred, reduced to a living dead man. D'Hubert, on the other hand, because he has never lost control of his passions, not only finally wins the duel but also lives to return to a happy, if somewhat subdued, life of domesticity. The superego prevails in the end.[3]

The officers' identification with passion and reason, respectively, appears even in their fighting styles. Feraud's sword strokes are broad and energetic, while D'Hubert's motions are more restrained, and he uses his opponent's strength against him. Their contrasting modes of combat are especially significant in the final fight, in which D'Hubert patiently lures Feraud into a vulnerable position by lying motionless and pretending to be dead. He defeats Feraud by using his intellect and self-control, entirely suppressing his emotions and physical movements to set his trap. Ironically, he becomes a living dead man in order to make Feraud one.

Scott employs additional visual contrasts to make viewers experience the absurd, jarring disconnection that ensues when reason and emotion are at war. The film's stunning photography employs two distinct styles that reflect the tension in the period between the eighteenth-century neoclassical Enlightenment that believed reason would produce more abundant, better governed, more orderly societies, and the newly emerging romanticism that recognized the limitations of pure reason and insisted on liberating the emotions. (Romanticism evolved in part from the French Revolution, which also spawned Napoleon's career.) Scott therefore pairs carefully composed, visually balanced, still-life shots with chaotic, motion-filled action scenes. He often jumps from one mode to the other without transition, thereby making the audience experience visually and viscerally the abrupt movement in D'Hubert's life from moments of tranquil harmony to violent chaos, and back again.

The jump cuts jolt us and cause us not just to acknowledge, but actually to feel the absurd discontinuity that the combat creates. For instance, after the first duel, which is shot with an unsteady, hand-held camera, the picture jumps from Feraud's maid lunging at D'Hubert to a static still life of a glass of wine, a bottle, and an open book on a wooden table, from which the camera slowly pulls out. Scott likewise cuts from Feraud threatening D'Hubert after the inconclusive second duel to a gentle shot of Laura nursing D'Hubert's wounds as he rests in a steamy bathtub. The still life evokes paintings by Rembrandt, whose soft but revealing lighting Scott emulates in peaceful moments throughout the film, often by illuminating them in candlelight. Scott, who served as his own camera operator but not as director of photography, studied the seventeenth-century Dutch masters, along with European painters from the Napoleonic era and the photography in Stanley Kubrick's then-current period film, *Barry Lyndon* (1976), as part of his pre-production research for conveying the period's atmosphere and its neoclassical ideal of harmony and balance (Sammon, *Ridley Scott*, 43–44). But the French Revolution and Napoleon's subsequent reign helped provoke the cultural transition from rational, temperate neoclassicism to vigorous romanticism, whose preoccupation with human passion Scott transmits by keeping the camera in constant motion. In particular, he films the fight scenes with tracking shots, panning shots, and a hand-held camera to emphasize the wild, dynamic, unrestrained energy that fuels the sword play.

Scott's camera work also contrasts the grandeur of nature to the relative bleakness and insignificance of human affairs. Exterior scenes set in town or in the army camps are typically shot in dull grays and earth tones. By contrast, nature spans the color spectrum. The opening scene establishes the visual contrast between nature and men, as an army officer on his way to witness a duel intrudes upon an idyllic shot of a little girl herding a flock of geese along a verdant country lane. The close-ups of the girl and the geese contrast with the subsequent long shots of the duelists and their attendants, who are dwarfed by the countryside behind them. Moreover, while the initial sequence highlights lush, life-affirming springtime colors, the attendants at the duel are dressed in black and look like undertakers. The hand-held and tracking shots of Feraud fighting introduce a new element of confusion.

Yet, if the landscape appears passive, its vastness overwhelms the human characters, to whom it seems indifferent. Both awesome and tranquil, fecund and constrained, the landscape subsumes everything yet appears peaceful and orderly. Unlike the humans, the countryside appears in harmony with itself, powerful yet temperate. Although Scott shot outdoors during the dead of winter as well as in more fertile seasons (he shot the scenes from the Russian retreat at a ski resort in Scotland), he never shows the weather storming or otherwise interfering with human activity. But though static, the natural backdrops overwhelm the human characters, suggesting that human affairs are comparatively insignificant.

Just as he varies his camera work, Scott manipulates the soundtrack to make us feel the abrupt swings between moments of chaos and order. In particular, Howard Blake's rich, contemplative flute score that plays over the opening credits and the final shot of the defeated Feraud frames the action in tones that express tranquil harmony. The flute reappears in other warm moments during the film. But the fight scenes sound raw and visceral. Music rarely accompanies the fighting; we hear mostly the grunting of the combatants and the clang of their swords or discharge of their pistols. Aurally, as well as visually, Scott stimulates our senses to make us feel the disjuncture between D'Hubert's domestic experience and his experience of the duels.

More than Conrad, Scott shows how the women in D'Hubert's life suffer from Feraud's passion for fighting and D'Hubert's compulsion to stand up to him. Though Scott's Adèle remains blissfully ignorant of her husband's final duel, the director adds the character of Laura both to demonstrate the steep price D'Hubert pays for his honor and to show how third parties are also victimized by the insane feud. Laura, who is not in the novella, appears in the film as D'Hubert's first love interest. A camp follower, she reunites with D'Hubert shortly before his second duel. She has been with many soldiers and is even engaged to one, but she loves D'Hubert, who, in turn, seems to care for her. Removing her engagement ring, she declares, "With this ring I renounce love and make due with you," confessing that he is the one she always wanted, but accusing him of placing her second in his affections to his career: "You, you Hussar!"

Laura accepts that D'Hubert honors his military duty above his feelings for her, but she cannot abide his dueling, which, merely to appease some abstract notion of honor, keeps her in a state of ongoing dread and robs her of control over her life. She nurses him after the second duel but is unable to convince D'Hubert to give up the fighting. She leaves before the third contest after a fortuneteller instructs her to follow her instinct and travel alone. She reappears somewhat improbably five years later, before the fourth fight. Dressed in black she tells D'Hubert of her husband's death and his dying advice for her to "go to that fool, Armand. He'll take you in again." But when D'Hubert silently rejects her, she runs away for good, bitterly predicting, "This time he'll kill you."

By introducing the Laura subplot Scott increases the price D'Hubert pays for literally sticking to his guns. Laura's past promiscuity is never an issue between them, and her devotion to him is clear. They share affection, and she tolerates his devotion to the army. If she is not the love of his life, they nonetheless accept and enjoy each other. Yet D'Hubert sacrifices Laura's warmth, caring, and camaraderie without hesitation in order to protect his "indescribable, unchallengeable" honor from possibly being sullied by a "lunatic." The high price D'Hubert pays for such an ephemeral goal lends an additional element of absurdity to the story.

The Laura subplot also introduces the feminist thread that runs throughout Scott's work, as we become acutely aware of how the absurd dueling destroys her life. Along with sacrificing his own happiness in order to protect his honor, D'Hubert undermines Laura's hopes for a love-filled life. The sacrifice is a choice for D'Hubert, but for Laura it is a condition imposed upon her. She has no input into D'Hubert's decision to answer Feraud's ridiculous challenges, a decision that affects her deeply by introducing continual dread into her existence. Only by leaving D'Hubert can she free herself from the fear that Feraud may at any time, without warning, tear her life asunder by calling out D'Hubert and killing him. The feud thereby compels her to sacrifice her love in order to preserve her sanity and emotional well-being. Yet even when she does that, the restricted opportunities for women of the period leave Laura dependent on men for her sustenance, and her only viable option after D'Hubert rejects her for the last time is to become a camp follower again. The absurd feud has robbed this strong, warm, compassionate woman of control over her life, taken away her best chance for happiness, and driven her back into a life of prostitution.

Scott also uses Laura's female perspective to expose a double standard in the gentlemen's code of honor that dominates D'Hubert's existence. When she confronts Feraud in his barracks, he immediately draws his sword, and tells her he once knew a man who was fooled by a woman who stabbed him to death. "It gave him the surprise of his life." Laura replies that she knew a woman who was beaten to death by a man. "I don't think it surprised her at all." In addition to making viewers think about male-on-female violence, the exchange underscores the absurdity of a code of conduct that responds literally with overkill to verbal insults but tolerates physical harm to defenseless women.

Although D'Hubert never criticizes Laura's sexual liaisons, and she remains a sympathetic figure in the story, the film conforms to Hollywood's predilection for punishing sexually active women and rewarding virginal girls, instead. Laura is consigned to a life of prostitution after D'Hubert rejects her. Eight years later, D'Hubert marries Adèle, the young, innocent daughter of neighboring aristocrats. She is far less D'Hubert's equal in maturity and experience than Laura, and is less compatible. But Adèle does lighten his spirits after years of hard campaigning, and unlike Laura she comes from a socially desirable background.

Yet, if by having D'Hubert reject Laura and choose Adèle the film implicitly endorses both the social caste and the conventional Hollywood view that an older man will find greater joy with a much younger woman than with an equal, D'Hubert's genuine concern for Adèle's happiness within their marriage stands out as exceptional. D'Hubert fears that she is an innocent whose joy and prospects for love are being sacrificed to convention and protection of property rights. His sensitivity to Adèle's situation and to her feelings elevates him in our eyes and further heightens our awareness of how women are affected by events that are primarily regarded from a male perspective. Fortunately, Adèle truly loves D'Hubert too, and in the film her pregnancy brings him even greater joy. Yet, even so, he risks his own happiness and the well-being of Adèle and his unborn child because Feraud's scruffy-looking seconds insinuate that he will not be acting like a gentleman if he spurns Feraud's latest challenge.

The upbeat ending suggests that perhaps the final duel is necessary for D'Hubert to be able to enjoy his domestic bliss, but the absurdity of risking harm to himself and everyone he cares for in order to appease a "madman" makes his decision to participate appear foolhardy. He had already saved Feraud's life when, after the fall of Napoleon, he interceded to save Feraud from execution by the restored monarchy. But because his code of honor required that he receive no credit for his anonymous good deed, he still believes his honor might be sullied if he does not offer Feraud further satisfaction. His obsessive fear for his reputation thus provokes him to commit his final act of absurdity.

Fortunately, D'Hubert's code of honor does not require him to relinquish his rational abilities and emotional restraint. In their final duel he employs these neoclassical virtues to execute a rouse that foils Feraud and ends the insanity at last. Scott underscores the final triumph of reason over passion and the restoration of domestic order by reintroducing the rich, contemplative flute score that opened the film. The final shot shows Feraud, a living dead man, standing alone, dwarfed by his surroundings, staring into the vast, mountainous distance. Like Napoleon in St. Helena, his spite has been rendered insignificant.

NOTES

1. Conrad's paradoxical picture of reality is similar to that of the ancient Greeks who regarded such opposite pairings as good and evil, reason and passion, and beauty and ugliness as co-dependent, not mutually exclusive. Thus, Medusa, the hideous, snake-haired Gorgon, gives birth to the beautiful winged horse, Pegasus; the same divine thunderbolts that kill Zeus's mistress, Semele, also confer immortality on their son, Dionysus; the same pride and rage that provoke Achilles to abandon the Greek army lead to his best friend's death and the near destruction of the Greek fleet, on the one hand, and the death of Hector and the final conquest of Troy, on the other; and Apollo, the god most associated with reason and emotional control, shares his sacred shrine at Delphi with Dionysus, the god most associated with ecstasy, lust, and passion.

For additional discussion of the cinematic treatment of Conrad's story, see Allan Simmons, "Cinematic Fidelities in *The Rover* and *The Duellists*," in *Conrad on Film*, edited by Gene M. Moore (New York: Cambridge University Press, 1998).

2. Scott returns to this theme in *Thelma & Louise*, where Louises' earlier mistreatment by the Texas judiciary makes her lose all faith in the legal system and provokes her to become a fugitive after she shoots the man who had attempted to rape Thelma.

3. Stephen Crane, in one of his Black Rider poems (1895), reveals the essence of the sort of distorted, embittered personality that Feraud exhibits. The narrator describes meeting a naked, bestial creature who is squatting on the ground, eating his own heart:

> I said, "Is it good, friend?"
> "It is bitter—bitter," he answered;
> "But I like it
> Because it is bitter,
> And because it is my heart."

Alien

(1979)

CAST

Ripley	Sigourney Weaver
Dallas	Tom Skerritt
Lambert	Veronica Cartwright
Brett	Harry Dean Stanton
Kane	John Hurt
Ash	Ian Holm
Parker	Yaphet Kott
The Alien	Bolaji Badejo

PRODUCTION

Director/Camera operator	Ridley Scott
Producers	Gordon Carroll, David Giler, and Walter Hill (a 20th Century Fox release of a Brandywine-Ronald Shusett production)
Screenplay	Dan O'Bannon (based on a story by O'Bannon and Ronald Shusett)
Director of photography	Derek Vanlint

"Alien" design	H. R. Giger
"Alien" head effects	Carlo Rambaldi
Art directors	Les Dilley and Roger Christian
Special effects	Brian Johnson and Nick Allder
Set decoration	Rand Sagers
Costumers	John Mollo and Roger Dicken
Production designer	Michael Seymour
Editors	Terry Rawlings and Peter Weatherley
Music director	Jerry Goldsmith
Sound	Derrick Leather

SYNOPSIS

Alien tells the story of how the crew members of a futuristic spaceship fight to survive against a vicious, constantly mutating, alien life form after they answer what they have been told is a distress call on a distant asteroid. The film opens with a view from space of the asteroid, over which are typed the basic data about the spacecraft. It is a commercial towing vehicle called the *Nostromo*. (*Nostromo* is the title of a 1904 Joseph Conrad novel that vilifies a company's exploitive practices.) The vessel carries a crew of seven and is returning to earth with a cargo of mineral ore. Establishing shots of the *Nostromo* make it appear vast, powerful, and quiet. A view of a long interior hallway and other interior shots reveal only machines and computers, no people. Finally, in another room the crew members emerge from their sleeping capsules, apparently awakening from a state of suspended animation. They talk among themselves over breakfast, but the dialogue is indistinct and fragmented. Finally, we hear Parker demanding a full share. He is a large black man who, along with Brett, performs manual labor. Dallas, the captain, replies that Parker will get what he contracted for, but Brett interjects that everyone else gets more than they do. The argument is suspended when Ash, the uniformed science officer, tells Dallas that Mother wants to speak with him.

Mother proves to be the ship's computer, whose access is restricted. Dallas learns that they are only half-way home because the flight has been diverted to check out a transmission of unknown origin—it may or may not be human. When Dallas informs the crew, Parker and Brett complain that this is a commercial vessel, not a rescue ship, and that they did not contract for the detour. Then they reiterate their demand for larger shares. But Ash reminds them of a clause in their contract that requires them to investigate any transmission that might be of intelligent origin—under penalty of total forfeiture of their shares. Parker and Brett submit to the threat, and the ship is diverted to the asteroid. It experiences a rough landing and requires repairs that Brett estimates will

take about seventeen hours to perform. However, Parker reports an anticipated twenty-five-hour delay.

The landscape outside the ship is bleak and severe; there are sounds of howl-
ing wind. Dallas, Kane, and Lambert, the female navigator, set out as a landing
party, leaving behind Brett, Parker, Ash, and Ripley, another woman who is
next in command after Dallas and Kane. Ripley, who becomes the film's protagonist, passes her first test when she stands up to Brett and Parker, who refuse to repair the ship unless they receive full shares. Finally, she tells them to
"fuck off" and returns to her work.

Meanwhile, the landing crew enters the wreckage of a reptilian-looking
spaceship that has apparently been abandoned on the asteroid. We see the im-
posing vessel only in fragments. Clearly not of human origin, its vast, misty,
cavernous interior dwarfs the humans walking within. It looks like the skeleton
of a dinosaur or some other huge, lizard-like creature. They discover a fossil-
ized life form that Dallas concludes died when it exploded from the inside out.
Kane sees something below and goes to investigate. Lambert is scared and
wants to leave, but Kane calls Dallas over to investigate. Meanwhile Ripley,
who took over the effort to decipher the transmission after Ash had failed to
obtain results, concludes that it seems to be a warning, not a plea for help. She
wants to go after the rescue party, but Ash convinces her that if it really was a
warning, it is too late for her to help.

Examining his discovery, Kane descends into the bowels of the alien ship
and falls into a nest of eggs. Scooping up a handful of the gooey matter, he sees
tiny, living creatures and identifies them as organic life. Then, as he examines
another gooey, viscous mass of tissue, it suddenly unfurls and lashes out at him,
affixing itself to his helmet. Lambert and Dallas carry Kane back to the decom-
pression chamber aboard the *Nostromo*, but citing the standard quarantine
rules for interstellar travel, Ripley refuses to allow Kane into the ship, even
though she knows he might die. She adamantly defies Dallas's direct order to
let them enter but is undermined by Ash, who manually opens the door and
admits the entire landing party.

Dallas removes the stingray-shaped creature from Kane's helmet but discovers that it has attached itself to his face and neck and inserted a tube down
Kane's throat that keeps him alive by feeding him oxygen. Despite Ash's urging not to disturb the Alien, Dallas tries to saw it off of Kane. But it bleeds a potent acid that threatens to eat through successive decks and ultimately through
the entire hull of the ship. After they contain the acid, Ripley confronts Ash
over his reversal of her order. She accuses him of risking everyone's life by defying standard procedure, but when she tries to assert her rank, he replies that
she should let him do his job, and she should do hers.

Ash goes to see Kane and calls Dallas to report that the creature has disappeared; it is no longer affixed to Kane's body. The crew can find no sign of the
Alien, but after a suspenseful search, a dead baby Alien falls from the ceiling
onto Ripley. As this is the first time this life form has been encountered, Ash

wants to preserve the corpse and send it back to earth for analysis. Ripley wants to dispose of it immediately; after all it bleeds acid. But Dallas leaves the decision to Ash, because he is the science officer. When Ripley objects, Dallas maintains he is following Company policy. He then reveals that the Company replaced his regular science officer with Ash just two days before their mission began. Ripley states that she does not trust Ash, and Dallas replies that he does not trust anyone. He adds that he wants to leave the asteroid right away, even though the repairs are not complete.

The next scene shows the *Nostromo* successfully taking off, and everything seems fine. Even better, Kane appears to have recovered spontaneously. Able to recall only "some horrible dream about smothering," he joins the crew for dinner and eats voraciously. But suddenly he begins convulsing and falls onto the table. In the most memorable scene in the movie, a baby Alien abruptly bursts through his chest, splattering blood upon the crew members who are hovering over him. The tiny lizard- like creature shows its sharp teeth and then runs away and hides. The crew searches for it unsuccessfully before returning to eject Kane's body from the spacecraft. Dallas asks if anyone has any final words to say on Kane's behalf, but no one does.

Dallas then orders the crew to form two teams and remain in constant communication with each other. They arm themselves and employ a detection devise that Ash has constructed. Their plan is to drive the creature into the airlock and then blow it into space. Ripley, Parker, and Brett engage in a suspenseful search that is filmed with special visual effects that alter the lighting. The anticipation is heightened when they detect something and catch it. But there is a sudden emotional release when it turns out that they have only found Jones, the ship's cat, who runs away. Brett follows Jones into another room, where we see the cat hiding and hissing. Shifting to the cat's point of view, the camera reveals a huge Alien hanging down from the ducts above Brett. Here, and elsewhere, however, we never receive a full view of the creature, only partial glimpses. The cat growls and retreats. Brett looks up and stares at the creature, which reveals its sharp teeth before snatching him away with its tongue, like a lizard snagging an insect. The scene closes with a reaction shot of the cat, who watches wide-eyed.

The Alien takes Brett into the air shaft, and Ripley volunteers to hunt the beast through the air ducts and drive it into the airlock, where they can blow it into space. However, Dallas overrules her and insists that he will go instead. He seeks logistical assistance from Ash and Mother but receives only vague replies. The crew arms itself and Lambert monitors a detection device. She locates the Alien as a blip on her screen and directs Dallas, another blip, toward it. But she loses the signal, and when it returns, the Alien is moving toward Dallas. He tries to escape but becomes disoriented and runs into the monster instead. His death becomes apparent when the two blips merge and the screen goes blank.

Lambert advocates that the survivors abandon the *Nostromo* and take refuge in the shuttle, but the shuttle can accommodate only four people. Lambert wants to draw straws, but Ripley asserts her authority as ranking officer and insists that they stick together and try to kill the creature as Dallas had planned. She then requests information from Ash about the Alien, based on his scientific findings, but he replies that the data are still being collated. Ripley accuses Ash of doing nothing and tells him that she now has direct access to Mother (because Dallas is dead), and she will get her own answers. She enters the white room that houses the massive computer, and after overcoming some initial intransigence, finally learns of Special Order 937, which only the science officer is authorized to read. The directive has rerouted the *Nostromo* to the asteroid with instructions for it to investigate the alien life form and gather a specimen. Its overriding priority is that the organism be returned to earth for analysis. All other considerations are secondary, and the crew is deemed expendable.

Ash appears beside her and tries to offer an explanation, but Ripley vents her anger instead and shoves him aside. She tries to leave, but Ash locks her in Mother's room. Ripley notices that Ash is bleeding a white liquid and realizes that he is an android, not a person. He then assaults her, overpowers her, and tries to kill her by shoving a rolled-up magazine down her throat. But Parker suddenly intervenes and crushes Ash, who degenerates into a wildly out-of-control machine. Parker knocks off Ash's head, but the robot manages to assault him anyway, until Lambert administers the knock-out blow. A close-up shows that Ash's innards look similar to the nest of Alien eggs Kane discovered, except that Ash's body parts are synthetic.

Ripley surmises that the Company must have wanted the Alien for its weapons division and concludes that Ash "must have been protecting it all along." They reassemble Ash's head, plug it in, and interrogate it. (The visuals of the disembodied head on "life support" evoke scenes from *The Brain That Wouldn't Die*, [1960].) Ash tells them that they cannot kill the Alien, that it is "a perfect organism." Lambert accuses Ash of admiring it, and Ash acknowledges that he admires the Alien's "purity." Ash concludes by expressing sympathy for the survivors, but Ripley responds by smashing and then unplugging him. She then decides that they should take their chances in the shuttle and blow up the *Nostromo*. On their way out, Parker incinerates the head with one of the flamethrowers they are using to hunt the Alien.

Ripley goes to prepare the shuttle but then becomes concerned when she cannot find Jones and returns to the ship to search for him. Meanwhile, Lambert and Parker set the charges in another part of the vessel. In a sequence that mirrors the scene where Jones first surprises Brett, Ripley sees movement and becomes concerned. But it turns out to be the cat, not the Alien. Ripley picks it up, hugs it, and puts it in a carrying box.

The Alien suddenly appears before Lambert, who freezes in terror. Parker, standing behind her, implores her to move so he can shoot it with his flamethrower, but she remains frozen. Parker then rushes at the monster, which shoots a tentacle into his chest and kills him. The Alien then slowly curves its tentacle behind Lambert's leg and lifts it toward her crotch. Just as it thrusts at her in a gesture suggesting vaginal rape or sodomy, the camera shifts to Lambert's terrified face.

Hearing the screams over the intercom, Ripley rushes to investigate and discovers the remains of her dead comrades. She then proceeds to Mother's room to activate the auto-destruct mechanism. This gives her ten minutes to escape in the shuttle before the *Nostromo* explodes. Carrying Jones with her, she heads for the shuttle, but between flashes in the strobing lights she glimpses the Alien. Perhaps because she thinks her path to the shuttle has been blocked, Ripley then returns to Mother's room and tries to cancel the auto-destruct command. However, Mother impassively replies that the ship will blow up in five minutes. Calling Mother a "bitch," Ripley lifts a chair and smashes Mother's computer screen. Then, with her flamethrower in one hand and Jones's carrying case in the other, Ripley returns to the shuttle as Mother explodes behind her.

Ripley takes off in the shuttle, and moments later the *Nostromo* explodes, yielding a spectacular display of colors. Ripley watches and then removes Jones from his box and embraces him. She declares, "I got you, you sonofabitch." Jones seems upset, so she places him inside her sleeping chamber and closes the lid. Then she removes her clothes. Standing in her undershirt and panties, she adjusts the instruments. Suddenly, the Alien leaps at her from the instrument panel. As Ripley runs to hide, the camera appears to adopt the perspective of the monster. It focuses on her buttocks and heaving breasts and then pans down her body to her crotch, while Ripley slides away. With a determined look on her face, she dons a large, bulky space suit so she will be able to breathe and arms herself with the flamethrower. To bolster her spirits, she sings to herself, "You are my lucky star." The Alien leaps at her, but she opens a hatch and the creature is sucked out into space, where it clings to the outside of the shuttle. But Ripley ignites the thruster engines and dispels it. The film concludes with Ripley dictating to her diary that in about six weeks she will enter the frontier, where she expects to be rescued. She then enters the sleeping chamber with Jones, and the final shot shows her peacefully at rest, like Sleeping Beauty.

RECEPTION

Alien is now regarded as an innovative classic in the horror film genre. However, despite a very strong showing at the box office, it was a critical failure upon its release. Many of its first reviewers found *Alien* derivative of both 1950s horror movies, such as *The Thing* (1951) and *Invasion of the Body Snatchers* (1956), and of more current space films, especially Stanley Kubrick's *2001* (1968) and George Lucas's *Star Wars* (1977). The *New York Times*'s Vincent Canby praised *Alien* for its cast, direction, special effects, and set de-

sign but complained that it was "an extremely small, rather decent movie of a modest kind set inside a large, extremely fancy physical production." He went on to dismiss the film as "an old fashioned scare movie." *Alien* won an Academy Award for its visual effects and was nominated for art direction. But many critics concurred with Canby's assessment that the plot lacks complexity and the character development is shallow. Other critics complained that in contrast to *2001*, *Alien*'s view of scientific exploration is bleak and uninspiring. Several reviewers complained that Sigourney Weaver's character is a typical, hysterical horror film heroine; *Newsweek*'s Jack Kroll compared her to Fay Wray from *King Kong* (1933) and other old-time damsels in distress.[1]

However, despite these complaints from professional movie watchers, the public flocked to see the film. *Alien* benefited from an extensive $6 million advertising campaign that packaged it as a "blockbuster." Moreover, the shock value of the horror scenes made it a widely discussed topic of conversation and stirred considerable word-of-mouth interest. Benefiting from repeat viewers, *Alien* became the fourth largest grossing film of 1979. It cost approximately $9 million to produce and grossed some $12 million in its first six weeks (Bell-Metereau, 21). Its box office success prompted two sequels: James Cameron's *Aliens* (1986) and David Fincher's *Alien 3* (1992).

DISCUSSION

Prior to starting on *Alien* Scott had been working on plans to film the medieval legend of Tristan and Isolde, but after Sandy Leiberson at 20th Century Fox's United Kingdom division approached him with the science fiction script, he asked Paramount to release him from the Tristan project, which, he claimed, had "lost its momentum." Scott maintains that he stepped into *Alien* "almost by accident. . . . I had been burying myself in the area of *Heavy Metal* comics and graphic novels and other similar things, and *Alien* seemed well suited for those types of design possibilities" (Sammon, *Ridley Scott*, 53–54).

Scott's overriding concern when he first took on the project was to create a credible looking monster. "In the few horror films I've seen . . . the creatures haven't been terribly good. As soon as you accept a script like this, you begin to worry about what you're going to do with 'the man in the rubber suit.' So the alien became our first priority. We had to make it repulsive and yet scary as hell." Scott could not find a suitable design until writers Shusett and O'Bannon showed him a copy of *Necronomicon*, a book of demonic, erotic, marginally pornographic drawings by the Swiss surrealist painter H. R. Giger. "I found a painting of a demon with a jutting face and long, extended, phallic-shaped head. It was the most frightening thing I'd ever seen. . . . That 1976 painting [Necronom IV] was the basis for the monster" (Carducci and Lovell, 12). The studio then hired Giger to design all of the Alien's incarnations—egg, "facehugger," "chestburner," and adult—and to create the look for the surface of the asteroid and for the wrecked spaceship that preceded the *Nostromo*.[2]

Scott has commented, "People sometimes talk about how Giger molded a real human skull into his full-scale *Alien* sculpture as an example of how frightening his stuff is. What I think that observation misses is because Giger used real human and animal bones throughout the film, such materials added to the realism of what he did. What I find most frightening about Giger's work is the extra quality of reality he brings to his dark fantasies. It's the realism that makes Giger's work strong, not the fantasy" (Sammon, *Ridley Scott*, 55–56).

The various interviews with Scott, the cast, and other members of the production crew reveal that the filming was arduous and emotionally intense.[3] According to the producers, Yaphet Kott became "so wrapped up in his unconscious hatred of the alien that he actually tried to pick a fight with Bolaji Badejo, the seven-foot black actor who played the monster" (Sulski, "An Interview with Gordon Carroll and David Giler," 39). Veronica Cartwright, who as a child appeared in Alfred Hitchcock's *The Birds* (1963) and later in Philip Kaufman's remake of *Invasion of the Body Snatchers* (1978), was genuinely shaken when the Alien burst through Kane's chest and splattered blood onto her face. According to Cartwright, "They had three cameras so they could get all of our first reactions—our gut reactions. That's what you see in the film. Those reactions are totally raw. Nobody quite anticipated what was going to happen. I was told that I'd get some blood on me. I had no idea the hose was pointed on my face. I felt very queasy afterwards" (Sulski, "An Interview with Veronica Cartwright," 38). Weaver, who made her film debut in *Alien*, also found the scene unsettling: "Just to see John [Hurt] not whole was upsetting to me. But by the time it actually came out of his chest, it was especially awful. Plus I knew the special effects men were trying to rig the blood so that it would hit me. I was absolutely green. There had been a huge vat of kidneys and livers and intestines floating around on the set for two days and the stench was awful. All the cameramen were covered with blood" (Sulski, "An Interview with Sigourney Weaver," 35).

The interviews also reveal how the script evolved and the shooting proceeded. Producers Hill and Giler made considerable alterations to the screenplay. Most significantly, they added women to the cast; in O'Bannon's original version the crew was all male. In order to avoid excessive comparisons to HAL in *2001*, Hill and Giler removed Mother's spoken lines and gave them to Ash. They also pared down and sharpened the dialogue.[4]

Eleven minutes were eliminated from the rough cut because, according to Scott, it was "just too intense." One of the deleted scenes shows Ripley discovering Dallas alive in the Alien's cocoon, half-consumed by the monster. He is begging to be killed. Scott maintains, "Originally, there was a stronger degree of terror. Just subtle things, half-seen, half-heard things earlier in the picture. Consequently, you have the audience holding on from the beginning. That's no good. There's no break in the tension, as Hitchcock provides in *Psycho*." A romantic scene between Ripley and Dallas was also shot but cut because it was a distraction. According to Scott, "that's not the purpose of the film." He adds, "The viewer may assume that on a spaceship it's a question of 'sex for all' or else it's bromides. One thing's sure, melancholia is the end effect of space travel. Ripley does a modest strip once in the shuttle, but we kept that in to stress the vulnerability of a lady who's pretty much a ballsy sort" (Carducci and Lovell, 12).[5]

Apart from his overriding interest in creating a genuinely scary monster movie, Scott has articulated some of his other artistic concerns. He maintains he was initially attracted to O'Bannon's script because "I saw something new in *Alien*. I was attracted to the theory of over-powering industrial influence, the conglomerate mass control, the Big Brother syndrome. Most of all, though, it was the thrilling aspect of the unseen, inescapable force of evil" (Carducci and Lovell, 12).

Many scholars have analyzed Scott's critique of capitalism. Others discuss the feminist and anti-feminist elements in the film, the significance of the Alien's sexual androgyny, the meaning of the disparate images and events associated with birth, and the psychological dynamics that fuel the terror. Harvey Greenberg points out that the Alien's extraordinary mutability makes it especially scary: "none of its forms can ever be presumed to be its last" (Greenberg, "Fembo: *Aliens*' Intentions," 171 n. 7). These discussions reveal much about the social and psychological dynamics operating within and around the film. However, few of these discussions directly address the question of evil.

The greed, militarism, and amorality of the Company that owns the *Nostromo* is the main basis for the anti-capitalist readings. They are further supported by the clear division of labor into social classes, in which Brett and Parker represent the working class, and Dallas and the other officers appear as middle managers of the future. Significantly, in Scott's vision of the future, as in Marx's, the workers will set aside racial differences and unite behind their common economic interests. (It remains unclear whether blacks will be mostly relegated to manual labor and lower echelon jobs; the *Nostromo* is, after all, a sample of only one small crew.) But in Scott's view even the combined strength of the workers will be no match for the powers of the unseen Company, which actively seeks to fragment the work force. Thus, although it remains an invisible presence, the Company emerges as the real monster in the film, an invisible, amorphous, but extraordinarily powerful villain that operates through the machinations of a supercomputer named "Mother." It heartlessly sends a civilian commercial ship into harm's way without warning the crew, with whom viewers identify but whom the Company considers expendable. It invokes legal loopholes to compel the crew to do its dirty work, and in its quest for power, dominance, and profit, the Company tries to violate international law and endangers all forms of terrestrial life by smuggling onto earth a dangerous alien creature.

The positioning of a greedy corporation as villain is characteristic of other films from the era, for example *Network* (1976), *The China Syndrome* (1979), and *Silkwood* (1983). But *Alien* stands out because it transfers the anti-corporate sentiment from a realistic context to a science fiction setting, much as 1950s horror films featuring creatures from outer space absorbed and expressed the Cold War anxieties of that era. Because Scott envisioned the Company as being Japanese owned and uses Japanese-looking designs on the costumes and ship's logo, he further tries to draw on then-growing fears of Japan as an economic rival. By subtly evoking economic anxieties that many viewers were experiencing, he heightens feelings of anxiousness that intensify the horror in his horror movie. Simultaneously, Scott uses his viewers' fear of Japanese business practices to give greater emotional punch to his attack on multinational corporations. However, his efforts to identify the Company as Japanese may have been so subtle that most viewers do not make the connection.[6]

One of the first academic treatments of the film, the 1980 "Symposium on *Alien*," edited by Charles Elkins, features six papers that discuss the movie from a Marxist perspective. Jackie Byars notes that "we must see cultural documents [i.e., films] in their industrial environment as well as in their cultural context. We must examine not only the ways in which a document internalizes and transmits ideology, we must examine the transmission of that document" (Elkins, 279–80). By way of examining the process of transmission, Byars explains how the demise of the Hollywood studio system in the 1960s and 1970s altered the economics of film making. Previously "blind booking" by the studios had compelled theaters to screen both top-flight "A" movies and cheaply made "B" films. Their control over the means of production—actors, writers, and directors were bound to them by restrictive contracts—and their control over distribution eliminated the necessity for high-earning "blockbusters" that, according to Byars, "were not relevant to the economics of the studio system." The rise of independent film studios and the corresponding dissolution of the studio system, on the other hand, have led investors to seek out movies that will bring a large return on their investment. However, as most independent films require a distribution agreement with a major studio, "in effect, the studios still control the industry" (Elkins, 282). Byars thus suggests that *Alien*'s financial success and its emergence as a cultural phenomenon result from its appearance at a time when the economic demands within the film industry made it especially attractive. A film with strong visual imagery and visceral appeal, it was well suited for packaging and promotion as a blockbuster.

In a separate article, Harvey Greenberg places *Alien* in its historical/social/economic context. He maintains that the film appeals to the post-Watergate, post-Vietnam, anti-capitalist, anti-government sensibility that was especially strong in the United States during the late 1970s. "Through the obscure cybernetics by which movies translate collective *angst* into extravagant scenarios, Hollywood delivered in *Alien* an outerspace ghoulie matching the proper paranoia of the day" (Greenberg, "Fembo: *Alien*'s Intentions," 166). By contrast, Greenberg notes, its first sequel, James Cameron's *Aliens*, endorses the pro-capitalist, pro-military values of the Reagan era.

According to Greenberg, "Director Ridley Scott portrays the film's future culture as a corrupted democracy, concealing a galactic oligarchy. The spaceship *Nostromo*'s crew are skilled, well-paid technicians with a narrowly conforming middle- or working-class ideology" (165). But they are revealed to be fundamentally greedy and self-interested. "An unrepentant lust after gain has struck hurtfully at the center of the social contract" (Greenberg, "Fembo: *Aliens'* Intentions," 165).

Like other observers, Greenberg notes, "The crew—as symbolic family—is overtly menaced by the Alien, but the film's authentic monstrosity is the Company they serve" (165). However, Greenberg argues that *Alien* and other anti-establishment films of the 1960s and 1970s are "sullied jeremiads, collective artistic derivatives of capitalism, deeply embroiled in the very practices they presume to attack" (Greenberg, "Fembo: *Aliens'* Intentions," 170).

Writing in the "Symposium on *Alien*," Jeff Gould observes that the Alien, whom Ash has described as the "perfect organism," is "self-replicating, it can adapt to any environment, recognizes no morality . . . participates in no social order, and is, of course, implacably hostile. It is in all respects a superior product of competitive evolution and resembles nothing so much as that other superorganism, itself victor in an evolutionary struggle: the multinational (soon to be interstellar) corporation. In the system of the narrative, the Alien is the double, we might say the *biological analogue*, of the Company" (Elkins, 283).

In another Marxist reading, Peter Fitting places the film in the context of such earlier science fiction and horror films as *The Thing, Invasion of the Body Snatchers*, and *The War of the Worlds* (1953). He concludes that the threat by the Alien derives from "the context of two filmic traditions: the monster in the horror film as the return and revenge of the repressed psyche, on the one hand; and on the other—from the filmic legitimizations of the imperialist exploitation and expropriation—the portrayal of the world's non-white peoples and cultures as ignorant and barbaric savages. . . . In these terms, the *Nostromo* and its crew suggest the US's own current self-image." Fitting suggests that the *Nostromo* is "a threatened ship" and that Americans in 1979 also saw themselves as threatened, specifically from rampant "third world" immigrants whose "suffering and poverty is an integral part of our own comfort and satisfaction. . . . For in everyday linguistic practice *alien* does not refer to the European visitor, but . . . to those other, undesirable foreigners—the 'illegal aliens.' Ripley's triumph over the alien is thus a victory for some new and enlightened capitalism, as well as the resolution of the spectators' xenophobic fears and anxieties by means of a redefinition of the problems which threaten it." Fitting adds that *Alien* explores the theme of "collectivity and what binds differing interests and competing individuals together in a system of social relations based on inequality and exploitation." He notes that the characters are united not by common values and goals, as they are in 1950s science fiction films that project values of love, family, and community traditionally articulated by the American middle class. Instead, the crew members on the *Nostromo*, like the Company itself, share only their desire for profit. Fitting thus concludes that the movie's ending "seems to contradict the ideal of group effort in favor of an older, more ruthless struggle for survival" (Elkins, 288–89, 292–93).

Judith Newton also notes how the ending celebrates the individual over the collective. "The film expresses two fantasies. The first is that individual action has resolved economic and social horrors, for all the anxieties the film evokes about the dehumanizing force of late-capitalist labor have been deflected onto the Alien. The second fantasy is that white middle-class women, once integrated into the world of work, will somehow save us from its worst excesses and specifically from its dehumanization." Acknowledging that on one level *Alien* offers to a white middle-class audience "a utopian fantasy of women's liberation," she ultimately concludes that the final scene "reinvests Ridley with traditionally feminine qualities" and that the movie degenerates into "wish fulfillment and repression of a familiar order. . . . Ripley, though in many ways a fine and thrilling hero, is robbed of radical thrust. . . . Unallied with minorities, with the working class, or with other women, she is also—and in contrast to Conrad's *Nostromo*—a Company Woman to the last" (Elkins, 294, 296–97).

Rebecca Bell-Metereau amplifies on some of these points. After noting how the initial reviewers responded more to the female stereotypes in their minds than to the character of Ripley on the screen, she reiterates some of the Marxist concerns, observing that "the film calls into question the validity of efficiency as an ideal by taking the concept to its logical extreme." Bell-Metereau concludes by describing how the Company is the source of the horror in the movie, that the films reveals "a monster unleashed by a business gone too far." Nonetheless, Bell-Metereau believes that although *Alien* derives from earlier science fiction, it introduces "a new kind of science fiction heroine set in a social system that may be too real for the genre. We see her [Ripley's] ability to fend for herself as clearly as we see the pores in her skin, but what she has lost in beauty, sex appeal, and dependence on others is amply recompensed by her readiness to stand on her own—without even falling down" (Bell-Metereau, 17–18, 22–23).

Susan Jeffords is less upbeat about the feminist values in the film. She argues that Ripley's feminism, "like the popular images of feminism promoted by contemporary American cultural ideology, is victorious only because it accepts the point of view of a corporate masculism at the expense of relations between women. . . . Severing any ties she might have with other women, these films [the *Alien* series] succeed in recreating Ripley's 'community' as a revised nuclear family supplied and supported by a corporate structure" (Jeffords, 73). Jeffords also points out that because the Company plans to profit from the

Alien, it commodifies survival. Any profit the Company might make from obtaining the Alien would enable it to survive as a business enterprise. And she notes that Ripley's survival requires her not only to disassociate from the other woman on board, Lambert, but also to act like a man. Lambert, who reacts stereotypically to the monster, becomes hysterical and freezes in terror—and she dies. Ripley remains calm, figures out a strategy, and initiates action—activities stereotypically associated with male heroes and with the male principle, or *animus* in Jungian psychology—and she prevails.

Ros Jennings discusses Ripley from a lesbian point of view and suggests that her lack of sexual definition makes her a rare heroine with whom lesbians might identify. However, she maintains that the final scene in which Ripley undresses before the camera and the Alien introduces an element of male voyeurism to the film that reimposes a level of patriarchal control onto the female figure. Other commentators have also criticized this scene as inherently sexist and exploitive, though some, including Bell-Metereau and Sigourney Weaver, herself, have justified its inclusion. Bell-Metereau notes how it complements the opening scene that features Kane emerging from prolonged sleep in a similar state of nudity, and she justifies it in terms of structure and plot (Bell-Metereau, 21).

Weaver asks, "What could be more natural than to take off that sweaty thing I was wearing [while hunting down the Alien]. . . . When we wake up [at the beginning], we were supposed to be naked. It was a very provocative visual concept to see these people moving through such a very harsh environment in just their natural state" (Sulski, "An Interview with Sigourney Weaver," 35). Moreover, the scene mimics to some extent the terrifying shower scene in *Psycho* (1960), a film whose pacing Scott admires. Both scenes begin with a moment of relaxation after the apparent resolution of a critical problem: Marion decides to return the stolen money just before she showers, and Ripley has seemingly escaped safely from the Alien and the exploding spaceship. Both scenes climax with an unexpected, violent attack on the naked or nearly naked, and therefore sexually vulnerable, woman. And both achieve surprise and terror by revealing that what seemed to be an objective narrative point of view has in fact been the subjective viewpoint of the unseen assailant. Thus our own secure belief that we know the truth of the situation is shattered, and the viewers, too, experience an unsettling loss of control.

Chad Herman connects the anti-capitalist interpretation with a psychological perspective. He argues that "Kane's fate unfolds like a man's worst physical/sexual nightmare: he is (orally) raped, emasculated, impregnated, forced to endure excruciating labor pains, only to die giving birth." Herman adds, "Underscoring the film's obvious and active critique of capitalism we find an anxiety over the possibility of a world or a time when men's responsibility may shift from modes of production to modes of reproduction. . . . This is an interesting variation on the Oedipal myth: men give birth [as Kane gives birth to the Alien egg], then are systematically hunted, pursued, raped, and killed by their own male offspring. Such are the self-fulfilling and self-contained horrors of *Alien*'s paternity (Herman, 38–39).

Krin and Glen Gabbard fuse the anti-capitalist motif with a psychological reading based on the work of psychoanalyst Melanie Klein. Klein maintains that we never completely overcome the *angst* of our earliest childhood fantasies, and the Gabbards argue that *Alien* evokes our "early but imperfectly repressed anxieties about nurturing figures that can turn against us, about our own aggressive tendencies that can punish us from within or without, and about our tenuous relation to bodies with no discernible beginning and end" (Gabbard and Gabbard, 171). They maintain that "the future that *Alien* creates is not just the dehumanizing computer culture of *2001* in which man must outwit his machines in order to climb to the next rung in the evolutionary ladder. As a revisionist science-fiction film, *Alien* creates a genuine dystopia in which urban decay and frustration have expanded into outer space and in which a sinister 'company' blithely declares its employees expendable at the whim of its 'weapons division.'" The authors add that the only "real human feelings" are directed by Ripley toward her cat (Gabbard and Gabbard, 174–75).

The Gabbards show how the viewers' sense of foreboding and anxiety is accentuated by characters' behaviors, and they suggest that certain sequences are shot in ways that mirror infantile behaviors and elicit anxieties similar to those described by Klein. In particular, they point out how Scott uses incoherent dialogue, sounds that emanate off-camera from unidentifiable sources, numerous close-ups, and incomplete views of the Alien to create feelings of uneasiness. They go on to suggest that the filming makes the audience share the paranoid/schizoid position that Hanna Segal, one of Klein's interpreters, maintains is "a normal phase in the first several months of infantile development" (Gabbard and Gabbard, 177).

The Gabbards' main contention is that *Alien* enacts Klein's theory that "the infant turns all of his libidinal desires and all his destructiveness onto his mother's body" (Gabbard and Gabbard, 176). In their reading of the film, the crew becomes analogous to the infant, while the computer, Mother, and the Alien, itself, become manifestations of the "bad mother" who desires to kill the child. They point out the birth imagery of the opening sequence and suggest that the spatial disorientation in those shots may parallel the infant's early cognitive experience. The heartbeats and breathing we hear off-camera throughout the film echo the first few months of life when the mother's heartbeat and breathing dominate the infant's consciousness.

Noting Segal's observation that infants have "fantasies of scooping out and possessing all of [their mother's body's] contents, particularly . . . her babies," the Gabbards point out that when Kane disturbs the eggs "he realizes the fulfillment of the scooping out fantasy as well as its punishment when the Alien leaps out of an egg and attaches itself to his face" (Gabbard and Gabbard, 176). The Gabbards continue, "Once the infant has projected his aggression into the mother's breast, he then lives in terror that the prosecutory object will get inside him [as it gets inside of Kane] and destroy both him and his good internalized object" (Gabbard and Gabbard, 177). This, they argue, creates anxiety characteristic of the infant's paranoid/schizoid position. They further note that the destruction of all father figures within the film intensifies the paranoid anxieties, and that the remaining action reflects this intensified paranoid/schizoid position. Finally, "the movie ends by fulfilling the audience's wish to master its infantile anxieties." Ripley's ultimate expulsion of the Alien enables the audience to vicariously master their paranoid anxieties and achieve "the nonambivalent, all-good, blissful union with the good mother" (Gabbard and Gabbard, 179).

Anthony Ambrogio and John L. Cobbs also discuss the birth imagery and implied parent-child relationships in the movie. Ambrogio describes the birth metaphor in largely Freudian terms: "The *Nostromo*'s crew members enact dual symbolic roles, as children and as homunculi—unborn fetuses scurrying about the womb, waiting to be born, while some rough beast slouches after them. Caught between Scylla and Charybdis—penis and vagina in the violent throes of copulation—they become unwilling, uncomprehending performers in a primal scene" (Ambrogio, 170).

Ambrogio explains the extended metaphor of the crew as family, with crew members likened to children under authority of their parent, the computer Mother. He observes that the crew do not appear to be sexually involved with one another, ostensibly because they are professionals doing a job, but metaphorically because they are like prepubescent children. In contrast to the crew, "the one markedly sexual, thoroughly non-innocent character in the film is the Alien. Its only purposes are self-preservation and reproduction, and it accomplishes this through penetration and violation, symbolic rape. In all its sentient incarnations it is almost pure phallus" (Ambrogio, 173). Mother, the computer working at the behest of the Company, "has sent her children to procure the Alien—the invading penis for which she betrays them—for her" (Ambrogio, 175).

For Ambrogio, the film climaxes when Ripley experiences a symbolic birth after she severs all connections with Mother (and by extension with the Company). Mother "seems heartless and unfeeling in her final rejection of Ripley. . . . Ripley cannot understand that Mother must force her to cut the apron strings, the umbilicus—to achieve finally a true, timely birth, the only one in the film. The screaming klaxons, strobing lights, and streaming gases represent the anguish of labor for Mother and child alike and cannot be stopped once set in motion. The split-screen explosion marking the *Nostromo*'s destruction is 'feminine': labia opening to expel a child" (Ambrogio, 177).

Ambrogio then likens the expulsion of the Alien from the side of the craft to "a stellar douche." He compares the birth metaphor to *2001* but concludes, "it is more important here because the birth is earned through a stark, life-or-death confrontation the audience can comprehend, because the heroine has matured through her experience, not beyond humanity, but into a self-sufficient human being" (Ambrogio, 178).

Cobbs, on the other hand, likens Ripley's killing of the Alien to an abortion. He argues that *Alien* is fundamentally about gestation and birth and that "the sexuality of the film has strong reproductive overtones that distinguish it from the kind of garden variety titillation of most thrillers. . . . *Alien* achieves a strange balance between the cold, steely world of technology and forms constantly evocative of flesh—erotic flesh in particular. Not since *Flash Gordon* has the world of science fiction been so erotically evocative. Vaginal doorways, cervical mazes on the walls, phallic sculptures on the alien starship, and bulbous mammary projections everywhere—virtually every scene works itself out within a matrix of sexual suggestiveness." Overall, Cobbs argues that we witness the gestation process of the Alien as it "advances through its hideous and progressively lethal stages of maturation," and he thus likens Ripley's killing of the creature to an abortion (Cobbs, 198–201).

While these social and psychological readings shed considerable light on the values the movie projects and on how its rhetorical composition plays off of unconscious human anxieties in order to evoke an experience of horror among viewers, few critics address Scott's other stated objective—to explore "the thrilling aspect of the unseen, inescapable force of evil." Among those who do, Tony Stafford argues that *Alien* presents the conflict between science and humanism, and that at the "extreme end of science lies the abyss: the Alien." Stafford points out that Ash, the robot science officer, is "misrecognized" as being human, that his "desire to know—the desire of science—is responsible for the entry of the Alien into the spacecraft," and that the "pure quest for knowledge results in evil" (Elkins, 297).

The dualism between science and humanism, and the belief that the unbridled quest for knowledge results inevitably in destruction, if not damnation, are not new to literature. Christopher Marlowe's *Dr. Faustus* (circa 1587) and Mary Shelley's *Frankenstein* (1817) come quickly to mind; even Sophocles' *Oedipus Rex* (circa 439–412 B.C.) addresses the theme. The topic was particularly prominent in Cold War-era literature, especially in science fiction, as the end result of science at that time threatened to become nuclear annihilation. In this regard, several critics have noted parallels between *Alien* and *The Thing*. In both movies the scientists want to preserve the dangerous creature from outer space, while the protagonists seek to save people by destroying it. However, the scientist in *The Thing* is truly motivated by Faustian-like intellectual curiosity, while Ash is merely doing the bidding of the Company.

Although *Alien* appeared in the relatively calm period of detente that characterized the Cold War in the late 1970s, its projection of average people being manipulated by and ultimately sacrificed to an unfeeling military-industrial complex nonetheless appealed to Cold War anxieties. Moreover, *Alien* appeared at a time when social critics were deconstructing the view of science that had prevailed during the 1950s—that science had allowed the Allies to win World War II, was saving the free world from communist domination, and was improving the standard of living through technological innovation. Instead, in the 1970s environmentalists and feminists, in particular, attacked science for what they perceived was its attempt to dominate nature. They believed that the fundamental quest of science was not driven by a value-neutral passion to satisfy intellectual curiosity, as virtually every American had been taught in school, or by a passion for improving the well-being of humanity. Instead, they insisted that self-interested domination of nature was the ultimate goal of science. Marxist-oriented critics further pointed out that such control was intended to serve the needs of corporate interests, while feminists often analogized scientific and technological control over the environment to patriarchal domination of women. At its extreme, this domination of nature and women takes the form of rape. In the analogy, science is characterized as having masculine traits: its orientation is hard (phallic); it is dispassionate, rational, aggressive, domineering, and life denying, while nature is depicted as feminine: passive, fecund, live giving, and soft.

Alien reflects these attitudes about science and its relationship to the military- industrial complex. Certainly the Company's interest in the Alien is not value-neutral. The *Nostromo*'s scientific expedition is not, as Ash suggests, to learn more about another life form. Instead, it is motivated by the Company's desire to capture and control this creature from a different natural environment and use it to dominate earth's political and economic landscape. Significantly, Ripley surmises that the expedition has been ordered by the Company's weapons division.

Moreover, there are several moments of real and symbolic rape that are directly or indirectly linked to science and capitalism. Some feminists liken mining to rape because mining involves forceful penetration of the passive Earth Mother. We learn that the *Nostromo* is returning from a mining expedition, and it is possible that the crew's implied violation of other planets is intended as a sort of original sin that leads to the horrors that they endure. Certainly, our first impression of the crew is that they are essentially mercenaries who care little about the consequences of their actions, except how they may profit from them.

A scene that more closely connects science and rape shows Ash, the science officer who is actually a computerized piece of technology, trying to force a rolled-up magazine down Ripley's throat, an act of "oral rape" according to one critic (Bell-Metereau, 10). Judith Newton, who calls it simulated rape, observes that Ash uses a girlie magazine (Elkins, 295).

The Alien, itself, is neither a product of science nor scientific in its orientation. But it can be regarded as the agent that effects the Company's rape of the crew. As noted above, Herman has likened the Alien's penetration of Kane to a rape, one that Herman maintains has anti-capitalist implications because it expresses anxiety that men's responsibility "may shift from modes of production to modes of reproduction." And Bell-Metereau points out that the Alien's attack on Kane "carries the idea of sexual violation. What is worse, the penetration happens not to a woman, the usual victim of such attacks, but to a man" (Bell-Metereau, 10). When the Alien "takes" Lambert, we see its tentacle ascending behind her leg in a slow, exploratory, essentially erotic motion that seems to conclude off-camera with a forceful thrust into her crotch—an act of vaginal rape or sodomy. Finally, the scene where Ripley unknowingly undresses before the Alien, who then attacks her, also has qualities of both voyeurism and intended rape, as the subjective camera passes over her body toward her crotch, which she exposes for both the camera and the Alien as she lifts her leg to slide into the spacesuit.

Rape, then, becomes Scott's dominant metaphor for the action of evil. Evil violates and exploits with complete indifference. It is greedy, relentless, and entirely self-centered. Insensitive to the pain and suffering of others, it needs to dominate and assert its control. Evil shows two faces. The most pernicious is super-rational and dispassionate, the other completely irrational. Ash, Mother, and the Company manifest evil's dispassionate, rational form. This kind of evil is cerebral and calculating. It will deceive and manipulate to get its way. The Company proves to be especially pernicious because it operates according to a system of logic that assigns no value at all to human needs. Human well-being has no way of being figured into the bottom line. Instead, the basis for all of the Company's action is a single corporate axiom: maximization of profits overrides all other considerations. This system of values makes the Company the most dangerous alien monster in the film. Like the voracious creature from outer space, its unrelenting pursuit of profit knows no limits.

Moreover, the Company, which exists only as a legal entity, appears in the film as an intangible, unseen presence. Its lack of definition or concrete image makes the Company especially terrifying, as it deceives and manipulates the crew, who operate in a fog, without any clear understanding of what is really going on until much too late. Like the Alien, which is filmed so we see only incomplete fragments, the Company is shown only indirectly, through the commands issued by Mother and Ash. It is a larger-than-life form of evil that cannot be directly confronted because, unlike the Alien, it has no physical presence.

The other form of evil Scott presents is impulsive, not calculating; it responds viscerally and emotionally, not cerebrally. The Alien is of this type. It cannot be reasoned with or appealed to, only opposed; it exists solely to consume and destroy. For the crew, who are accustomed to dealing with entities that behave rationally, according to their own best self-interests, the Alien's unrelenting aggression poses a special problem. Weaver thus describes Ripley as "a woman who lived her life very much by the book and believed that rules existed for a reason. But when the alien appears there's nothing in the book to go by and she has to react only from instinct, and that's very hard for her (Sulski, "An Interview with Sigourney Weaver," 35).

So the crew is caught between two forms of evil, one super-rational, the other completely visceral.[7] All but Ripley and Jones, the ship's cat, succumb. Ripley survives only through a combination of luck, courage, alertness, and perseverance; Jones survives because he is a cat. But although these qualities may be sufficient for combating an irrational form of evil, which may fall victim to its own impulses, the denouement showing Ripley and Jones peacefully at rest inside their capsule leaves only the Alien defeated. The Company, after all, has lost just one cargo vessel and its crew, a small tax write-off in its debit ledger. Otherwise, it remains undiminished by the *Nostromo*'s adventure and impervious to Ripley's victory over the creature from outer space.

NOTES

1. For a more extensive analysis of *Alien*'s initial critical reception, see Rebecca Bell-Metereau, "Woman: The Other Alien in *Alien*," in *Women Worldwalkers: New Dimensions of Science Fiction and Fantasy*, ed. Jane Weedman (Lubbock: Texas Tech Press, 1985). In particular, Bell-Metereau observes and tries to account for why so many of the first reviewers failed to recognize the extent to which Ripley departs from the stereotypical female roles in early horror films.

2. Giger's work has appeared in *Omni* and avant-garde European art magazines. According to John L. Cobbs, it is reminiscent of the drawings of Aubrey Beardsley, but it "consistently borders on pornography." Giger's drawings often center on male and female genitalia. His *Penis Landscape*, which shows ten sets of copulating male and female genitals, was distributed with the Dead Kennedys' rock album *Frankenchrist*. Cobbs notes that Giger's work often shows the violation of women, and that he uses reptilian-like creatures to show horror (Cobbs, 199).

3. Mark Patrick Carducci and Glenn Lovell's 1979 interviews in *Cinefantastique* with Scott, producers Walter Hill and David Giler, artist H. R. Giger, and other members of the production crew provide firsthand accounts of the process of making the film, as do James Delson's two-part interview with Scott in *Fantastic Films* and Jim Sulski's interviews with actors Weaver, Skerritt, and Cartwright and producers Carroll and Giler in the same issues. Paul M. Sammon also describes the production process in *Ridley Scott Close Up: The Making of His Movies* (New York: Thunder's Mouth Press, 1999).

4. Despite their considerable contributions to the screenplay, the Writer's Guild declined to credit Hill and Giler as co-writers because, as producers, they were required to write 65 to 70 percent of the filmed material to receive a screen credit. Had they not been producers, they would have been required to write only 33 percent of the filmed material to earn co-credit (Carducci and Lovell, 18).

5. Scott elaborates on his concern that space travelers will need to combat boredom and melancholia: "I think that unless people's minds are controlled with drugs, one of the big things any spaceman is going to come up against is melancholia. Deep melancholia. I think this will become a massive problem. You see, most of the time there's nothing very much to do. Everything is being done for you. Suddenly, in a way, the human being becomes the automaton and the machine becomes the human being. One is either going to be sleeping or somehow be put on a programme to keep the body and mind fit" (Delson, "Interview with Ridley Scott, Part 1," 21–24).

6. In an interview with James Delson, Scott states, "The owners of the *Nostromo* are Japanese. Look at their crew uniforms, and all the other things with the ship's name on it" (Delson, "Interview with Ridley Scott, Part 2," 27). He returns to the notion of a future dominated by dispassionate Japanese corporations in *Blade Runner* and *Black Rain*, which deals with corporate-like organized crime and is set mostly in Japan.

7. Scott addresses both aspects of evil in several of his films. His first movie, *The Duellists*, presents the problems that a reasonable person faces when confronted by an irrational, passionately obsessed enemy who allows no middle ground or compromise. D'Hubert, like Ripley, must either defeat his foe or succumb to him. *Blade Runner*, like *Alien*, vilifies the large, impersonal corporation and mirrors its cruel dispassionate efficiency in the behaviors not only of Roy Batty and the other replicants, but also in Tyrell, the replicants' creator, and in the protagonist Deckard, whose re-connection with his emotional, nurturing, "human" side defines the happy ending. Drawing on settings and images from mythology, fairy tales, sagas, and medieval romances, *Legend* depicts the mythic struggle between good and evil. Although our sympathies lie decidedly with the forces of good, the film advances the premise that good and evil need each other, and that good cannot exist without evil. *White Squall* presents nature as an awesome, inspiring source of exquisite beauty that is also a wild, relentless, irrational force capable of frustrating the best efforts of rational humans. But it is depicted as value-neutral, not evil. Most of Scott's other films also address the destructive nature of excessive rationality and/or excessive passion.

Blade Runner

(1982; Director's cut released 1992)

CAST

Deckard	Harrison Ford
Batty	Rutger Hauer
Rachael	Sean Young
Detective Gaff	Edward James Olmos
Bryant	M. Emmet Walsh
Pris	Daryl Hannah
Sebastian	William Sanderson
Leon	Brion James
Tyrell	Joe Turkel
Zhora	Joanna Cassidy
Chew	James Hong
Holden	Morgan Paull
Bear	Kevin Thompson
Kaiser	John Edward Allen
Taffrey Lewis	Hy Pyke

PRODUCTION

Producer	Michael Deeley (a Ladd Company release in association with Sir Run Run Shaw through Warner Brothers of a Michael Deeley-Ridley Scott production)
Screenplay	Hampton Fancher and David Peoples, based on the novel *Do Androids Dream of Electric Sheep?* by Philip K. Dick
Director of photography	Jordan Cronenweth
Art director	David Snyder
Costumers	Charles Knode and Michael Kaplan
Set Designers	Tom Duffield, Bill Skinner, Greg Pickrell, Charles Breen, Louis Mann, and David Klasson
Production designer	Lawrence G. Paull
Supervising Editor	Terry Rawlings
Editor	Marsha Nakashima
Music	composed, arranged, and performed by Vangelis

SYNOPSIS

Ever since a bloody "off-world" mutiny by a replicant combat team in the early twenty-first century, the presence on earth of human replicants has been illegal and punishable by death. The replicants—genetically engineered androids that look, think, and act like people—have been built to perform hazardous jobs in outer space, serve as personal slaves, and give sensual pleasure to the humans who have fled earth and now live in "off-world" space colonies. Nexus 6 replicants are stronger, more agile, and at least as intelligent as their creators—"more human than human" but without emotions. They are built with a limited, four-year life span as a "fail safe" against the possibility that in time they might begin to develop emotions. *Blade Runner* tells the story of the return to earth in 2019 of a Nexus 6 contingent that has begun to feel emotions and is seeking their manufacturer in an effort to extend their lives. Rick Deckard, a "Blade Runner" policeman, has been assigned to destroy them. In the process, he finds love, regains his humanity, and experiences spiritual regeneration.

The band of renegade replicants has abducted a spaceship, killing twenty-three people in the process, and returned to Los Angeles to compel their manufacturer to extend their lives. Their initial attempt to infiltrate the Tyrell Corporation has failed, but four replicants remain. While undergoing a security check for a job at Tyrell, one of them, Leon, has shot the best Blade Runner on active duty.

When we first see Deckard, he has retired from the Blade Runner unit that "retires" illegally returned replicants and is alone on a dark, rainy Los Angeles street, dwarfed by the buildings and crowds around him. As he orders from a Japanese food stand, the Japanese-speaking Detective Gaff arrests him and returns him to his former boss, Captain Bryant. Insisting that Deckard is the best at tracking down replicants, Bryant declares that this group of renegades is "the worst yet." Bryant then coerces Deckard to take the job, reminding him that "if you're not a cop, you're little people." However, Deckard's job becomes complicated when he falls in love with Rachel, a highly advanced replicant who works as an assistant to the founder of the Tyrell Corporation.

Deckard first meets Rachael when he goes to interview Tyrell about the Nexus 6 model. Initially hostile, stark, and severe, she asks accusingly if he has ever retired a human by mistake. Deckard replies unequivocally, "No." Tyrell then enters and insists that Deckard test Rachael to ensure that the standard police test does not improperly mistake humans for replicants. Deckard administers the test, which records the changes in the dilation of her eyes as he describes scenes that for humans should be emotionally upsetting. Because replicants are supposed to have no emotions, their eyes dilate little in comparison to people. Tyrell dismisses Rachael from the room before Deckard reports his results—she is a replicant. Tyrell admits that he is correct but adds that Rachael does not know.

Deckard and Detective Gaff, whom Bryant has sent along more to keep an eye on Deckard than to assist him, go to Leon's hotel room and find a scale from an artificial snake and some well-hidden photos. At the same time Roy Batty, an Aryan-looking combat model who leads the Nexus 6 renegades, learns the identity of Sebastian, the genetic engineer who designed their brains and who, Batty believes, would know when the replicants were conceived and how long they have been programmed to live.

When Deckard returns home, he finds Rachael in his apartment, waiting to ask him about the results of her test. When he tells her she is a replicant, she tries to disprove him with a picture of herself as a little girl with her mother. But he tells her how Tyrell has implanted those memories to deceive her into believing she had a childhood. When Deckard proves he is correct, Rachael is devastated. Moved by her distress, Deckard shows compassion and feeling for the first time. As he tries to console her, he begins to fall in love. However, Rachael soon leaves and Deckard drinks alone in a melancholy funk, first looking over her childhood photo and then reviewing the ones he collected from Leon.

Meanwhile, Pris, a replicant designed for conferring sexual pleasure, waits outside Sebastian's building and tricks him into believing she is homeless and needy. Although he lives in an otherwise abandoned building, Sebastian assures Pris that he "makes friends." Then he brings her into his apartment, which he has populated with toy soldiers and other robots that he has genetically engineered.

Still alone in his apartment, Deckard sits at the piano, pensively tapping on the keys. (In the Director's Cut, but not in the originally released version, Deckard now has a reverie of a white unicorn running outdoors through a white fog.) He looks up and notices something in one of Leon's photos. After examining the picture closely through computer enhancements, Deckard is able to track down Zhora, a replicant who is apparently Leon's lover and who works as an exotic dancer in Chinatown. Deckard calls Rachael from the club where he has found Zhora, but she refuses to join him in such a sleazy place. He then confronts Zhora in her dressing room and kills her as she runs away. Bryant and Gaff appear to congratulate Deckard on his success, but then Bryant informs him that he must also kill Rachael, as she is a replicant too.

When the officers leave, Leon appears and overpowers Deckard. While beating him, Leon taunts, "Painful to live in fear, isn't it?" But just as Leon prepares to kill Deckard, Rachael shoots him.

Rachael and Deckard return to his apartment, where he tells her that he will not hunt her down, because "I owe you one," but that somebody else will. The scene concludes with their falling in love and Rachael telling Deckard, at his insistence, that she wants him.

Batty comes to Sebastian's apartment and, after kissing Pris passionately, reports sadly that she and he are the only ones still alive. When Sebastian proves unable to give them the information they need, Pris and Batty convince him to take Batty to Tyrell.

Tyrell immediately recognizes Batty as his creation, and Batty declares with double meaning, "It's not easy to meet your Maker." When Tyrell asks what his problem is, Batty answers, "Death." Calling Batty his prodigal son, Tyrell tries to convince him to accept his shortened life span: "Revel in your time. The light that burns twice as bright burns half as long. And you have burned so very, very brightly." In response, Batty kisses Tyrell on the mouth and then kills him with his bare hands. We learn later that Batty also kills Sebastian, off-camera.

Upon hearing about the murders, Deckard goes to Sebastian's apartment, where he finds Pris and shoots her. She dies literally kicking and screaming. Batty soon returns and, kissing her corpse, grieves over her. Deckard tries to shoot him as he walks away from the body, and Batty taunts him for not being a good sport. "Aren't you supposed to be a good man?" he demands. Physically superior, Batty takes Deckard's gun, breaks two of the fingers on his right hand—one for Zhora and one for Pris—and then returns the gun. Shirtless, he chases Deckard through the building to the rooftop. Trying to leap across to the neighboring edifice, Deckard falls short and dangles from a protruding beam. Suddenly holding a white dove, Batty appears and successfully jumps to the adjoining roof, where he stands above Deckard taunting, "Quite an experience to live in fear, isn't it? That's what it is to be a slave." Batty then pulls Deckard to safety, as his own life ebbs out. He bemoans the fact that all his experiences in outer space—far more incredible than anything Deckard has known—will be lost "like tears in rain." Saying, "Time to die," he releases the dove, and falls dead.

Gaff suddenly appears on the roof and, speaking in English for the first time, congratulates Deckard. As he tosses Deckard his gun, Gaff tells him, "You've done a man's job." Then he adds, "It's too bad she won't live. But then, again, who does?"

Deckard returns to Rachael in his apartment. When he finds her, she is lying motionless and he fears that her life has run out too. But Rachael is merely asleep. When she awakes, she tells Deckard that she loves and trusts him. They leave together, walking past an origami unicorn that Gaff has left behind. The Director's Cut concludes as the elevator door closes behind them, but, in an effort to give the movie a more upbeat ending, the original release includes a final shot of the couple driving through a pristine wilderness.

RECEPTION

Blade Runner had two major releases, both of which were preceded by limited viewings and sneak previews and then altered prior to the full theatrical release. The film officially premiered on June 25, 1982, in 1,290 theaters. Although it garnered over $6 million during its opening weekend, it faced fierce competition for science fiction audiences, and grossed only $14 million in its initial theatrical run (Sammon, *Future Noir*, 318). Among its competitors were *Star Trek II: The Wrath of Khan, Conan the Barbarian,* John Carpenter's remake of *The Thing,* and, most importantly, Steven Spielberg's *E.T.* As Paul M. Sammon points out, *E.T.* dominated the science fiction genre that season. Moreover, its upbeat attitude "took over the sensibility of audiences" and left little room for *Blade Runner*'s more depressing view of the future (Sammon, *Future Noir*, 317).

For the most part, viewers either liked *Blade Runner* very much or disliked it intensely. Supporters raved about the stunning sets and other visual effects, but detractors ripped the storyline as confusing and inconsistent, the characterizations as shallow, and the pacing as slow; the critic for the *Los Angeles Times* suggested calling the movie *Blade Crawler.* The *New York Times* dismissed it as "muddled"; Pauline Kael derided it in the *New Yorker;* and Roger Ebert complained that the special effects technology overwhelmed the story. Another reviewer agreed, labeling the film "science fiction pornography: all sensation and no heart" (Sammon, *Future Noir*, 313–15). On the other hand, *Variety* was more generous, calling *Blade Runner* "the most riveting—and depressing—vision of the near-future since *A Clockwork Orange.*" It praised the special effects and "sheer virtuosity of the production," but speculated that "unrelenting grimness and vacuum at the story's center will make it tough to recoup [the] reported $30,000,000 budget." *Variety* further criticized Deckard's passivity and the film's overall narrative structure. Like several other reviews, it specifically attacked Harrison Ford's narrative voice-over, which the producers imposed just prior to the final release in order to create the *film noir* tone of a Raymond Chandler hard-boiled detective movie (Sammon, *Ridley Scott*, 136–37). Other critics objected to the upbeat final scene, also tacked on at the last minute, because it conflicted with the *film noir* sensibility. (The wilderness background in the concluding sequence was compiled in post-production from out-takes from Stanley Kubrick's *The Shining*.) Both of these last-minute additions were dropped from the 1992 Director's Cut, and Deckard's unicorn reverie was restored.

Although the film's first theatrical run was disappointing, *Blade Runner* benefited immensely from the cable television and home video markets that were newly emerging in the early 1980s. It frequently appeared on HBO and other channels seeking to fill their time slots with exciting movies featuring major stars. Perhaps as a result of the cable exposure, *Blade Runner* also became one of the most popular video rentals of all time. In addition, according to Sammon, by 1994 the film had sold almost 500,000 video cassettes. As Sammon also points out, its success in the home-viewing market helped establish *Blade Runner* as a science fiction cult film that was embraced by Cyberpunk, a 1980s literary analogue of hard rock. Cyberpunk champions intricate, detailed, fast-paced narratives that create sensory overload as they address future social problems that might ensue if consumer capitalism, mass media, and high technology continue to dominate the culture (Sammon, *Future Noir*, 321–29). Additional interest in the film followed the 1987 release of the Criterion Collection's high-resolution, wide-screen laser disk that shows the somewhat more violent International Cut.

These factors combined to generate sufficient enthusiasm for Warner Brothers to release *Blade Runner: The Director's Cut* on September 11, 1992. Initially screened in fifty-eight theaters nationwide, the Director's Cut performed well at the box office, garnering the highest per-screen gross of any film during its first weekend. Its critical reception was again mixed. Supporters still admired the movie for its visual effects and mythic aspirations, and detractors still criticized the inconsistencies in the plot, though most acknowledged that deleting the voice-over narration and upbeat ending had improved the film.

DISCUSSION

Scott's ability to render his own artistic vision was impeded by the film's financial backer, Tandem Productions, which continually pressured him about budgetary overruns. (The filming ran some $5 million over budget.) Tandem fired Scott and producer Michael Deeley two days after the principal filming was completed, and although they continued to work on the post-production,

Scott lost artistic control. Therefore, even the Director's Cut does not fully actualize Scott's final intention. But as it comes closest, it serves as the basis for the discussion below.[1]

Along with *Alien* and *Thelma & Louise*, *Blade Runner* has attracted the most critical analysis of Scott's films. Scholars have analyzed the movie's vision of the future (Kaveny, Lev, Silverman, and Kerman, "Technology and Politics in the *Blade Runner* Dystopia"); its contemplation of human nature and human identity (Gwaltney and Shapiro); its representations of women and ethnic populations (Barr and Desser, "Race, Space and Class"); its connections to Mary Shelley's *Frankenstein* and John Milton's *Paradise Lost* (Desser, "The New Eve"); its use of *film noir* and the hard-boiled detective genre (Carper, Doll, and Gray); its place within science fiction (Desser, "Blade Runner: Science Fiction and Transcendence," Doll, Slade, and Romero); its adaptation from its source novel, Philip K. Dick's *Do Androids Dream of Electric Sheep?* (Kaveny, Landon, Rickman, Kolb, "Script to Screen" and "*Blade Runner* Film Notes"); its visual indebtedness to Fritz Lang's 1927 silent masterpiece, *Metropolis* (Neumann); and the effectiveness of its musical score by Vangelis (Stiller).

Among the most provoking discussions are Judith Kerman's introduction to her critical anthology, *Retrofitting* Blade Runner, and Joseph Francavilla's "The Android as *Doppelgänger*," which appears in that anthology. Kerman argues that in the near future moral issues will be framed by a social context in which the government exercises authoritarian control through police state tactics, and capitalism and technology have exaggerated the Reagan-era social divisions and further stratified the economic classes. She further asserts, "*Blade Runner* considers what it will mean morally, technologically and politically" to live in a future in which genetic engineering and computer science have created "new kinds of people or intelligences, entities physically and emotionally different from historic humanity but who are arguably entitled to be considered persons." She underscores the importance of asking these questions by placing them in the context of the Holocaust: "The question of how people treat other people when they define them as non-human, or consider their own political ends more important than the humanity of the enemy, was made newly urgent by the technology and political will which make genocide and mass warfare possible" (Kerman, *Retrofitting* Blade Runner, 1).

Francavilla regards the moral complexity of human-replicant interactions from a psychological perspective. He suggests that Batty functions as an archetypal shadow figure who embodies Deckard's repressed traits and is both a feared harbinger of death for Deckard and his guardian savior. Using a concept initially advanced by Sigmund Freud and his disciple Otto Rank, Francavilla argues that Batty is Deckard's double, or *Doppelgänger*. Quoting Freud, he defines the *Doppelgänger* as a class of phenomena that is "in reality nothing new or alien, but something which is familiar and old-established in the mind and which has become alienated from it only through the process of repression

... [it is] a secretly familiar thing which has undergone repression and then re-turned from it" (Francavilla, 5). Associated with uncanniness and intuition, the *Doppelgänger* represents "the return of the repressed part of the personal-ity torn apart by its irreconcilable elements" (Francavilla, 6). Francavilla argues that, ironically, Batty's entrance into the Blade Runner's life revives Deckard's most human qualities, his long-repressed capacity for compassion, empathy, and love.

Taking Francavilla's point a step further, we can see that, in archetypal terms, *Blade Runner* is the story of how Deckard mends his fractured spirit by reconnecting to his repressed anima when he confronts Batty, his *Doppelgänger*, and empathizes with Rachael. Or, to state it in terms of 1980s popular culture, Deckard becomes fully human only when he gets in touch with his feminine side. Either way, *Blade Runner* gains much of its power and appeal from this play of unconscious archetypes, which takes place in the futur-istic environment Kerman describes. So, finally, the film is about the problem of remaining attuned to one's anima, or feminine side, in a futuristic America dominated at every level by corporate capitalists who wield power through mass marketing, high technology, and police state tactics.

The same political, technological, and economic forces that have created luxury-laden space colonies, swift hovercraft, versatile computers, and over-whelming corporate edifices have also rendered the city sterile, denuded it of foliage and other signs of nature, and fractured the spirits of the humans still living on earth. Indeed, all the humans we see seem jaded or broken, with the exceptions of Sebastian, who has learned to cope by "making friends," and Tyrell, who enjoys a position atop the corporate ladder.[2] For Carl Jung, the human spirit is healthy and complete when the anima, the female aspect, and animus, the male aspect, are each healthy and in balance with one another. But the corporate-dominated police state of the future promises to compel citizens like Deckard to repress their animas, the nurturing, compassionate, intuitive part of the spirit that Jung associates with femininity.[3] In repressing their animas, people become disconnected from humanity, nature, and all living things. In their emotionally disconnected state they lose the capacity to love, the desire for morality and social justice, and other empathetic qualities that have historically been credited with separating humans from wild beasts.

In both the movie and Dick's source novel, *Do Androids Dream of Electric Sheep?*(1968), the ability to experience empathy, a function of the anima, sepa-rates humans from replicants. The test for detecting replicants is based on this key difference, as only replicants fail to respond viscerally, or through their ner-vous systems, when abhorrent situations are recounted. It is suggested that any person who could manage entirely to suppress his or her capacity for empa-thy would cease to be truly human. In fact, to ensure that the replicants remain nonhuman, Tyrell has programmed them not to have animas and has limited their life spans lest they spontaneously develop emotions and become essen-tially indistinguishable from people. In *Do Androids Dream of Electric Sheep?*

the androids' incapacity for empathy remains their definitive quality. But in *Blade Runner*, the Nexus 6 models have begun to develop aspects of the anima, notably their loyalty to one another and Leon's heartfelt love for Zhora and Batty's for Pris. Already in possession of many traits that Jung associates with the masculine animus, such as physical prowess, rational thought, strategic planning, and other capabilities associated with the left side of the brain, when they develop their animas, the replicants essentially possess a human spirit.

Ironically, the replicant rebellion, an act of their assertive, action-oriented animus, revives Deckard's long-repressed anima, awakening his capacity for love and empathy. So, in confronting his *Doppelgänger* Deckard ultimately heals his shattered spirit. At the end, he ceases to operate as an agent for the political power structure that insists that he repress his anima. The ending imposed by the producers in the original release underscores this point not only by showing Deckard and Rachael together in love but also by emphasizing their return to pristine nature. Connection to nature is a characteristic of a healthy anima. And though Scott removed this scene in the Director's Cut, he insisted on restoring another important, nature-oriented sequence, Deckard's unicorn reverie.

The reverie takes place after Deckard has revealed to Rachael that she is a replicant. In response to her distress he has begun to feel compassion for her. In other words, his reemerging capacity for empathy has begun to restore his anima. After Rachael leaves, Deckard sits alone at the piano, pensively tapping on the keys, in a state between unconscious sleep and conscious alertness. This state between sleep and wakefulness leaves a person particularly receptive to communications from the unconscious—it is the state cultivated for the practice of hypnosis, which seeks to establish a connection to the unconscious. Thus, the dreamlike image of a strong, healthy white unicorn running freely through a forest begs to be read as a message from Deckard's unconscious, encouraging him to rediscover the life force that he has so long repressed. The virile unicorn suggests male sexuality and hints at Deckard's suppressed lust for Rachael. Thus, by reconnecting to his anima by feeling compassion for Rachael, Deckard also regenerates his animus, as his masculinity resurfaces.

Although it does not result in any overt action, the unicorn dream actually serves as a plot point that inaugurates the second phase of the story, where Deckard moves from passively studying the replicants to actively hunting them. Immediately following his reverie, Deckard experiences a sudden, intuitive revelation, as he looks up from his thoughts and notices something in one of Leon's photos. This burst of insight enables Deckard finally to engage the replicants, as he tracks down and kills Zhora. After Rachael saves Deckard from Leon, they return to his apartment, demonstrate their desire for one another, and presumably make love. For both of them, the off-camera act of lovemaking literally reestablishes their connection to another being. It is a quintessential act of empathy that helps actualize Rachael and Deckard's animas.

Moreover, because the same act also requires Deckard to manifest his masculinity, it completes his spirit by uniting his animus and anima.

Rachael enables Deckard to experience love and compassion for a soul mate, but for his spirit to be fully restored, he must empathize with others, as well. He achieves this in his confrontation with Batty, his *Doppelgänger* who, according to Freud, represents the Other. Deckard first encounters the replicant leader when Batty returns to Sebastian's apartment after killing Tyrell and Sebastian. Ford plays the fight sequence stoically, so we cannot specify Deckard's feelings as he goes through his life-and-death struggle with his *Doppelgänger*. We see no direct evidence that his love for Rachael has sensitized Deckard to Batty's grief over Pris, but he must certainly recognize when Batty saves his life that this is a noble action, as Batty is under no compulsion to rescue his enemy.

Furthermore, Batty's final glorious speech in which he bemoans the imminent loss of both his life and his spectacular memories establishes an empathetic bond between the character and the audience, too. We most identify with Deckard's point of view, so we project the pity and respect we have acquired for Batty onto Deckard and infer that his capacity for empathy has broadened. In being able to appreciate and respect the Other, he can now fully actualize his own life. He thus returns to his apartment to run off with Rachael, the replicant woman who completes his spirit but whose death is also imminent. Ironically, then, their respective attempts to come to terms with their own mortality and the mortality of those whom they love finally establish a connection between Deckard and Batty and occasion their most profound feelings of being human.[4]

Though Deckard's story concludes on a more or less upbeat note, the happy ending is predicated on his rejection of the futuristic society and tempered by Detective Gaff's cynical observation, "It's too bad she won't live. But then, again, who does?" In the long run, it may not be viable for Deckard to disassociate from the police state, because in Scott's futuristic picture of America, "If you're not a cop, you're little people." Moreover, even if he does manage to exist apart from his society, Deckard knows that Rachael's life span is severely limited. But although these considerations temper our response, we nonetheless experience a sense of fulfillment in the union of Deckard and Rachael and in our knowledge of the personal growth it required of each.

If the story's main plot centers around the reintegration of Deckard's shattered spirit, its subplots present Rachael and Batty's struggle to cope with their identities. Rachael is challenged by her knowledge that she is a replicant, Batty by his awareness of his own mortality. Arguably, Rachael develops a fully human spirit after she learns she is a replicant. She seems more horrified by discovering that she is not a real human than by knowing she will die soon. In general, her basic response is to become more emotional and act in other ways that are uniquely human. Ironically, when she believed she was human, she behaved most like a replicant. Nothing about her was nurturing or encouraged human contact. Unfriendly and severe, she dressed in black in clothes that fully shielded her body and diminished her sensual appeal; her hair was pulled back tightly, and her expression showed no warmth. Until she learns she is a replicant, she exhibits no feelings. But her first response when Deckard proves she is a replicant is to experience emotion—she breaks down crying. Though she runs from his apartment, she apparently also begins to develop affection for Deckard, who had been solicitous of her feelings. Her growing affection accounts for why she changes her mind and comes to meet him in the sleazy strip joint in Chinatown, and why she then saves Deckard, the replicant assassin, by shooting Leon.

In killing Leon, Rachael demonstrates her allegiance to humanity and her repudiation of her replicant "roots." Afterward, she connects to her femininity for the first time, playing the piano, letting her hair down, and acknowledging her desire for Deckard, with whom she then presumably makes love. We regard their lovemaking as an act of mutual passion, and not the detached experience we imagine for most replicants of the "pleasure model," who are designed to give but not receive sexual fulfillment. Thus, just as it restores Deckard's humanity by reanimating him, their lovemaking penetrates the barriers to her humanity and consummates Rachael's transformation into a completely human spirit. Consequently, even though we, like Deckard, remain acutely aware of her impending death, we feel that her plot line concludes in a positive way, because, for all practical purposes, she has become what she most wanted to be.

If Rachael repudiates her replicant aspect, Batty embraces his. Like her, he experiences such emotions as loyalty, love, and grief, but his compassion extends only to other replicants, not to humans—until he saves Deckard's life at the end. A host of moral questions arises at the prospect of tribes of competent, rational, physically powerful and adept non-human biological beings that have strong emotional ties among themselves but not with humans. Most importantly, should we try to coexist with such creatures or dominate them, lest they dominate us? After all, the renegades *are* murderers; they killed twenty-three people off-world when they mutinied, and at least three more since their return—Tyrell, Sebastian, and Holden, Leon's interrogator in the opening sequence.

Officially, the state policy is to treat replicants as dangerous wild beasts. Like wild animals, they are physically empowered entities that lack compassion for humans and will completely disregard human interests to get what they want. (Interestingly, sociopaths fit this description, too.) Thus, Blade Runners like Deckard are assigned to hunt them down and kill them, much as human hunters slay wild animals that threaten the safety of their communities. The pronounced absence of animal life in the film (and the book) further invites us to make this analogy between replicants and wild beasts, and to reconsider the consequences of this deadly policy. Or, as Kerman observes, "the larger question of the film which is related to genocide is the ability of the state to define the human and to destroy those who fall outside that definition" (Kerman, "Technology and Politics in the *Blade Runner* Dystopia," 23).

The humanization of Batty makes Kerman's question especially relevant. Batty's transformation, however, is first anticipated by Leon's. Despite the neutral expression he maintains, Leon is clearly anguished by Zhora's death. The revenge he exacts by torturing Deckard and his taunt, "Painful to live in fear, isn't it?" exhibit both his empathetic bond with Zhora and his desire for retribution, which, after all, is an entirely emotional response. But Leon seems slow witted, unattractive, and dull, and, regrettably, such matters of appearance do influence how people respond to the "humanness" of others. Though we may have some momentary sympathy for him, most viewers, like Deckard, are not compelled by the suffering that we infer he experiences, especially as we witness his sadistic side.

Batty, on the other hand, appears youthful, virile, alert, and blessed with Nordic good looks. As several commentators have observed, Tyrell, who seems to have fascistic proclivities, has designed his ideal replicant to conform to the Nazi ideal of manhood. Indeed, as a blond, white-skinned man with superior mental and physical attributes, he approximates the *Übermensch*.[5] But despite these associations Batty remains pleasing to the eye; therefore, audiences are more receptive to the prospect of his humanization.

Batty is not only handsome, he is also clever and eloquent. His sharp mind, facility with language, and ability to produce powerful visual images also contribute to our willingness to accept his humanity, especially as word-based speech is a uniquely human capability. His verbal acuity is most evident during his encounter with Tyrell and in his death speech. Batty's ability to pun demonstrates his mental dexterity, along with his despair. His first words to Tyrell are, "It's not an easy thing to meet your Maker." Literally, of course, Batty is meeting his manufacturer. But the phrase also alludes to death, and, taken this way, Batty's remark is especially poignant, because he is desperately seeking to extend his life. The pun further makes us aware of how Tyrell has presumptuously, if not blasphemously, assumed the role of God. But if Tyrell becomes God, then by the same analogy Batty and all replicants are equated to humans. Thus the single opening sentence in their dialogue calls attention to Batty's connections to humanity. Moreover, the rich imagery he invokes to describe the memories of his lifetime, "c-beams glittering near the Tanhauser gate [and] attack ships on fire off the shoulder of Orion," makes his life seem not only human but extraordinary.

Of course, as Francavilla notes, Batty's rescue of Deckard, who is dangling helplessly from the rooftop, represents the strongest expression of Batty's human identification (Francavilla, 11). In fact, his compassion toward an enemy who has just murdered a loved one is not simply human, it is saintly. But at the same time the rescue also serves Batty's own purposes by compelling Deckard, the Blade Runner, to acknowledge that replicants are not subhuman; they have it in themselves to be as good as the best people. Therefore they should not be hunted down like wild beasts, programmed with unnecessarily short life spans, or used as slaves. That Batty's lesson was effective and that Deckard now recognizes the replicants' essential humanity are implied by his subsequent decision to save Rachael and begin life anew with her.

Finally, the white dove that Batty releases as he dies suggests that Batty is giving up his spirit. That he has a spirit to surrender underscores that he is a living entity and not simply a machine. Moreover, in Christian symbolism, the white dove is associated with the Holy Ghost, and Batty's connection to the divine spirit is the most compelling acknowledgment of his fundamental humanity. Though the point is not explicitly made, the logical inference is that Christ died for Batty's sins too, sins that Batty had earlier confessed to his Maker, Tyrell.

But if Batty expires as a candidate for Christian salvation, he also dies a mass murderer, and his newly developed humanity does not excuse him from answering for his crimes. Ultimately, it is for this reason, and not because he is a replicant, that Batty's death remains a fitting ending to the plot. However justified from the replicants' point of view, the story cannot conclude with a murderer on the loose. Such an ending would offend both the viewers' moral sensibilities and their narrative expectations. After all, *Blade Runner* remains a detective story whose formula requires that criminals be punished in the end, regardless of how corrupt or morally twisted the society against which they rebel may be. So, even though we may sympathize with Batty and begin to understand the perpetual terror experienced by those deemed subhuman, in Scott's moral universe victimization does not legitimize murder. And so, both the story's moral and narrative requirements hold Batty accountable. (Scott returns to this issue in *Thelma & Louise*.)

Even though they remain accountable, we sense throughout the film that both Deckard and Batty are playing out roles to which they have been consigned and that neither is solely responsible for the murders he commits. Our sympathy for the replicants' plight and our growing acceptance of them as humans provoke us to look for the original sin that created in Batty the need to become a criminal, or for Deckard to become an assassin, in order for them to live freely as humans.

The original sin proves to be the corporate decision to institute an updated version of slavery. By developing emotionless humanoids to serve as slaves (the equivalent of giving lobotomies to existing people and rendering them emotionless), Tyrell reduces human life to mere property. Until Deckard's compassion for Rachael changes him, he too shares this perception. When he first arrives at Tyrell Corporation, he says that he regards replicants "like any other machine. They're either a benefit or a hazard. If they're a benefit, it's not my problem." Once this view of the replicants becomes institutionalized, the showdown between Batty and Deckard becomes inevitable.

Tyrell also exhibits *hubris*, the tragic flaw in Greek tragedy, when he arrogantly overestimates his own powers. Like Dr. Frankenstein, to whom he has been compared, Tyrell believes that his scientific genius can enable him to maintain complete control over the creation to which he has given life. This intellectual pride blinds him to the possibility that the highly advanced Nexus 6 replicants might spontaneously develop emotions sooner than he predicted. As in classical tragedy, Tyrell has his moment of recognition when Batty confronts him. But even then his arrogance does not diminish, and instead of showing some sympathy for Batty as a suffering person facing death, he continues to regard Batty only as his most brilliant creation. The price Tyrell pays for his self-centered arrogance is his life.

Blade Runner thus reveals Scott's emerging preoccupation with sustaining a healthy spirit in a world that is increasingly driven by corporate capitalists who use technology, mass media, and police state tactics to maintain power. Remaining attuned to our fundamental humanity requires us to conduct ourselves morally, in ways that respect the lives of others, regardless of the political and economic forces that encourage other behaviors. It further requires us to nurture our anima, as well as our animus, to be attuned to our feelings, feel compassion for others, and remain connected to nature.

NOTES

1. William Kolb details the numerous changes the Director's Cut underwent prior to its premiere ("Reconstructing the Director's Cut"). Kolb also provides an extensive, annotated bibliography ("Bibliography"). In *Future Noir* Sammon describes Scott's differences with the studio and questions Scott about them in an interview (202–15, 386–87). Sammon also lists additional releases since the Director's Cut (*Future Noir*, 369–70, 396–408). In general, *Future Noir* provides a detailed account of the production history of the film, including evolutions in the script and changes made in response to early screenings. It also contains a short bibliography.

2. The film's audio and visual components also communicate Scott's vision of a twenty-first century in which people on earth will be dwarfed by their man-made environment and the institutions that created it. In most scenes, the sets dominate the people, filling the majority of the screen. Interior scenes are frequently shot with a wide-angle lens that gives less prominence to the characters in the middle. The high ceilings and intruding props further reduce them in our visual experience. The panoramic exteriors diminish the individual to virtual insignificance. The opening shot makes the city seem alive and volatile; a dramatic panorama shows fire exploding from smokestacks, as hovercraft cruise through the canyons between office towers. This is apparently an era of abundant energy and high technology, as lights shine brightly from countless sources throughout the vast cityscape, and huge billboards flash advertisements. The airborne camera approaches the Tyrell building from below, causing the corporate headquarters to fill our field of vision and thereby appear immense. The first voice we hear comes not from a human but from a loudspeaker, and throughout the film loudspeakers literally give police and corporations a "large voice" capable of

drowning out people. Thus architecture and electronic sound amplification appear in the film as means by which the corporate police state exercises power.

By contrast, the first human we see, Holden the interrogator, stands alone in a smoky, empty room that dwarfs him. When Leon enters, he is shown alone, and throughout the scene, until Leon shoots Holden, the men appear in separate frames. Visually, they are isolated from each other, a technique that hints at the emotional isolation that pervades the film. On the other hand, the street scenes are packed with people. But instead of creating a sense of community, these shots make individuals appear insignificant. (Deckard's willingness to shoot into a crowd while chasing Zhora reiterates the point.) Moreover, even the teeming masses are small in comparison to the buildings surrounding them. The cumulative effect of these audio and visual techniques is to bypass the viewers' cognitive thought processes and communicate by direct sensory experience how, in the near future, individuals will be dominated by their artificial environment.

3. See Carl Jung, "Aion: Phenomenology of the Self (The Ego, the Shadow, the *Syzgy*: Anima/Animus)," in *The Portable Carl Jung*, ed. Joseph Campbell (New York: Viking, 1971), 139–62.

Although a large electronic image of an attractive Asian woman selling Coca Cola looks down upon the city, the only living women we see for any extended time in this futuristic city are replicants: Zhora, Pris, and Rachael. They and the robots that populate Sebastian's apartment are also the most colorful and animated beings in the film. Visually, the physical absence of women communicates through direct sensory experience the repression of the anima in the futuristic police state.

4. The moral context of the film becomes somewhat more complicated when we consider the possibility maintained by Scott, but not Harrison Ford or producer Michael Deeley, that Deckard too is a replicant (Sammon, *Future Noir*, 359–64, 376–77). This possibility gives special significance to the unicorn origami that Gaff leaves in Deckard's apartment at the end, suggesting that like Deckard, who read the file and knows Rachael's dreams, Gaff has read Deckard's file and knows his dreams. Such an interpretation also accounts for Deckard's preoccupation with photographs, something shared by Leon and Rachael, and for the way his eyes glow in one of his scenes with Rachael. Reading the film in this way also lends considerable irony to the ending, as Deckard realizes his life is an illusion. Moreover, it makes the police state appear even more pernicious for having manipulated the protagonist throughout, so that he turns against his own kind. But, as Sammon observes, regarding Deckard as a replicant also has potential drawbacks. Audiences will quickly cease to identify with Deckard once they regard him as an android and then lose interest in his story. "What's the point of Deckard's spiritual awakening, they will ask, if *Blade Runner*'s android hunter turns out to be an android himself?" (Sammon, *Future Noir*, 360). Ultimately, the audience's failure to identify with Deckard if he is a replicant would undermine the main theme of the movie, which is to empathize with the Other.

In either case, the film's fundamental point about the need for connection to the anima remains the same. Whether Deckard is a replicant who spontaneously develops his anima by learning compassion and empathy, or whether he is a human who had repressed those qualities but regained them in his confrontation with his *Doppelgänger*, the fact remains that he achieves wholeness of spirit as a result of his experiences, and that spirit constitutes the true essence of humanity.

5. Perhaps because Scott introduces this Aryan element into the story, he names the corporate head Tyrell instead of Rosen, the Jewish-sounding surname of the manufacturer in the book.

Legend

(1985)

CAST

Jack	Tom Cruise
Princess Lili	Mia Sara
Lord of Darkness	Tim Curry
Gump	David Bennent
Blix	Alice Playten
Screwball	Bill Barty
Oona	Annabelle Lanyon
Meg Mucklebones	Robert Picardo
Brown Tom	Cork Hubbert
Nell	Tina Martin
Pox	Peter O'Farrell
Blunder	Kiran Shah

PRODUCTION

Director	Ridley Scott
Producer	Arnon Milchan (a 20th Century Fox release of a Legend Production; re-

leased in the United States by Universal Pictures)

Screenplay	William Hjortsberg
Director of photography	Alex Thomson
Editor	Terry Rawlings
Music director	Jerry Goldsmith
Production design	Assheton Gorton
Costumes	Charles Knode
Special effects	Nick Allder
Special make-up supervisor	Rob Bottin
Choreography	Arlene Phillips

SYNOPSIS

Legend attempts to relate the archetypal struggle between good and evil. A written introduction states that before time existed, the world was shrouded in darkness. But with the appearance of light, life and love entered the universe and the Lord of Darkness retreated deep into the shadows of the earth, where he plotted to obliterate light and regain his power. His efforts have been thwarted by unicorns who protect light and, because they know only love and laughter, are immune to the Lord of Darkness's evil machinations. Unicorns can be touched only by the purest of mortals, such as Jack, a young man who lives alone in the forest with the animals. Jack loves Lili, a beautiful princess, but in their innocence they believe that only goodness exists. However, their experiences teach them that the universe depends on eternal balance, that good needs evil, love needs hate, and light needs dark. The introduction concludes with the declaration that legends result from the struggle to maintain the balance between these opposites.

The film opens with a shot of a forest bathed in white light. However, the soothing sights and sounds of nature are interrupted by the footsteps of the goblin Blix, who approaches a dead swamp. Across the wasteland is a barren mountain that houses the underground kingdom of the Lord of Darkness. Patterned after conventional images of Hell, the underworld is filled with demons torturing their human captives as their leader looks on. But Darkness is not content. He complains to Mother Night that he is an impotent exile tormented by an unsettling force in the forest that he had almost forgotten. This force is the power protected by the unicorns, which is so potent that anyone possessing it could rule the universe. Ordering Blix to kill the unicorns and bring him their horns, Darkness advises his henchman to take advantage of innocence in order to fulfill his task.

The camera cuts to Lili walking through a field of brightly colored flowers on her way to a cabin in the forest where she visits Nell, a nurturing maternal figure who lives a simple but good life. Nell tells Lili she should not waste her time visiting poor people in the woods, but Lili replies, "This place holds more magic for me than any palace in the world." Nonetheless, Lili cuts her visit short to return to the forest, where she seeks Jack.

Unbeknownst to them, goblins watch as Jack jumps down from a tree to surprise her. They kiss and lie down together, although there is no suggestion of lovemaking. Jack teaches Lili to talk to the birds and then promises to show her something special: the unicorns frolicking. "Nothing is more magical," he tells her. "As long as they roam the earth, evil can never harm the pure of heart. . . . They express only love and laughter. Thoughts are unknown to them."

Over Jack's objections, Lili walks up to the unicorns and pets the male. As she does, a goblin shoots him. Lili returns to Jack and tells him touching the beast was lovely, like a dream, but Jack insists the act was forbidden and she risked her immortal soul.

As the goblins chase the unicorns in another part of the forest, Lili tries to make up with Jack, who she says is as dear as life to her. She removes her ring and vows to marry whoever finds it. But she inadvertently tosses it over a cliff and into the river below. Jack dives after it, but as he does the sky darkens, winter comes on, the unicorn weakens, and Lili calls out desperately. Lightning strikes and the wounded male unicorn falls to the ground. At the same time, the river freezes over Jack, who breaks through the ice just as the goblin cuts off the unicorn's horn.

Jack calls out to Lili but she has run back through the sudden blizzard to Nell's cottage, where she discovers Nell dead and the house trashed. She hides as the goblins gloat over how Lili enabled them to kill the unicorn, and they brag about how they would like to eat her brains and suck her bones. After they ride off, Lili vows to make right the unintentional evil she has committed.

In another part of the woods forest sprites find Jack asleep. Gump, their leader, demands an explanation from him of what has happened, and he admits taking Lili to see the unicorn. "Do you think you can upset the order of the universe and not pay the price?" Gump demands. But when Jack says he did it for love, Gump is appeased, and the sprites toast Jack, a "loving fool and fairy friend." Nonetheless, after they find the fallen unicorn, Gump declares that they are cursed and doomed to stay in darkness unless they reclaim its horn. To achieve this, they need a champion bold of heart and pure of spirit. Gump nominates Jack, who protests that he knows nothing of weapons. But Gump says he can learn, and that they have access to the best weapons.

Oona, a Tinkerbell-like spirit who usually appears as a point of light, leads Jack to a trove of golden armor and swords. Oona then assumes a girl's form and tells him that she can be anything he wants her to be, "even your heart's desire."

The camera cuts to Lili, who stumbles upon a goblin gloating over the magic horn. He declares that he will make himself ruler of the universe, but he squanders his power on cheap tricks, like building a bonfire. The Lord of Darkness appears and takes the horn from him. Darkness then learns that only the male unicorn has been killed. The goblins say that the female has no power, put Darkness retorts that she has the power of creation and commands the goblins to kill her too, for as long as she lives his power will not be complete. The rising sun at dawn is testimony to this.

After they leave, Lili continues wandering through the forest until she stumbles upon one of the forest sprites, Brown Tom, and the female unicorn. She begs forgiveness and then warns that the goblins will soon be coming. When they arrive, Brown Tom tries to hold them off while Lili and the unicorn escape, but the goblins shoot him in the head and capture Lili and the mare.

After they depart, the forest sprites return and discover Brown Tom, who has only been knocked out. They go to a barren, swamp-like place where the wicked once went to sacrifice. Goblins attack them, but are defeated due to Jack's heroics. The group then stumbles into a cave that leads to a prison inside the palace where Lili and the mare are incarcerated in a separate dungeon. Oona offers to help them, if Jack will kiss her passionately, but he cannot make himself do this. Oona leaves angrily but then returns and frees them, and they make their way through fire and fog in search of the dungeon.

Darkness confesses to his father that Lili troubles and fascinates him. He is told that this is because her soul is pure, but that Darkness can win her over by charming her, hypnotizing her, and changing her spirit. Subsequently, Darkness tempts Lili with a glimmering diamond necklace. He dances up to her, and although she initially resists, she finally dances with him and reaches out to him. After she does, she becomes clothed in a black gown like his. But as Darkness beckons her to him, Lili collapses. He goes to possess her, but she runs away. As she flees, he declares she will be his, that "beneath the skin we are already one. . . . Even now the evil seed of what you've done germinates within you." In reply, Lili calls him an animal, but Darkness counters that we are all animals. He then vows that the remaining unicorn will die tonight and there will never be another dawn.

Jack and the sprites fight and defeat more goblins, and Gump hails Jack as their champion. Meanwhile, Darkness proposes to Lili, offering his heart, soul, and love, but he becomes infuriated after she rejects his offer of food, and he chases her. Finally, Lili says she will marry him, if he will let her slay the unicorn. Darkness is delighted by the proposal.

Jack and Gump arrive at the room where the unicorn is chained, and they are prepared to shoot Lili with an arrow to prevent her from killing the mare. But at the last minute Jack refuses to shoot because he still trusts Lili. His instinct proves correct, as Lili, at the last instant, smashes the chain and frees the animal instead of killing it. Jack then swings down and fights the Lord of Darkness. Jack seems overpowered, but he manages to seize the horn that Blix had cut from the male. He throws it into the heart of Darkness, who vanishes in an explosion of light. As he disappears, he declares that he is part of them all.

"What is light without dark. . . . You can never defeat me. We are brothers eternal."

However, Lili has fallen into a deep sleep. She remains unconscious until Jack returns to the river where she had cast her ring and retrieves it. She awakens as he kisses her and places it on her hand. Meanwhile, Gump affixes the severed horn to the male unicorn, who springs back to life. As he does, springtime returns and the sun rises. As Jack and Lili kiss, they watch the unicorns run off together and then wave farewell to Gump and the other forest spirits who go off with them. The final shot, however, shows the Lord of Darkness laughing.

RECEPTION

Like *Blade Runner* that preceded it, *Legend* was poorly received upon its initial release but has since attracted a following. The film closed in American theaters after just a week or two, and in Europe it did not fare better. It grossed only $15.5 million. Vincent Canby of the *New York Times* dismissed the film as "fluff"—both literally, in reference to the excessive number of dandelions and cherry blossoms that fill the air, and in terms of the movie's content. He called the story confusing and dismissed the mythology as a "slap-dash amalgam of Old Testament, King Arthur, *The Lord of the Rings*, and any number of comic books." *Variety* was somewhat more generous. Its reviewer praised the visuals, especially the Lord of Darkness, who is "the most impressive depiction of Satan ever brought to the screen." But the reviewer dismissed the premise as "alarmingly thin" and criticized the "rather insipid hero, as played by Tom Cruise." However, the performances by David Bennent (Gump) and Annabelle Lanyon (Oona) received praise (Sammon, *Ridley Scott*, 138–140).

Since its re-release for the home video market, *Legend* has attracted something of a cult following, and Scott is now reportedly considering reissuing a Director's Cut that would restore his original, bleaker intention and the full, original musical score (Sammon, *Ridley Scott*, 85).

DISCUSSION

Like *Blade Runner*, the final cut of *Legend* does not represent Scott's actual artistic intention, which would have presented the much darker, more paradoxical vision that is suggested by the prologue. In that view, the symbiotic relationship between good and evil would have been brought out; whereas in the final cut good and evil remain polar opposites. Scott originally conceived scenes showing Lili's actual seduction by Darkness and her subsequent transformation into a creature half-woman, half-cat because, "despite how she comes across now in *Legend*, which is innocence personified, Lili was nevertheless conceived as being very manipulative. . . . I'd always felt it was Lili's manipulative streak that let her be seduced to the side of evil" (Sammon, *Ridley Scott*, 78). However, following dismal reactions from preview audiences, Scott re-edited the film and cut it from 113 minutes to eighty-nine in the American release and ninety-four in the European version, which was longer because he felt European viewers would better appreciate what he was trying to achieve.[1] Scott also allowed himself to be persuaded to replace Jerry Goldsmith's original romantic score in the American release (but not the European) with a New Age version by the German group Tangerine Dream, because the producers at Universal feared audiences would find Goldsmith's music too sweet.

In retrospect Scott regrets the changes, which he attributes finally to his "crisis of confidence" following the disappointing reception of *Blade Runner*. "I cut a lot of interesting stuff . . . that I'm now sorry is gone. Basically, I got afraid of the film's rather ingenious fairy-story emotion." Scott still prefers the original score and its darker conception. Moreover, as the European version was also poorly received, he believes "all the re-editing and score changes were really for nothing." He also regrets the bad feeling that resulted between himself and Goldsmith, who "had given me exactly what I asked for," and that *Legend* was ignored by the Academy Awards, despite his belief that the film is "a masterful piece of scenic design" (Sammon, *Ridley Scott*, 83–84).

Scott, who had previously begun an unfinished treatment of the Tristan and Isolde legend, began the project because he wanted to do a medieval fantasy set outside of any specific place and time: "the type of fantasy that would lie somewhere between Cocteau's *Beauty and the Beast* (1946)—which I love and is truly esoteric—and the Hollywood version of *A Midsummer Night's Dream* (1935), with James Cagney and Mickey Rooney. I also wanted to make something a little lighter, since my first three films were rather intense and heavy" (Sammon, *Ridley Scott*, 76). After reading William Hjortsberg's story *Symbiography* (1973), he contacted the novelist, and they went to work on a script for a film originally to be called *Legend of Darkness*.

Hjortsberg wrote some fifteen drafts between 1982 and 1984 and drew on myths and legends from numerous cultures. Foremost is the creation myth from Greek mythology, in which the sudden appearance of light dispels the cold, chaotic darkness.[2] This, of course, is mirrored in the Old Testament story of creation that also begins with the introduction of light. *Legend* also draws on Norse and Germanic myths, especially tales about rings of power, such as *The Nibelungenlied*, the source for Richard Wagner's operatic tetralogy, *Der Ring des Nibelungen* (1853–74), and for J.R. Tolkien's *Lord of the Rings* trilogy (1955). Scott maintains that Wagner's *Siegfried* from the ring cycle inspired the forest setting. Gump and the other diminutive forest sprites seem loosely patterned after Tolkien's hobbits and their friends. Persephone's abduction by Hades in Greek mythology appears to be another influence in the script, especially where Lili rejects the food Darkness offers her and spurns his marriage proposals. Unicorns, of course, were popular mythological figures during the Middle Ages and Renaissance. Scott maintains Darkness's physical appearance was predicated on the satanic figure in the "Night on Bald Mountain" segment from Walt Disney's 1940 animated film, *Fantasia* (Sammon, *Ridley Scott*, 79). The final scene where Jack awakens Lili with a kiss evokes the story of *Sleeping Beauty*, and Oona has close connections to Tinkerbell from Disney's *Peter Pan* (1953).

Scott is always at least as concerned with the visual and aural sensibilities he creates as with the story he relates, and this is perhaps more true for *Legend* than for his other movies. Indeed, its greatest appeal comes from his evocation of a mythical, magical place in an indeterminate time. The musical score(s) contribute to this effect, as do the lush, colorful springtime forest; the harsh, monochromatic winter blizzard; the interiors lit by fire; and such props as the necklace Darkness offers Lili, the golden sword Jack acquires, and the black gown that Lili dons, which is reminiscent of that worn by the wicked queen in Disney's *Snow White and the Seven Dwarfs* (1937).

Legend continues the exploration of pure evil that Scott began with *Alien* and that appears in many of his films. However, although his original intent was to show the interconnectedness of good and evil, this aspect of the story is largely absent from the final version, where they appear as polar opposites. As in *Alien*, evil is predominantly concerned with power and domination, as the Lord of Darkness seeks to gain ultimate control over all of creation. His motivation is vague, apart from his being tormented by the presence of the fun-loving unicorns and his general nostalgia for the good old days before "the perfect void of darkness was corrupted by light . . . [and] all the brethren fled in terror."

The interconnectedness of good and evil is more consistent with ancient Greek mythology, Eastern philosophy, and modern notions of a universe built on paradox and complementarity than with Christianity. Scott seems to have intended to treat the theme by playing off the legendary belief that unicorns can be handled only by pure-hearted virgins. Lili and Jack kiss and lie down together in the woods before he reveals the unicorns to her, and although there is no suggestion that they have consummated their passion, their experience of limited sexual pleasure may account in part for why her touch renders the unicorns vulnerable. Nonetheless, the greater reason appears to be Lili's manipulation and other spiritual impurities to which Scott has alluded. But these have been largely cut from the final version.

However, the dance between Lili and Darkness, a dance of good and evil, does underscore the interdependence of sexuality and spirituality. When Lili accuses Darkness of being an animal, he replies that we all are animals. Whereas Jack's attraction to Lili is essentially spiritual, Darkness is motivated by lust. His remark that "even now the evil seed of what you've done germinates within you" evokes an image of Lili pregnant with his essence, and their dance appears to be a symbolic seduction. It thus not only creates emotional tension for concerned viewers, it also makes us especially aware that she is a sexual creature as well as a spiritual one. Like light and darkness, and good and evil, Scott uses these scenes to suggest that spirituality and sexuality are both essential parts of the human psyche.

Scott also makes the point that naive innocence can be exploited for nefarious purposes.[3] Darkness tells Blix that he can kill the unicorns by taking advantage of innocence, and the story does show the harm that follows Lili's well-intended act. She and Jack apologize repeatedly, but even though Gump and the forest sprites forgive them because they acted from love, the peril resulting from her ignorant behavior nonetheless proves almost devastating. On the other hand, because her innocence is never truly compromised, Lili remains sufficiently innocent and pure hearted to rescue the unicorn mare.

Both Jack and Lili evolve somewhat over the course of the story, and their evolution enables them to overcome their innocence to forge a happy ending. Both figures go from being essentially passive and socially disconnected to being active and aware of their responsibilities to the world at large. They also acquire limited self-knowledge. Lili discovers that she can be tempted by material things (the necklace and gown) and by the seductive nature of Darkness's masculine power. Jack, who at the beginning is attuned primarily to his anima—his gentle female side—learns that the capacity for self-defense and even for aggressive action is necessary for survival. Thus he develops his animus—his assertive male aspect—and becomes a warrior and a champion. Lili, too, strengthens her animus as she acts decisively to save the unicorn. Ironically, it is Darkness, himself, who reminds us of the essential nature of the female aspect. When Blix objects that they need not kill the mare because she is powerless, Darkness corrects him, pointing out that she has the power of creation. So, even though the film does little to show the mutual dependence of good and evil, it depicts the interdependence of opposites by suggesting that both Jack and Lili must develop both the assertive male and nurturing female aspects of their personalities.

NOTES

1. Both the European and American versions are currently available on video, along with a 1990 laserdisc that was released in Japan with the Goldsmith score and a running time of ninety-one minutes.

2. In the ancient Greek creation myth, Chaos, a rather indeterminate divinity, ruled over a shapeless, indistinct realm with his black-clad wife Nyx (Night). Their son, Erebus (Darkness), eventually usurped his father and married his mother, thereby inaugurating a theme in Western culture that extends from the Oedipus myth to the Oedipus complex. Paradoxically, the dark union of Erebus and Nyx gave issue to two light-filled offspring, Aether (Light) and Hemera (Day). These children eventually supplanted their parents and bore a child of their own, Eros (Love).

The Lord of Darkness appeals to Mother Night at the beginning of *Legend*. She is also a major figure in Mozart's opera about purity and innocence, *The Magic Flute* (1791).

3. John Barth explores the dangers of innocence at length in his novel, *The Sot-Weed Factor* (New York: Doubleday, 1960).

Someone to Watch over Me

(1987)

CAST

Mike Keegan	Tom Berenger
Claire Gregory	Mimi Rogers
Ellie Keegan	Lorraine Bracco
Lt. Garber	Jerry Orbach
Neil Steinhart	John Rubinstein
Joey Venza	Andreas Katsulas
T.J.	Tony DiBenedetto
Koontz	James Moriarty
Win Hockings	Mark Moses
Scotty	Daniel Hugh Kelly
Tommy	Harley Cross

PRODUCTION

Director	Ridley Scott
Producers	Thierry de Ganay and Harold Schneider (a Columbia Pictures release of a Thierry de Ganay production)

Screenplay   Howard Franklin
Director of photography   Steven Poster
Production design   Jim Bissell
Set decoration   Linda de Scenna
Costume design   Colleen Atwood
Music director   Michael Kamen
Editor   Claire Simpson

SYNOPSIS

Someone to Watch over Me tells the story of Mike Keegan, a New York police-man and dedicated husband and father whose first assignment as a detective compels him to choose between his family and a wealthy murder witness with whom he unexpectedly falls in love. The story begins in a working-class neighborhood in Queens where Mike, his wife Ellie, and his friends are celebrating his promotion to detective and assignment to a posh, upper Manhattan district. The next scene shows another party, with elegantly dressed men and women chatting among strobe lights in the expansive, richly furnished home of Win Hockings. Win greets Claire with an exaggerated kiss. His longtime friend (and perhaps former lover), Claire introduces him to her wealthy boyfriend, whom Win privately calls "constipated." She defends Neil as dependable—unlike Win. Later, Claire chances upon Win arguing downstairs with gangster Joey Venza; then she sees Venza kill her friend. When she shrieks in horror, Venza spies her, but she escapes and becomes an eyewitness for the police. Mike's first assignment is to protect Claire until she can officially identify the murderer.

Lt. Garber, Mike's boss, tells him that Claire is in considerable danger. But because they do not want her to become fearful and refuse to testify, they assure her that the risk is minimal. Mike is uncomfortable with the duplicity but complies with his orders. However, because of his role in the deception, his sense of responsibility for Claire's safety and his guilt over the betrayal eventually intensify and leave him emotionally vulnerable.

When Mike, as junior detective, is assigned to the late night shift, Ellie is supportive and understanding. After all, as the daughter of a cop, she became a cop, married a cop, and believes their son Tommy will probably become a cop too. But over time, Ellie becomes lonely, feels vulnerable in their high-crime neighborhood, and comes to resent Mike's time away from home and his growing devotion to Claire.

Mike's first day on the job accentuates the difference in social class between Claire and her bodyguards, who are awed by the fancy apartment. Mike overhears Neil telling Claire not to risk her life by testifying, but she insists that she must—after all, she witnessed someone murder one of her friends. She cannot do nothing and just live with it. However, the next evening Claire asks Mike to reassure her, which he does despite his own reservations. These assurances make it difficult to justify extraordinary security measures, so Mike agrees to accompany Claire to a reception at the Guggenheim museum. Although Ellie likes the way Mike dresses, Claire finds his attire unsuitable for the occasion and stops off to buy him a dressy tie on the way. After they arrive, the other guests speculate about the man accompanying Claire while Neil is out of town, and a wealthy woman brazenly comes on to Mike, who politely deflects her coarse inquiries about whether his job makes him "hard." Claire convinces Mike not to accompany her into the ladies' room, even though standard procedure insists that he should. While she is in the commode, Venza enters and threatens to have her painfully killed if she identifies him in a police lineup. Mike spots Venza leaving the ladies' room and runs in to find Claire bruised and shaken but unharmed. He chases Venza to the street, where the criminal walks up to a uniformed policeman and surrenders.

That night Mike confides to Ellie that by not being straight with Claire, Lt. Garber has endangered her, but Ellie passionately insists that the only way to stop crime is to refuse to be intimidated by criminals. She admires Claire's insistence on testifying and proclaims that in the same situation she would too, but Mike says he might stop her. He adds that Claire seems like a nice person, and he worries that he might be setting her up to be killed. Ellie becomes a little jealous when she learns that Claire had taken Mike to a ritzy party and bought him a tie; however, their disagreement quickly dissipates and their mutual affection prevails. As with Neil and Claire previously, their argument about Claire's testimony apparently concludes with Mike and Ellie making love, as they go upstairs to check out the bedroom of a house they might buy.

On the night before Claire is due to identify Venza in a police lineup—presumably their last night together—she invites Mike out for cocktails. They have fun walking along the street while the police back-up watches enviously from a squad car. Over drinks, while the band plays "Someone to Watch over Me," Mike tells Claire how he fell in love with Ellie at first sight. He then asks Claire about Neil and tells her she could do better. She defends her boyfriend, but not too energetically, and they agree that they have enjoyed knowing each other. When they finally say good night back at her apartment there is a romantic spark, but neither acts upon it. Instead, Claire enters her bedroom alone and finds Neil waiting for her, upset because it is 3 A.M. and she has been gone.

The next day Mike escorts Claire to the police lineup; she identifies Venza, and the assignment seemingly concludes. Mike returns home, where he and Ellie are preparing to take Tommy to a ballgame. However, a phone call informs Mikes that Venza is out of prison on a legal technicality. At this point, Ellie feels the assignment has begun to harm their family and she tells Mike to take himself off of it, but Mike argues that he feels that Claire is his responsibility.

Mike returns that night for his shift at Claire's apartment. Claire feels angry and betrayed and accuses Mike of knowing all along that he could not protect her. He restrains her from leaving the apartment in anger, and she breaks down and cries. Claire accuses him, saying that she thought he cared for her, and he assures her that he does. They embrace and kiss, and then the camera cuts to Ellie alone in bed. Hearing a noise, she gets up to investigate. Their son Tommy hears it and is scared too. Then we see Mike leaving Claire's bed at the end of his shift. He returns home to find two policemen in the kitchen, reassuring Ellie. Mike reiterates an earlier opinion that Ellie and Tommy should stay with his mother until the case concludes, but Ellie is adamant about not living with her mother-in-law and insists that she can take care of herself. Later, however, she takes offense when Mike criticizes her for cursing, something she has done ever since they have been married, and she expresses renewed jealousy of Claire.

That night, Mike speaks to Claire in her bedroom and tells her that it was a mistake for them to sleep together. She agrees, but T.J. sees him leave the room. Mike tells his friend, "I'm all messed up." Back at home, Ellie insists that Mike change his assignment. She does not fault him, but she says he must recognize that it is not working. They go to dinner at a favorite restaurant, and Mike becomes angered when Ellie tells him she has asked his boss's wife to speak to her husband about changing Mike's assignment. The ensuing argument leads to Ellie's discovery of Mike's affair with Claire. Declaring that she has behaved like "the kind of lady you apparently prefer," Ellie checks her temper but commands Mike not to return unless he is coming back for her—not for their son or his mother or his job, but for her.

As T.J. enters the building to begin the night shift to which he has now been assigned, an assassin sneaks in with him. Subsequently, Mike, now off duty and expelled by Ellie, returns to Claire's apartment. Alone in her bedroom, he tells her he does not know what he wants to do, that he is tired. As T.J. guards them from outside, Claire watches over Mike while he sleeps. Later, he holds her as she sleeps beside him. Meanwhile, the assassin enters the apartment and, using a pistol with a silencer, shoots T.J. in the head. Mike senses something is amiss, hunts down the assassin, and kills him in a shootout. He then discovers T.J., who is rushed to a hospital. In the waiting room, Garber suspends Mike and orders him not to see Claire again until the case is closed. Ellie subsequently orders him to move out of their house. At the same time, Claire breaks up with Neil.

Mike moves in with a divorced friend who sings the praises of unmarried life. Claire then phones. After receiving assurances that T.J. will live, Claire invites Mike to a reception in Queens but tells him she will be leaving the country afterward. Mike answers that it would not be very smart for him to go, and Claire understands. But then he says he might show up.

Mike visits Tommy, who tells him that he and Ellie have been going to the shooting range. The camera shows Venza watching them from his car.

Mike appears at the reception after all and tells Claire that things would not work out between them; he misses his wife too much. She says he need not explain and that she is going away to forget about him. Then Mike receives an urgent phone call and learns that Venza is at his house, holding Ellie and Tommy hostage. Mike tells Claire that Venza wants Claire in exchange for his family. Her police escorts do not want her to go, but Claire leaps into Mike's car and insists he take her with him. He agrees, but only if she remains out of sight.

Venza insists on hearing Claire's voice and then takes Mike as his hostage in exchange for Tommy, who hides under the kitchen table. As a police officer borrows Claire's cloak, places the hood over his head, and enters the building to appease Venza's demand to see her, Tommy notices the pistol that Ellie has hidden beneath the table top. Seeing this, too, Ellie suddenly overturns the table, grabs the pistol, and shoots Venza as Mike rolls aside. Shortly afterward, Claire enters the room to see Mike and his wife embracing, and she leaves silently. Mike tells Ellie that he loves her and wants to come home; she says she loves him too. Claire departs in a police car after exchanging a final glance with Mike.

RECEPTION

Someone to Watch over Me was not well received, either critically or at the box office. It grossed only $10 million during the year of its release. In part, the film fell victim to a change in management at Columbia Pictures. The new studio heads were unenthusiastic about the movie, and they released it with minimal publicity. Moreover, fans of Scott's earlier science fiction/fantasy films were disappointed at the realistic story. Similarly, although the sets in *Someone* are often exquisite, the film lacks the massive scale, imaginative costumes, and expressionist designs characteristic of *Alien, Blade Runner,* and *Legend.* Therefore, many viewers who arrived expecting another visual extravaganza from Scott left disappointed.

The critics were lukewarm at best. *Variety* praised the acting and the sets but criticized the plot for the ease with which Mike cheats on his wife and for the improbable ending: "Though suspenseful and well-staged, the violation of police procedure is incredible and unconvincing" (Sammon, *Ridley Scott,* 141). The *New York Times*'s Vincent Canby also rejected the ending as absurd. He criticized the "comparatively easy-to-achieve effects that pass for style—smoky interiors often lighted from below, lots of reflecting surfaces . . . [and] a music track that contrasts cocktail-piano pop and high-toned classical tidbits." In short, Canby concluded that "beneath its elegant mask, *Someone to Watch over Me* is a common-place melodrama."

DISCUSSION

The movie holds up better than the reviews suggest. While the audience is required to exercise some willing suspension of disbelief, the characters' motivations are better developed than in many of Scott's films, and the plot is more tightly scripted. Moreover, the ending reaches a climax that brings about a satisfying emotional release, as it endorses working-class values and personal responsibility.

The story revolves around Mike's need to choose between Ellie and Claire. That choice, in turn, is driven by the danger to Claire's life posed by Venza, and the resolution of Mike's personal conflict coincides with the termination of Venza's threat. As each of the plot lines develops, the contrasts between Ellie and Claire become more pronounced, and we become more aware of the differences in the attraction that each holds for Mike. Therefore, the emotional release caused by this double climax is informed by an unstated set of priorities that finally endorses traditional values, such as family, friendship, integrity, personal responsibility, and the importance of sustaining enduring relationships.

Unlike many other stories in which the protagonist must choose between potential partners, the decision between Ellie and Claire does not reduce down to good and bad choices. In fact, both women are attractive characters. Both seem to love Mike but in different ways, care for his well-being, appreciate his playfulness, and value what he stands for as a person. Both live according to their convictions about what they believe to be right. They even respect each other. Ellie expresses her admiration not only of Claire's beauty but also of Claire's determination to testify against Venza. And despite her lapses, Claire recognizes that Mike belongs with his wife. Claire therefore not only makes plans to leave the country so she will not be tempted by him, but she ultimately risks her life to save Ellie and Tommy. In fact, the plot culminates only after both women perform acts that save their rival, along with saving themselves. By shedding her police escort and going with Mike to confront Venza, Claire helps rescue Ellie and Tommy. By shooting Venza, Ellie preserves her family and simultaneously eliminates the threat to Claire's life. Ironically, Mike, who begins the movie as the most assertive of the three, and the most in control, concludes the action as a passive figure, Venza's hostage. Venza dies and the plot is resolved only because both Claire and Ellie have the personal strength and integrity to act as they feel they must.

Because Mike tells Claire before the hostage crisis that he wants to go back to Ellie, her insistence on helping him save Ellie appears especially noble. We sense that she feels some responsibility for Ellie's predicament and wants to rectify the damage their affair has caused. Her willingness to risk her life for Ellie redeems her in our eyes. Moreover, Mike's declaration that he misses his wife proves to us that his ultimate choice of Ellie is not just an expression of gratitude and relief at the conclusion of a highly emotional crisis. Thus, as in *Casablanca* (1942), for instance, the final scene allows us to feel good for all three figures in the love triangle.

The plot develops in three stages: the first creates the circumstances that lead Mike, a committed family man, to choose between his wife and the woman for whose life he is responsible; the second creates uncertainty about both which woman he will choose and his ability to protect Claire; the third resolves the uncertainty. The initial section introduces the need for accepting responsibility, as Claire insists upon testifying, Ellie accepts her role as a detective's wife, and Mike assumes first professional and then personal responsibility for

Claire's life. The section further establishes a conflict between Mike's professional duty and his personal responsibility since, by obeying Garber's order to deceive Claire about the magnitude of the threat, Mike feels he has put her life at risk. Consequently, with each new deception he feels increasingly responsible for her safety. This, in turn, causes him to identify more fully with his role as guardian. This role is different from his role as husband to Ellie, who is self-sufficient and a trained police officer capable of protecting herself. Part of Claire's allure is that she seems more feminine and in greater need of protection. Claire, in turn, expresses to Win her need for someone dependable who can give her a sense of security, and as her bodyguard under extraordinary circumstances, Mike fills that role. He also offers the warmth that Neil lacks (a lady at the Guggenheim reception comments on the kindness of Mike's eyes), and his playfulness reinvigorates a spirit of fun and whimsy that Claire has seemingly repressed.

Ellie, on the other hand, expresses insecurity about her looks even before Mike is assigned to the case, complaining that her buttocks are falling. After seeing Claire's picture in the paper, and hearing Mike say Claire is even more beautiful than that, Ellie literally lays claim to her man, grabbing his cheek with hands dirty from car repair and marking her possession. (Venza similarly marks Claire when he roughly pinches her cheek in the ladies' room.) Though this and other incidents in this section are handled with humor, they indicate that Ellie is both jealous and protective of what she believes is hers. These scenes also underscore the differences between Ellie's more masculine working-class environment, in which she dresses in work clothes, fixes cars, and shoots guns, and Claire's world of wealth, which is softer and more feminine. At the same time, Ellie is a mother preoccupied with domestic and maternal matters, while Claire, unburdened by such distractions, is free to develop exotic interests.

The first section concludes with a return to harmony and order after Claire identifies Venza. The night before, as Mike and Claire share details of their lives with each other, their suppressed attraction becomes mutually apparent, even though it remains unspoken. Both implicitly understand that it would be inappropriate and pointless to act on the attraction. Instead, Mike returns to Ellie and Claire to Neil, who is also possessive but does not share with Claire the bonds of commitment that Ellie has with Mike. Neil's outburst turns us further against him—he has already insulted Mike and the other policemen. By contrast, we feel Mike and Claire have acted responsibly by not compromising either his marriage vows or his professionalism as an on-duty detective. As the section concludes, the threat from Venza has seemingly been resolved; Mike has returned to his family, and, except for a desirable rift between Claire and Neil, all are prepared to resume their lives as they had been before the murder.

According to Scott, one of the things that most attracted him to Franklin's screenplay was that Mike and Claire "are suddenly thrown together into a high-pressure situation which knocks their internal compasses off" (Sammon,

Ridley Scott, 88). The second section destabilizes their internal compasses and introduces uncertainty about the fates of Claire's life and Mike's marriage.

Venza's release on a legal technicality creates the plot reversal that violates the protagonists' sense of restored harmony and order. The phone call announcing this news provokes the first rift between Mike and Ellie that is not quickly mended with humor and affection. Ellie perceives that Mike's assignment is somehow threatening her marriage, and she reacts defensively, insisting that he demand to be reassigned.

But if protecting their marriage is foremost in Ellie's mind, protecting Claire becomes Mike's obsession. Because he feels he has betrayed Claire by understating her danger, and has thereby jeopardized her life, Mike's feeling of impersonal, professional responsibility for Claire's safety transforms into deeply felt, personal guilt. Seeing Claire consumed by pain and anger intensifies the guilt, and it seems that he wants to eradicate her pain as much to alleviate his unbearable guilt as to comfort her. For her part, Claire feels physically vulnerable and wants to feel safe and protected. Thus, the combination of her need to be reassured and cared for and his need to end her pain and squelch his guilt by making her feel secure again creates the unstable high-pressure situation that sends their internal compasses going every which way and makes their mutual attraction irresistible.

The instabilities mount as long as Mike remains torn between the two women, and the characters' fortunes plummet. First Ellie figures out that Mike and Claire are having an affair and orders him from their home. Then a would-be assassin nearly kills T.J., who has taken over the night shift at Ellie's prior insistence. As a result Mike assumes an additional burden of guilt. Any satisfaction he might have taken from successfully protecting Claire is negated by his concern for T.J. and his suspension and demotion from the position he so prized. Moreover, Garber forbids him to see Claire again until the case is closed. The lives of Claire and Ellie have also undergone upheaval. Claire now lives with the knowledge that despite police protection a killer has entered her apartment. Ellie, now a single mother, also fears for her personal safety and begins practicing her shooting skills and teaching them to Tommy.

After Mike and Claire independently conclude that Mike should be with Ellie, the plot reverses again, producing the climax that restores love, harmony, stability, and self-respect to the protagonists' lives. Ellie has already insisted that she will accept Mike back only if he returns for her—and not for Tommy, his job, his mother, or any other reason. When Mike violates Garber's order and attends the reception in Queens, he has already decided to return to his wife and uses the occasion to inform Claire. She, in turn, has already made arrangements to leave the country in order to terminate their affair. Having decided to do what is right not only because conventional morality dictates it but because they each recognize that Ellie really is Mike's greater love, both Mike and Claire enter the climax with greater insight into themselves and each other. And although they can never regain moral innocence, their voluntary renunciation of their love affair confers a degree of absolution that makes a happy ending possible.

When Venza takes Tommy and Ellie hostage, he reverses many of the dynamics shaping the characters' relationships. Now Ellie, not Claire, requires Mike's protection, and now Claire, not Ellie, must make personal sacrifices on behalf of the other woman. Moreover, Ellie is independent and active at the beginning of the film and Claire is dependent and passive. But during the hostage crisis Ellie sits motionless and utterly vulnerable in the kitchen chair, while Claire evades her police escort, commands Mike to take her with him, and places herself within Venza's proximity in order to fulfill her personal responsibility. In so doing, she demonstrates the strength of character she evidenced when she insisted on testifying, but that later diminished as her terror increased.

When Ellie and Tommy are taken hostage, Mike more properly redirects his nurturing instincts to his wife and child. Initially, Claire's vulnerability had both distinguished her from Ellie and made her attractive to him. But now he no longer needs to look outside his family to fulfill his need be a protector. Moreover, by offering himself as hostage to replace Tommy, Mike demonstrates the depth of his actual commitment to his family in the most convincing way possible. He thus truly earns Ellie's forgiveness.

The final role reversal comes at the peak of the crisis. With Venza's gun to his head Mike becomes a passive, vulnerable figure, and Ellie and Tommy become the active figures who engineer his rescue—and incidentally terminate the threat to Claire's life and her presence in theirs. In the long run, Ellie's fierce desire to preserve her family prevails over all else.

In having Mike choose Ellie over Claire, Scott implicitly endorses Ellie's earthy, passionate, maternal, direct, unpretentious, assertive character and her working-class lifestyle over Claire's emotionally reserved, highly cerebral personality and upper-class existence. The opening scenes contrast the two classes. At Mike's party, everyone dresses casually and comfortably, they dance enthusiastically, and demonstrate close bonds of friendship. Visually, Scott packs them together within the frames, literally showing them to be close. Their conversations are about matters of personal interest. These guests laugh a lot, drink too much, and become coarse and loud. The women make catty remarks about a sexy blonde dancing provocatively with one of the men.

Win's party, by contrast, is more sumptuous but less fun. Everyone is dressed elegantly; the chic strobe lights are harsh and distracting, and the conversations do not sound heartfelt. At the Guggenheim reception the guests also seem stiff and unfriendly. The blonde who matter-of-factly asks if Mike becomes sexually aroused when he shoots someone is not sophisticated, as she apparently imagines herself to be; she is simply tasteless—after all, shooting someone must have been emotionally wrenching for Mike, regardless of the circumstances. She acts as a cerebral foil to the earthy blonde at Mike's party, but that woman, at least, is open about her lasciviousness and having fun. By contrast, the blonde at the Guggenheim seems cold and coarse as she crudely hides her lust under the guise of dispassionate intellectual curiosity.

In general, in this film the working-class people show greater integrity than the wealthy. Neil, the least sympathetic character after Venza, discourages Claire from performing her duty as a citizen and a friend. Claire's friends at the Guggenheim reception subtly encourage her to have an affair with Mike, whom they have just met. Even Win, the murder victim, clearly owes his wealth to financial dealings with underground figures like Venza. By contrast, Ellie has a strong sense of her priorities and lives by them. Although she shows some insecurity about her looks, she stands up for herself. Ellie values her family most of all and she does what she needs to do to protect it. But she will not sacrifice her self-respect or pretend to be what she is not in order to keep Mike. Therefore, she defends herself against Mike's insinuation that she is vulgar because she swears, and when she learns of his affair, she insists that if he returns it is for her and not for any other reason.

The other police officers also demonstrate a clear sense of what is expected of them, and they do it. Unlike Neil and some of the other wealthy socialites, they always speak politely and behave professionally with the public. For instance, when Claire seems reluctant to permit her bodyguards inside her bedroom, Garber smoothly wins her approval by asking her to allow it as a favor to him. And Mike tactfully gets rid of Neil by telling him he can use the phone in the other room, where he will have more privacy.

The only lapses in professionalism among this blue-collar group appear when Garber orders his men to deceive Claire about the extent of the danger, and when Mike violates his commitment to Ellie and his code of professional conduct by becoming romantically involved with Claire. Though understandable, these exceptions prove harmful, much as Louise's greatly provoked but nonetheless improper murder of Harlan ultimately condemns the protagonists of *Thelma & Louise*. Indeed, the plots of both films are driven by understandable violations of responsible behavior that result from extraordinary emotional circumstances, and both suggest that we must pay the consequences of our lapses, even when circumstances create almost irresistible emotional pressures that confuse our internal compasses.

The need to temper emotion with reason, an enduring theme in Western literature, appears repeatedly in Scott's work, most notably in *The Duellists*. In *Someone to Watch over Me* Mike suffers the breakdown of his marriage, diminution of his professional status (and probably the loss of his job), and physical threats to himself and his family because he succumbs to emotional forces that overwhelm his reason: his own guilt, his need to nurture, Claire's need for comfort, and her other alluring qualities. He regains control of his life and repairs the damage to himself and his family only after his reason once again prevails and he regains a clear vision of himself and his life. In the long run, as in so many of Scott's movies, the characters prevail by being strong-willed and assertive, living according to their beliefs, and accepting responsibility for their actions.

Black Rain

(1989)

CAST

Nick Conklin	Michael Douglas
Charlie Vincent	Andy Garcia
Masahiro Matsumoto	Ken Takakura
Joyce	Kate Capshaw
Sato	Yusaku Matsuda
Ohashi	Shigeru Koyama
Oliver	John Spencer
Katayama	Guts Ishimatsu
Nashida	Yuya Uchida
Sugai	Tomisaburo Wakayama
Miyuki	Miyuki Ono

PRODUCTION

Director	Ridley Scott
Producers	Stanley R. Jaffe and Sherry Lansing (a Paramount release of a Jaffe/Lansing

	production in association with Michael Douglas)
Screenplay	Craig Bolotin and Warren Lewis
Director of photography	Jan DeBont
Production designer	Norris Spencer
Art direction	John J. Moore, Herman F. Zimmerman, and Kazuo Takenaka
Set design	Alan S. Kaye, Robert Maddy, and James R. Bayliss
Set decoration	John Alan Hicks, Leslie Bloom, Richard C. Goddard, John M. Dwyer, and Kyoji Sasaki
Costume design	Ellen Mirojnick
Editor	Tom Rolf
Music director	Hans Zimmer

SYNOPSIS

Black Rain tells the story of Nick Conklin, a New York police detective who is indignant because his department has charged that he stole money from criminals he arrested. He becomes further outraged when he and his friend, Charlie Vincent, are ordered to accompany the murderous Sato back to Japan after Nick witnesses Sato commit a murder, then pursues and captures him. But upon their arrival in Japan, Sato's accomplices trick Nick into releasing him into their custody, and the story centers around Nick's efforts to recapture Sato, a member of the Japanese Yakuza, or organized crime. He achieves this with the assistance of Masahiro Matsumoto, a Japanese detective. In the process, Nick acquires some Japanese notions of honor, and Masahiro learns the value of American individuality and personal assertiveness.

The opening credits roll against a red sun on a black background. The image, which evokes the Japanese symbol of the rising sun, dissolves into the large globe that was built in Flushing Meadows for the 1964 World's Fair, thereby foreshadowing the interplay between Japan and New York. The camera then follows Nick as he rides his motorcycle across the bridge into Manhattan. Nick joins a group of bikers and bets a younger man with a powerful motorcycle fifty dollars that he can outrace him. Nick wins after he performs a dangerous maneuver that causes the other man to wipe out. Then he returns to his apartment where he listens to a phone message from his ex-wife, who needs money for their child's private school, and from a lawyer, who advises him to wear a coat and tie today. A camera shot reveals Nick's holstered gun on the table.

Nick rides his motorcycle into town, where he picks up his son, whom he treats with affection. He also gives the money he has won to his ex-wife. After dropping off his boy, he rides through traffic and then pulls up before the precinct house, where Charlie greets him by pretending to play matador with his jacket. As Nick changes into more formal wear inside, we learn that he is a decorated detective who is being investigated by the department's Internal Affairs division. Charlie and Oliver, Nick's superior, encourage him beforehand. At the hearing, bureaucrats maintain that $8,000 is missing from a vehicle that Nick and one of his other partners impounded. Nick maintains his innocence and expresses his outrage that they seem willing to believe the criminals who have made the accusation. The officials note that his expenses, which include alimony and tuition for his child, are more than he can afford on his salary, and they accuse him of being "dirty." Indignant, Nick challenges them to charge him with a crime.

Afterward, Nick meets up with Charlie at a bar, and as they eat lunch they observe Japanese and Italian mobsters sitting together. Suddenly, armed men enter the room and Sato approaches the mobsters. He takes a box from one and then murders him with a knife. As Sato and his companion flee, Nick pursues and chases Sato through the city seats and into a refrigerated warehouse where they fight among hanging sides of meat. Nick finally subdues him and Charlie arrives to assist. Soon afterward Oliver informs Nick that Sato is being extradited to Japan and that Nick and Charlie are being assigned to deliver him. Nick objects, since he wants Sato to face justice in the United States, where he committed the homicide Nick witnessed. But Oliver insists that this has become a State Department matter, and he has no choice.

As Nick and Charlie accompany the unrepentant Sato on the plane to Osaka, Nick defends a fellow officer who has taken money illegally. Nick points out to Charlie that the man had a family to support and was "just trying to get by." When the plane lands official-looking men present badges and give Nick paperwork to sign. The paperwork is in Japanese, which Nick cannot read, but he signs it and delivers Sato to them. Moments after they depart, the real police officers arrive, and Nick watches from the window as Sato is driven off by the imposters.

At the Japanese police headquarters, Nick calls Oliver back in New York, explains what happened, and defends his action; after all, everything seemed legitimate. He insists on remaining in Osaka to salvage the situation. Masahiro, whom Nick treats condescendingly, takes Nick and Charlie into a room where they meet with the chief of police. When Masahiro tells Nick that the chief expects him to apologize, Nick becomes indignant. After all, the impostors had legitimate-looking badges and paperwork. The chief points out that the paperwork Nick signed was actually an insurance policy, but Nick remains unrepentant. The chief calls Nick and Charlie foreigners and maintains that they are now nothing more than casual observers. But Nick insists that until they sign off for real on Sato, the case is his. The chief allows them to work on it, but insists they surrender their guns. He then assigns Masahiro to work with them, as Masahiro speaks English. Though not pleased at the assignment, Masahiro approaches Nick with a formal politeness that contrasts with the American's crude, impatient brashness.

The three of them go to a club where they check out the body of a man who was recently murdered. Nick identifies him as one of the phony cops at the airport, but when he tries to make sense of the murder, Masahiro tells him and Charlie that they must now leave. Nick once more becomes indignant, but Charlie tries to smooth over the situation. Against Masahiro's wishes, Nick checks out the club, and, noticing blood on her dress, he approaches Joyce, an American from Chicago who is reluctant to speak for fear of reprisal, but at last informs him that there is a gang war between Sato and Sugai, the head of the Yakuza. Moreover, Sato had once been Sugai's lieutenant. When Nick asks how many people know about this rift, she answers that virtually everyone in Japan knows.

Nick and Charlie are upset that the Japanese police failed to inform them of such a basic fact. Nick demands that by the following morning they be given the police file on Sato and the details of the evening's murder. Then, disgusted with Masahiro, whom Nick regards contemptuously as just another bureaucrat, or "suit," they insist upon leaving the police car and walking home alone, even though they do not know where they are in this strange city that teems with activity throughout the night. As they walk, Charlie asks what Oliver told him, and Nick answers that "the suits back home think I cut a deal with Sato." The pair is then harassed by a menacing motorcycle gang, and after the bikers leave, Charlie suggests cutting their losses and returning home. But Nick insists that he cannot leave without Sato.

The following morning at the police station, they review the files they had requested. Masahiro remains evasive, and Nick asserts that even he and Charlie know that Sato used to be Sugai's lieutenant and that now there is a serious gang war going on. Masahiro provides some innocuous background information, but when Charlie notices a SWAT team arming itself, Masahiro initially tells them it is merely a drill. Only when they press him, does he finally admit they have a lead on Sato's last hide-out. As the SWAT team boards the bus, Nick and Charlie hop on, and Masahiro is compelled to join them.

During the raid Sato escapes, but one of the men who duped Nick at the airport is captured. Nick confronts and strikes him, but Masahiro reprimands him and reminds Nick that he is a foreigner, and he must abide by the rules. Nick spots a pile of cash on the table and surreptitiously takes some of the $100 American bills. But Masahiro notices. When Nick and Charlie are alone, Nick burns one of the bills to demonstrate that it is fake. They then return to the police headquarters to report the counterfeiting, but Masahiro calls Nick a thief and tells him that he has dishonored him. He adds that he has notified his superior, who will contact Nick's boss in New York. Nick then burns another bill and demonstrates to Masahiro and his boss that it, too, is counterfeit. He speculates that the box Sato took from the man he killed in New York contained the plates from which the bills were printed.

The three officers adjourn to a club, where Charlie, who has taken a liking to Masahiro, tries to make peace between him and Nick. "Everyone was doing the right thing," he says. But Nick complains that Masahiro violated protocol by not checking first with his teammates before going to the suits. In response, Masahiro states that Nick should think more like a member of a team.

Nick sees Joyce and goes off to speak with her. While he is away, Charlie and Masahiro form a friendship, as Charlie gives him his tie and invites him to come up to the microphone and sing an American rock-and-roll song with him. Meanwhile, Joyce points out Sugai in the crowd, but assures Nick that he would never help a foreigner. When she refuses to endanger herself by helping any further, Nick tells her that sometimes she needs to choose a side. She answers she did, hers.

As Nick and Charlie walk home, they are accosted by a motorcyclist. When Charlie takes off his coat and pretends to be a matador, the biker steals the coat, which has Charlie's passport. Charlie chases him into a parking garage, where several more bikers surround him. Nick follows, but cannot penetrate the security gate they have dropped behind them. He then watches helplessly as Sato approaches Charlie on a motorcycle and decapitates him with a sword. As he drives away, Sato looks back at Nick and gloats.

As Nick stands alone grieving on a bridge, Joyce approaches him and tells him to come with her. Masahiro watches them leave together. Later, he appears at her apartment and asks to see Nick. He expresses his sorrow and sense of responsibility for Charlie's death. After Nick thanks him, Masahiro gives him a box containing Charlie's belongings. Nick gives Masahiro Charlie's badge, and Masahiro allows Nick to retain Charlie's gun. Then they go back together to the hide-out they raided earlier. After trashing the place, Nick notices sequins that he associates with one of the girls from Joyce's club. He concludes that she is Sato's girlfriend, and that night they follow her through the crowded streets. During their stake-out Masahiro asks Nick about the charges against him in New York, and Nick answers that some of the men he worked with stole from drug dealers. Masahiro replies, "Theft is theft. There is no gray area," and Nick retorts, "New York is one big gray area." Masahiro then asks if Nick stole too, and Nick admits that he did. He is not proud of it, but he needed the money for alimony and for his kids. Masahiro asks if Charlie knew this, and Nick says he did not. Then Masahiro declares that Charlie was a policeman, and by stealing "you disgrace him and yourself and me." Nick simply but sincerely answers, "Thanks."

The next morning they follow the girl, who leads them to the man who set up Charlie. They follow him to a steel mill and, as molten metal erupts in the background, they secretly watch the leaders of the Yakuza, who have gathered to discuss their counterfeiting operation. Sato is there too, but he will not surrender the plate he stole unless they give him his own territory. Sugai complains that Sato knows nothing of loyalty and respect, and that his methods are cruel and disrespectful. But Sato answers that Sugai liked his methods enough when Sato worked for him. As Nick tells Masahiro to call the police, Sato and his companions leave. Nick confronts them, and Sato taunts him about Charlie's death. In the shootout that follows, Nick kills two of Sato's underlings, but as he chases Sato, the police arrive and arrest Nick, while Sato escapes. Nick is then told he is being deported for carrying a gun. If he returns, he will be arrested.

On the plane, Nick watches Charlie's coffin being loaded. Then he sneaks off and goes to Masahiro's apartment. Nick asks for help but learns that Masahiro has been suspended and demoted for providing the gun. Nick apologizes, but Masahiro says he knew what he was doing. Masahiro maintains that he belonged to a group that now will no longer have him, and when Nick tries to change his mind about helping, Masahiro orders him out. Nick then goes to see Joyce, who writes down where he can find Sugai.

Nick presents himself to Sugai, announcing himself with one of the counterfeit bills. As Masahiro secretly watches from his car, Sugai tells Nick that Sato might just as well be an American: "His kind respect just one thing, money." Nick asks Sugai what he is in it for, if not money, and he learns that Sugai wants revenge against America for the atom bomb that brought the "black rain" during World War II and for creating a new, materialistic Japanese society that produces men like Sato. When Nick replies that he will kill Sato if Sugai can get him close to him, Sugai answers that he has given his word to maintain the peace. But Nick presses on, declaring that he will do the dirty work, and Sugai will be clean. At last, Sugai agrees, and he takes Nick to a farm where the Yakuza heads will meet with Sato. He then arms Nick with a rifle. As Nick reconnoiters, Masahiro appears and saves him from one of Sato's men, who is dressed as a farmer. They realize that Sato plans to assassinate the other leaders.

Sato drives up and joins the other leaders inside the farmhouse. He vows that if they give him his own territory, he will surrender the plates and remain loyal to them. Sugai says he will agree to his terms, if Sato consents to apologize in the traditional fashion. Otherwise there will be no truce. Sato consents, and as his men begin their assault, he cuts off his little finger. Sugai then drinks to the truce, but Sato rises and impales Sugai's hand onto the table with the knife. As he does, his men appear and open fire on the other leaders.

As a battle breaks out among the Yakuza factions, Nick chases Sato, who hops on a motorcycle and drives away. Nick mounts a second bike and follows him through the rows of crops. Using the same maneuver he employed at the beginning of the film, Nick forces Sato to wipe out. They fight, and when Nick gains the upper hand, he threatens to impale Sato on a stake in the ground.

The scene cuts to the police station where Nick and Masahiro present Sato to the chief of police in a very public fashion. Later, as Joyce watches from the audience, Nick and Masahiro receive official commendations. Afterward, Nick thanks her for choosing a side, and they kiss briefly.

Masahiro accompanies Nick to the airport, and as they wait for the plane, he notes that the plates were never found. Nick answers that whoever has the plates will be set for life, since no one will ever know. They exchange gifts, and when Nick begins to bow, Masahiro insists on shaking hands. Masahiro seems disappointed, because he thinks Nick has the plates, but when he opens his gift, he finds that Nick has given them to him. They exchange smiles as the credits roll.

RECEPTION

Black Rain met a mixed reception. Some critics, such as the viewer for *Variety*, found fault with the drawn-out storyline and the superfluous romantic subplot between Joyce and Nick, but overall considered the film a "gripping crime thriller" in which the *film noir* atmosphere, characterizations, and thematic questions about morality and honor were meritorious (Sammon, *Ridley Scott*, 142–43). On the other hand, the *New York Times*'s Vincent Canby panned the movie, although he too liked its visual effects. According to Canby, the story, and even the title, are derivative, and his final assessment is that "*Black Rain* may be dumb but it's pretty" (Canby, Review of *Black Rain*). The disparate assessments about the movie's virtues were reflected in the box office. Neither a financial failure nor a raving success, *Black Rain* grossed a modest $45 million in its U.S. run.

DISCUSSION

Scott directed *Black Rain* but was not involved as a producer. In fact, he refers to himself as "a hired gun" (Sammon, *Ridley Scott*, 91), and this perhaps accounts for its relative lack of thematic exploration, especially when compared to other films in which Scott had a stronger voice in developing the script and other aspects of the project. The movie has attracted little scholarly attention. Paul M. Sammon notes that *Black Rain* "takes the audience on a tour of contemporary Japan rarely seen in Western films; it is a society seething with corruption and mob violence, with prostitution and the repression of the individual, a divided country whose sleek city life is counterpointed by an archaic, quasi-feudal rural culture." Sammon adds that the film also depicts homelessness, an urban phenomenon rarely shown in cinema of the time (Sammon, *Ridley Scott*, 96).

Pat Dowell takes these critical perceptions of Japan further and argues that the film reflects and reinforces Americans' anxieties in the late 1980s about Japan as an economic rival capable of displacing the United States as the dominant world power: "*Black Rain*'s furious contradictions reveal more insecurity about America than about Japan. Japan itself is conceived . . . as an alien nation, something of a monolith in its otherness. In fact I was reminded often of the

brutalizing respect John Ford paid to Native American tribes in his films."
Dowell concludes, "At the heart of Nick Conklin's hysterically threatening
brush with Japan is the nightmare, not of being bested, but of being trans-
formed: that 'we' will become 'them'" (Dowell, 10).

A case can be made that *Black Rain* plays off then-current concerns that the
introduction of Japanese business practices into the American workplace
would threaten the individual initiative and self-reliance Americans traditionally cherish. Nonetheless, Dowell's accusations of "Japan bashing" seem extreme. After all, the film's moral center resides not in Nick but in Masahiro,
who reminds Nick that his corrupt behavior dishonors not only himself but
also his late partner Charlie, Masahiro, and by extension all policemen. And if
Masahiro benefits from acquiring some Yankee independence and personal assertiveness, Nick has clearly become a better person for his association with the
Japanese Masahiro. Moreover, Dowell's conclusion that the film expresses
Americans' fear of becoming Japanese is simply not borne out by the story. On
the contrary, the plot is ultimately driven by Sugai's complaint that his country
has been deformed by American materialism. His hatred of how the Americans
have ruined Japan both accounts for the title and motivates him to undermine
the American economy by spreading counterfeit money. One could, therefore,
more readily argue that this movie, made near the end of the Reagan presi-
dency, indulges in "America bashing" more than "Japan bashing." (Michael
Douglas had two years earlier attacked the material excesses of Reagan-era
America in his 1987 film *Wall Street*, in which the unsympathetic corporate
raider he portrays promulgates Ivan Boesky's view that "greed is good.")

Timothy P. Hofmeister's argument that *Black Rain* invokes a story structure found in Homer's *Iliad* and other ancient "friendship literature" is more
useful. Noting how Nick feels alienated from the New York police department
in which he serves, because he feels it has lost "a simple intuitive correspondence between service and reward" and that it has become tougher on the
crime fighter than the criminal, Hofmeister maintains that Nick's reintegration into his society is initiated by the death of Charlie. According to
Hofmeister, "the death of the beloved friend catalyzes a profound, often final
transformation of the hero's social and spiritual dispositions," such as the
death of Patroclus does for Achilles in the *Iliad*. In addition, "just as the *Iliad*
tells the wrath of Achilles, of his withdrawal from a community of fel-
low-warriors and his return, so the film *Black Rain* depicts the isolation, cor-
rosion, and reconstitution of a modern warrior, a police detective named Nick
Conklin" (Hofmeister, 45–47). In particular, Hofmeister notes that Charlie's
death sparks vital self-confrontation and growth in self-knowledge that ultimately make Nick a better, less resentful person. Hofmeister also argues that,
like the ancient mythic hero, Nick must descend to the underworld before he
can reemerge to fulfill his quest. In this case, Nick's humbling himself before
and collusion with the "underworld" crime leader Sugai enables him finally to
exact his revenge on Sato and revive his own honor at the same time.

Indeed, honor emerges as the central issue in the movie. Nick's dissatisfaction with the New York police department stems from his feelings that the suits who run it dishonor him and his colleagues by caring more about the welfare of the criminals than that of the cops. These feelings of not being respected enable him to rationalize his acts of petty corruption. Unlike Charlie, Nick fails to show appropriate respect to the Japanese police after he inadvertently frees Sato. Failing to accept any responsibility for the act, he blames them and insults Masahiro to his face when he thinks Masahiro cannot speak English. But the Japanese police also fail to respect Nick and Charlie, whom they dismiss as foreigners. Until Charlie's death, even Masahiro goes along with their attempts to keep the Americans out of the investigation. He fails to give them the most rudimentary background information about the gang war between Sato and Sugai, and he lies to them, saying that the SWAT team's preparations to raid Sato's hide-out are just a drill. Nick feels further dishonored when Masahiro reports the money Nick has stolen to his superior instead of first confronting Nick about it. For these reasons, Masahiro appears to Nick to be just another suit, a bureaucrat who has no respect for the actual work of apprehending criminals.

As Hofmeister notes, Charlie's death initiates the plot reversal that brings about Nick's personal growth. And even though Masahiro embodies incorruptible virtue (like the older advisor who accompanies and teaches the epic hero), Charlie's death also facilitates Masahiro's personal growth by initiating a partnership between him and Nick, in which he learns the virtue of individual initiative. Masahiro takes the first step in forging this bond by bringing Nick Charlie's belongings. In doing so, he knowingly allows Nick to arm himself, even though his superiors have forbidden it. He thereby allies himself with Nick against the suits, for the first time. (Although Hofmeister does not mention it, this act corresponds to the arming of the epic hero, a convention found in the *Iliad* and elsewhere. It signifies the transformation of the hero from a relatively passive or submissive mode to an active, assertive one.) In return, Nick honors Masahiro by giving him Charlie's badge, a token of the professional bond that unites the men.

Once Nick is armed, he and Masahiro rely on personal initiative instead of Japanese teamwork, and this enables them to observe Sato's meeting with the other gang leaders at the steel mill. Ironically, Nick's efforts to capture Sato here are thwarted because he tries to use teamwork: Nick instructs Masahiro to call in the other police. But, like the suits in New York, the Japanese police come down harder on the crime fighters than the criminals. Not only does their rigid fidelity to regulations allow Sato to escape, but it also leads to Nick's deportation and Masahiro's suspension and demotion. Only because Nick persists in his personal initiative and Masahiro ultimately joins him are they able to capture Sato and, incidentally, assist in the action that wipes out the other gang leaders as well.

When Nick and Masahiro present Sato to the police in a very public display, they both regain their honor in the eyes of the Japanese and New York suits. But Nick's admission to Masahiro that he, too, stole from criminals has diminished Nick in Masahiro's eyes. To Masahiro, honor knows no gray areas, and when a police officer steals, he dishonors all policemen. Thus, when Nick gives the missing plates to Masahiro as a gift, he signals that he has understood Masahiro's sentiments and taken them to heart. In this way, he becomes honorable once again not only in Masahiro's eyes, but, more importantly, in his own.

Ironically, the other man in the film who is obsessed with personal honor is Sugai, the crime lord. He berates Sato for his disrespect and lack of personal loyalty, and he blames the Americans for introducing into Japan a culture that values only material wealth and thereby fosters dishonorable behavior among money-hungry Japanese youth. Sugai explains that his motivation for counterfeiting is not to enhance his own wealth, but to undermine the Americans who made the "black rain" fall on Japan, by both dropping the atomic bomb and tarnishing traditional Japanese values with greed. However, Sugai's sanctimonious position is undercut by the facts that he will profit from the counterfeiting (it is not as if he plans to donate the profits to charity) and that he is willing to allow Nick, the foreigner, to do his dirty work for him. Thus Sugai preserves his honor only in the most technical, legalistic sense, and his death remains part of the happy ending, not an exception to it.

Perhaps the most interesting facet of the film is how Sato emerges as a shadow figure for Nick. In fact, if Masahiro represents the honorable, self-respecting person Nick can be at his best, Sato embodies and exaggerates Nick's worst traits. He represents what Nick could become if he succumbed fully to his dark side. Preoccupied only by power and wealth, Sato is cynical, arrogant, cruel, lawless, and totally alienated from society. If Nick takes some portion of the missing $8,000 he and his cohorts have stolen from drug dealers, Sato stands to make a fortune by stealing the plates from other criminals and murdering them. If Nick is contemptuous of the suits who wield authority, Sato violently disregards all forms of authority, from the police to Sugai. If Nick believes in bending the rules and asserting personal initiative to get results, Sato shatters the rules and does whatever he pleases. If Nick takes satisfaction in asserting his power by smashing Sato with his elbow in Charlie's absence, Sato asserts his power over Nick far more forcefully when he gloats at Nick's inability to save Charlie from decapitation. Not incidentally, both men are brash and disrespectful, and both prefer the freedom and exhilaration of risk taking and motorcycle riding. At the beginning of the film, Nick is cynical, bitter, and isolated, and he risks succumbing fully to those personal qualities that would make him more like Sato. However, just as Deckard in *Blade Runner* emerges as a better person for his confrontation with his *Doppelgänger*, Roy Batty, Nick is redeemed and revitalized by his conflict with his shadow figure, Sato, and by his association with his better self, as embodied by the honorable and incorruptible Masahiro.

The Duellists. Photo courtesy of Photofest.

Alien. Photo courtesy of Photofest.

Blade Runner. Photo courtesy of Photofest.

Legend. Photo courtesy of Photofest.

Someone to Watch over Me. Photo courtesy of Photofest.

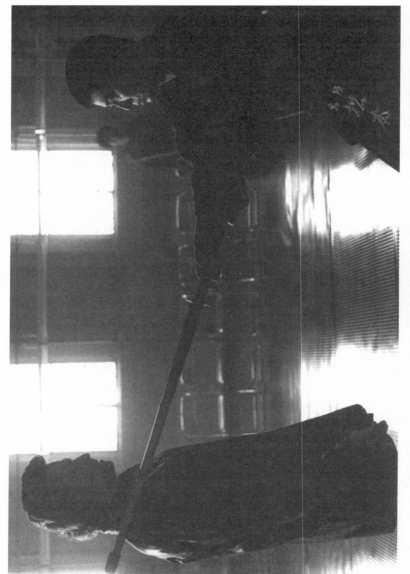

Black Rain. Photo courtesy of Photofest.

Thelma & Louise. Photo courtesy of Photofest.

1492: Conquest of Paradise. Photo courtesy of Photofest.

White Squall. Photo courtesy of Photofest.

G.I. Jane. Photo courtesy of Photofest.

Gladiator. Photo courtesy of Photofest.

Hannibal. Photo courtesy of Photofest.

Thelma & Louise

(1991)

CAST

Louise	Susan Sarandon
Thelma	Geena Davis
Hal	Harvey Keitel
Jimmy	Michael Madsen
Darryl	Christopher McDonald
J.D.	Brad Pitt
Harlan	Timothy Carhart
Lena, the waitress	Lucinda Jenny
Max	Stephen Tobolowsky
Truck driver	Marco St. John
State trooper	Jason Beghe
Bicyclist	Noel Walcott

PRODUCTION

Director	Ridley Scott
Producers	Ridley Scott and Mimi Polk (a Percy Main production)

Screenplay	Callie Khouri
Director of photography	Adrian Biddle
Production designer	Norris Spencer
Art director	Lisa Dean
Set design	Alan Kaye
Set decoration	Anne Ahrens
Editor	Thom Noble
Costume designer	Elizabeth McBride
Music director	Hans Zimmer

SYNOPSIS

The story of the misadventures of two small-town women who set out for an innocent three-day vacation together and find themselves fugitives from justice, *Thelma & Louise* begins with shots of the western landscape and empty dirt roads that lead to the mountains. It then cuts to Louise waiting tables in a small Arkansas diner and making plans on the phone with Thelma, who is browbeaten by her self-important but buffoonish husband, Darryl. In contrast to Louise's tidiness and sense of being in control, Thelma appears messy and subservient. She over-packs for the trip, bringing not only extraneous lanterns and camping equipment, but also, in case of bears or psycho killers, a pistol, which she gives to Louise to hold for her, as she is afraid of it. Louise tells her to put the weapon in her purse and then forgets about it. The women then photograph themselves together and drive away in Louise's 1966 Thunderbird convertible. Thelma mentions that she has never been out of town without Darryl and admits that she never told him she was going away with Louise, because he would never approve: "He never lets me do one goddamn thing that's any fun." Louise answers, "You get what you settle for."

Although Louise wants to keep driving until they reach their destination, a fishing cabin in the woods, Thelma convinces her to stop at the Silver Bullet bar for a drink. Louise is guarded and only wants to stop briefly, but Thelma is ready for a good time. She orders a strong drink and plays along with Harlan, a man who comes by their table to flirt with them. Thelma and Harlan drink and dance until Thelma becomes dizzy. Harlan then takes her outside, while Louise is in the ladies' room. Even though Thelma has just thrown up, Harlan comes on to her, and he slaps her when she resists his advances. She hits him to stop him from accosting her, and he strikes her back hard and then begins to rape her. Suddenly Louise appears and places Thelma's pistol to his head. Harlan complains that they were just having fun, but Louise replies, "You've got a real fucked up idea of fun. . . . In the future, when a woman's crying like that, she isn't having any fun." As Thelma and Louise walk away, Harlan says he should have "gone ahead and fucked her." Then he tells Louise to "suck my cock." Without hesitating, Louise shoots him dead.

Louise orders Thelma to get the car, and they careen away. The camera shows the bruises on Thelma's face as she drives. When Thelma says they should go to the police, Louise answers that no one would believe that Harlan was raping her against her will after so many people saw her dance with him cheek to cheek. "We don't live in that kind of world," Louise tells her. Instead, Louise cleans off Thelma's face and takes over the driving chores. They go to a coffee shop to compose themselves, and Thelma complains that she is not having any fun on this vacation. Louise rejoins that if she were not so concerned about having fun, the incident would never have happened, to which Thelma retorts, "So, this is all my fault, is it?" Louise looks angry and somewhat incredulous, but she refrains from blaming Thelma, who excuses herself to go to the bathroom. While she is up, Thelma tries to call Darryl, but no one is home.

Back at the Silver Bullet, Detective Hal Slocum interviews the waitress who served Thelma and Louise and who maintains they never would have committed the murder. She adds that she expected Harlan to die like this. She hopes it was his wife who killed him but expects it was some woman he fooled around with, or her husband. When the questioning concludes, she flirts with Hal, but he good-naturedly puts her off.

After Louise tries unsuccessfully to call her boyfriend Jimmy, they go to a hotel where the women continue to bicker, and Thelma cries. Louise asks for ideas, but Thelma says Louise rejected her only idea, which was to go to the police. So she suns herself by the pool while Louise phones Jimmy to ask for money. She tells him she is in "deep shit" but will not give any particulars. He agrees to help, but when she asks if he loves her, he hesitates before answering "yes." Afterward, Louise sounds more aloof, but he agrees to wire almost $7,000 to her in Oklahoma City.

Hal talks to his superior, Max, who suggests notifying the FBI, as the killer may have crossed state lines. Thelma tells Louise that she called Darryl at 4:00 A.M., but he still was not home. Louise tells her that she is going to Mexico, and she needs to know what Thelma will do, but Thelma cannot give her an answer. But when Thelma later calls her husband, instead of showing concern for her, he curses her and orders her to come home. Thelma replies, "You're my husband, not my father," and when he gives her an ultimatum, she tells him to go fuck himself and hangs up. As she leaves the phone booth, she stumbles into J.D., a young hitchhiker to whom she wants to give a ride, but Louise refuses.

Thelma now tells Louise that she will go to Mexico with her. Then she talks about how good looking J.D. is. Louise tells Thelma to find a route to Mexico using secondary roads that avoid Texas. When Thelma complains that Texas is the most direct route, Louise becomes adamant, but she refuses to tell Thelma what happened to her in that state.

Hal does a computer search that lists all the 1966 Thunderbirds with Arkansas license plates and locates Louise on the list. He then goes to her apartment, which he breaks into and explores. Meanwhile, having agreed to flee together, Thelma and Louise drive happily across the country, singing and waving to crop dusters. They pass J.D. hitchhiking, and Thelma pleads successfully for them to pick him up. While Hal interviews an incredulous Darryl, Louise drives through an oil field to avoid speeding police cars.

When Louise goes to pick up the money at the hotel where Jimmy has said he will send it, she finds him waiting there for her. He pays for an additional room, and Louise leaves Thelma in their room alone with the money, which she places in the night stand before joining Jimmy. Jimmy asks what is going on, but Louise refuses to answer. When he becomes frustrated and smashes items on the desk, she threatens to leave, and he calms down. Then he gives her an engagement ring. Louise asks why he is proposing now, and he says it is because he is afraid she will leave him for good, but she replies that this is not a good reason to marry. He answers that he thought this is what she wanted, and she replies that she did, but not like this. She then declares that they both got what they settled for and that she still loves him, but that it is time to let go.

Meanwhile, J.D. appears at Thelma's door and she admits him. They joke and play together. He tells her he is a robber and describes how he conducts himself when holding up a store. Afterward, they make love. In the other room, Jimmy and Louise reminisce. The next morning at breakfast in the hotel restaurant, Jimmy tells Louise he will not say anything to anyone. He offers to go with her, but she says she will catch up with him later. He declares that he just wants her to be happy and tells her to keep the ring. Then they kiss good-bye affectionately, and he leaves. The waitress tells Louise it is good that he left; otherwise, they thought they would have to extinguish a fire. Thelma then appears feeling great. She finally admits having had sex with J.D., and now "I finally understand what all the fuss is about." Louise is pleased that her friend "finally got laid properly," but she is horrified to learn that Thelma left J.D. alone in the room with the money. They hurry back, but J.D. and the cash are both gone. Louise is devastated, but Thelma asserts herself and insists that she will deal with it. She commands Louise to leave the room and they depart.

While Hal and other police officers set up in Darryl's house to trace any phone calls, Thelma robs a convenience store. We see Darryl watching the videotape from the store's security camera in stunned disbelief as he sees his wife pointing the pistol that she had previously been afraid even to touch and commanding the customers and employees in the same way J.D. had described.

The day is sunny and bright as Thelma and Louise drive cheerfully across the country. But their good spirits are temporarily dampened when they pass a trucker who makes obscene gestures at them.

Hal and Max interview J.D., and Hal holds J.D. responsible for forcing Thelma to commit the robbery, as he stole all their money. He demands J.D.'s cooperation so he can help the women, and he threatens to become J.D.'s nemesis if J.D. refuses. Louise tells Thelma to call Darryl, but to hang up immediately if he suspects anything. Thelma phones, and hangs up instantly after

Darryl answers sweetly. Then Louise calls back and asks to speak with the officer in charge. Hal talks with her, expresses concern for her well-being, tries to reassure her, and asks what happened, but Louise will not answer. After she hangs up, she is distraught because the police know they plan to go to Mexico; she infers that J.D. told them, and that Thelma told J.D. She says the two things they had going for them were that the police did not know either their location or where they were going, and now they have lost one of those two things. She commands Thelma, "We're fugitives now, right. Let's start behaving like that."

They drive at night and savor the beauty of the landscape and sky. As Thelma sleeps, Louise stops the car and gets out to watch the sunrise, but soon after, the beauty of the scenery is again polluted by the obnoxious behavior of the same trucker. Later, Thelma asks Louise if something like what Harlan did to her happened to Louise in Texas, but Louise becomes very angry and again refuses to talk about it. Soon after, a policeman pulls them over for speeding, but when he starts to call in information about their car, Thelma puts the gun to his head and the women lock him inside his trunk, apologizing all the while. The officer, who had been stern, breaks down crying, and Thelma tells him to be nice to his wife, or she might turn out like Thelma. She commands Louise to shoot out the radio, and they steal his gun and throw away his keys before driving on. As they drive away, Thelma declares that she "has a knack for this shit."

Louise fears that she has got them into a situation where they both might be killed, and she wonders why she did not go to the police in the first place. But Thelma reminds her that no one would have believed them, and they would still be in trouble. She says that her life would have been a lot worse, because at least she is having fun now. She only wished it had been she, and not Louise, who killed Harlan.

Louise calls to speak to Hal again, and she tells him that they are experiencing a snowball effect with the crimes. He asks if she wants to come out alive, but Louise mentions the alternatives—incarceration, electrocution, life in prison. Just before she needs to hang up to avoid having the call traced, Hal stuns her by telling her he knows what happened in Texas. After Louise freezes momentarily, Thelma hangs up for her, but it is too late. Louise's moment of hesitation has enabled the police to discern their whereabouts. Thelma asks Louise if she is going to give up, but Louise tells her that she is not. Thelma maintains that "somethin's like crossed over in me, and I can't go back. I mean, I just couldn't live." She adds that she now feels wide awake. "I never remember feeling this awake. . . . Everything looks different." For the first time, she feels like she has something to look forward to, and they imagine a good life together in Mexico.

Encountering the obnoxious trucker for the third time, they pretend to want to have sex with him. But when he pulls over and leaves his cab, they lecture him about how to behave properly with a woman. When he still does not get the message, they take out their pistols and blow up his gas truck. Then Thelma steals his cap and puts it on as they drive away. Afterward, a police helicopter surveys the still-smoldering fire, while a Rastafarian bicyclist blows marijuana smoke into the trunk of the police car in which the trooper has been locked.

Thelma and Louise spot a line of speeding police cars and drive off the road to avoid them. The police give chase, and although the women temporarily escape them, they are forced to stop when they suddenly reach the edge of the Grand Canyon. They pause momentarily to admire its beauty before a helicopter carrying Hal suddenly rises from the gorge before them. They back up, but a phalanx of police cars waits behind them. Louise declares, "All this for us," as the officers load their weapons and prepare to fire on the women if they do not surrender. Hal urges his boss to adopt a less hostile course of action. But Max reminds him that the women are armed and that this is standard procedure.

Thelma tells Louise, "Let's not get caught. . . . Let's keep going." Louise asks what she means, and Thelma commands, "Go." They look into each other's eyes, kiss, and then drive forward as Hal runs helplessly after them. They hold hands and, as they go over the cliff, the photo they took of themselves at the beginning of their adventure flies from the car. The frame freezes just as the Thunderbird begins to descend into the gorge. Then, as the credits role, we see clips from earlier, happier moments.

RECEPTION

Thelma & Louise has aroused more passion and provoked more widely ranging opinions than any of Scott's other movies. Although Scott, himself, was more concerned with celebrating the American landscape, developing the script's humor, and providing solid entertainment than with making a social statement, the film tapped into a reservoir of strong emotions among viewers. *Thelma & Louise* was praised by feminists and others for depicting how women are routinely demeaned by men on an almost daily basis, and it was condemned for male bashing. An unlikely smash hit of 1991, the movie became the subject of many reviews, commentaries, and even a television documentary on the Movie Channel, *When Thelma Met Louise*. Moreover, the story quickly transcended cinema to symbolize, in the minds of many, ongoing conflicts in American society over women's rights, social roles, and modes of behavior. Linda Frost, for instance, notes how the characters were widely adopted as "guardians of women's rights or as representations of women's political anger," and she cites how women at a pro-choice rally in Washington, D.C., in April 1992, wore buttons declaring, 'Thelma and Louise were right' and 'Graduate of the Thelma and Louise Finishing School,' even though abortion rights were never mentioned in the film" (Frost, 152–53).

Many viewers, especially women, recognized in their own lives the provocations that fueled the protagonists' violent odyssey, and many of them maintained that the characters' reactions were justified and acceptable. Others pointed out the film's proclivity for showing men as uniformly crass, predatory, and insensitive—a representation they deplored as distortive—and they condemned the protagonists' violence against men as unwarranted, despite the provocations. Still others responded more to the film's humor and regarded the movie in cinematic terms rather than political ones, noting similarities to other "road movies" and to buddy films like *Butch Cassidy and the Sundance Kid* (1969). *Variety*'s reviewer, for instance, declared that "despite some delectably funny scenes between the sexes, Scott's latest pic isn't about women vs. men. It's about freedom, like any good road picture. In that sense, and in many others, it's a classic" (Sammon, *Ridley Scott*, 144). Jane Maslin, writing in the *New York Times*, also enjoyed the humor and praised the film for its writing, acting, cinematography, and characters (Maslin, May 24, 1991). In a second review, she defended the movie against charges of excessive violence and "antisocial depravity" by comparing it to other current films with male protagonists that showed far more violence and received no criticism for it (Maslin, June 16, 1991).

The film, which was featured on the cover of *Time* magazine, did well both critically and at the box office. It cost $16 million to produce and grossed $46 million in the United States alone. Khouri won an Academy Award for best screenplay; Scott was nominated for best director, Biddle for best cinematographer, and Davis and Sarandon for best actress. *Thelma & Louise*, Brad Pitt's third movie, catapulted him to fame.

DISCUSSION[1]

Reflecting the popular debate over the film, most of the academic criticism regards *Thelma & Louise* in terms of the feminist issues it raises. However, while these concerns are clearly integral to the movie, the feminist perspective typically fails to fuse them to larger questions about our expectations for individual responsibility and moral behavior, not just for victimizers but for victims as well. Other criticism that seeks to place the film within the cinematic traditions of buddy films, outlaw films, road movies, and screwball comedy comes closer to addressing the larger questions of proper action raised by *Thelma & Louise*. But these central questions come into clearest focus when we regard the movie in terms of Shakespearean tragedy.

Among the feminist voices, the film's writer, Callie Khouri, maintains that she wrote *Thelma & Louise* to delight and empower female spectators. "I wanted to write a movie that I could go to as a woman and not be really upset and offended by. . . . I really wanted to write a movie where women were going to go in there and feel good about being women. I myself have experienced going into movies where so often I'm *embarrassed* . . . by the behavior of the women on the screen . . . by the audience's response to the women on the screen. And I just don't think that most of the things that I see represented in women on the screen are in any way indicative of the reality of most women's lives or most women's psychologies or personalities or emotions or motivations" (Winter, 8). Khouri adds that most representations in mainstream media of women's relationships are undignified: "You always see women as adversaries. It's as if the interesting relationship between women is adversarial; they're in competition for a man . . . or their characters are just so weak that they naturally are aggressive towards other females. I have never found that to be true in my own life—ever" (Winter, 6).

Lillian Robinson compares the movie to Herbert Biberman's *Salt of the Earth* (1954), arguing the films are mirror images of one another. *Salt of the Earth* foregrounds class struggle, gender divisions of labor, and women's lack of power within their households, while ignoring matters of sexuality, domestic violence, and rape. *Thelma & Louise*, by contrast, "centers on the institutionalization of violence against women and . . . as a consequence, the film's other observations about marriage, family, and work in or outside the home become 'background' surrounding and reinforcing that center, not organically connected parts of a single oppressive system. . . . *Thelma & Louise* examines social conditions chiefly as a way of explaining the motives and actions of the particular individuals" (Robinson, 173, 174).

Pat MacEnulty argues that Thelma and Louise are "two ordinary women governed by rage and finally empowered by violence. They are feminists in the way that all women are. They only expect the dignity and freedom that all humans deserve. They are not de-sexed man-haters" (MacEnulty, 104). Pat Dowell observes the role reversal in which the women are active and the men are comparatively passive. However, the failure of Thelma and Louise to survive their experience leads Dowell to maintain that the movie is finally about the impotence of women who "seek to wrest such magic items as guns, fishing rods, cash, and fast cars from the guys who normally wield them in our Hollywood consciousness" (Kamins et al., 28).

Cara J. MariAnna argues that the movie's structure imposes seven layers of mythology that are tied to femininity. In her reading the film progresses from opening shots that begin in darkness and then draw our attention to the land, which possesses "the spirit, power, and intelligence of the Earth" (MariAnna, 84). Thus the movie is rooted in a "foundational mythic cycle" of Planetary Intelligence/Mother Earth. The subsequent cycles are Cosmic Balance/Truth and Justice, Male Dominance/Rape, Female Sexual Autonomy/Female Freedom, Fire/Transformation, Return, and Dawn. Like MariAnna, Lizzie Thynne also finds meaning in the film's preoccupation with the landscape. She argues that "the desert suggests the freedom to become autonomous. . . . Other recent features looking at the relationship of two women have put them into open spaces—suggesting a new place for female desire beyond the confines of domestic interiors. The landscape previously colonized by men trying to conquer nature and native peoples, often designated as feminine, becomes the arena of women: Thelma and Louise speed across the desert on the run from patriarchal law" (Thynne, 139).

Jack Boozer also notes the importance of the setting, but he places it more in the context of genre than feminism. In particular, he regards *Thelma & Louise* as a road outlaw film and notes that "associations with the promise of the West and the problems of western migration have been fundamental to the history of road outlaw films as they are to most Westerns. Both genres look to a mythical natural world. . . . In the classical road film, social attitudes and authority usually appear at best injudicious, although the male protagonist's method of confrontation and escape also seems doomed, as does the enrollment of a woman, [as] fellow fugitive, who might point to an alternative family/community base in the future" (Boozer, 189). Boozer finds especially strong connections between *Thelma & Louise* and *Easy Rider* (1969). But he notes that "*Easy Rider* glorifies the wide open spaces of the Southwest that can support an alternative family farm or struggling communal experiment, but nature in *Thelma & Louise* is at best a last vestige of mother earth under stress, capable only of a metaphorical promise of reintegration. . . . [The protagonists'] physical isolation within the big frame is related to their inability to escape their social experience, which has further distanced them from anything transformational in nature" (190). Noting how Louise reiterates her belief that "you get what you settle for," Boozer maintains that the film "turns the trajectory of its road film duo not so much into a male bashing spectacle as into a metaphor of the longing for a more active and assertive feminine principal of subjectivity" (Boozer, 192). Finally, he concludes that the movie transforms the road outlaw genre "by forcing its central narrative conflicts into the perceptual terms of contemporary sign culture. . . . Scott's images suggest the impact of a voracious consumerism, which has buried the old frontier under an interconnected urban grid of commerce, signified here by food and motel chains, strip malls, and redundant bi-ways and parking lots where even the Lone Ranger isn't safe" (Boozer, 195).

Like Boozer, Peter N. Chumo II recognizes the indebtedness of *Thelma & Louise* to earlier road outlaw films. Chumo notes that Louise's shooting of Harlan expresses a common situation in the outlaw movie in which "the outlaw is on the side of society's underdogs and on their behalf takes revenge on society's oppressors." He adds that by killing Thelma's would-be rapist, Louise was probably also, in her own mind, "righting the wrong done to her" in Texas (Chumo, 4, 5). Chumo draws specific parallels to *Bonnie and Clyde* (1967), noting the two-character title and the facts that Bonnie had been a waitress before joining Clyde, that their first robbery took place in a small grocery store, that they capture and humiliate a police officer, and that they become associated with their photographs of themselves. Chumo also points out how the film generalizes Thelma and Louise's predicament and applies it to all women. "By showing that a more sophisticated woman like Louise, not just a somewhat naive woman like Thelma, can be a victim, the film suggests that all women are potentially in danger. *Thelma & Louise*, then, like *Bonnie and Clyde*, offer the viewers vicarious revenge" (Chumo, 5).

However, despite these affinities with outlaw road films, Chumo finds an even greater indebtedness to the screwball comedies of the 1930s. He identifies "road screwball" as an important subgenre, best exemplified by Frank Capra's *It Happened One Night* (1934), "in which madcap couples would forsake the constraints of authority for the freedom of the open road, play out new roles, and ultimately shed old identities for new ones. Like *Thelma & Louise*, the screwball tradition of the 1930s exhibited its own feminist streak as it featured female characters who were the equals or superiors of their male counterparts; moreover, the most consistently smart and witty characters of screwball were the women, played by actresses like Myrna Loy, Claudette Colbert, Irene Dunne, and Carole Lombard" (Chumo, 3). But Chumo concludes that the sense of freedom the protagonists acquire creates a generic problem "since the screwball couple is supposed to achieve a clarity of vision on the road that leads to reintegration into society. . . however, Thelma declares, 'somethin's, like, crossed over in me, and I can't go back. I mean, I just couldn't live,' and Louise concurs." Chumo thus concludes that, by driving over the cliff, "Thelma and Louise reject the 'dead or alive' options and instead choose the freedom of the American landscape. . . . Moreover, the decision at the end is not framed in terms of suicide but rather in terms of continuing the journey. When they realize they are trapped, Thelma . . . urges Louise onward: 'Let's not get caught. . . . Let's keep goin'. . . . Not only do Thelma and Louise escape the authorities . . . but the film itself has escaped the generic constraints of the outlaw tradition by ending with an image of flight and freedom" (Chumo, 10, 11).

The efforts by Chumo, Boozer, and others to place *Thelma & Louise* within a generic context highlight the conflict between the protagonists and the figures of social and legal authority in the film. As in outlaw road films, this conflict drives the plot. But whereas the protagonists in *Easy Rider, Bonnie and Clyde, Butch Cassidy and the Sundance Kid*, and other outlaw films voluntarily elect a life of crime, circumstances push Thelma and Louise into it, and this makes a critical difference. The women are seemingly driven by fate, not by their own volition, into their acts of murder and robbery. As Robinson observes, "*Thelma & Louise* . . . proceeds according to a tragic sense of perceived inevitability" that is rooted in sexual violence and "attendant questions about women as sexual objects and as sexual subjects" (Robinson, 184). This sense of tragic inevitability gives the protagonists more in common with Hamlet and Romeo than with Bonnie and Butch. In fact, *Thelma & Louise* works like a modified Shakespearean tragedy in which the protagonists are sacrificed to preserve social order. Yet, as in Shakespearean tragedy, the characters mature, acquire self-knowledge, and become better human beings from the experience that ultimately dooms them.

Shakespeare typically builds his tragedies around tensions between fate and free will, passion and reason, individual ambitions and social restrictions, excess and restraint. Frequently, protagonists must choose between pursuing their own best interests or strictly adhering to human and divine law and social authority. Flourishing at the juncture in English history between the Middle Ages and the Renaissance, Shakespeare was able to view these issues with a double vision. He often seems attracted by the celebration of the individual will that emerged during the Renaissance and by its open pursuit of personal gain. These, however, conflicted with the medieval insistence that individuals subordinate themselves not only to divine law but also to social authority. The Great Chain of Being posited that the sovereignty of the king within the political and legal sphere and of the husband within the familial realm was an integral part of God's plan. Thus to violate either sacred or secular law or to challenge the social authority was to blaspheme.

Shakespeare builds several of his tragedies and history plays around situations where the needs of a sympathetic protagonist conflict with the demands of a rigid and sometimes corrupt social authority. *Romeo and Juliet*, *Antony and Cleopatra*, *Hamlet* and those history plays dealing with the House of Bolingbroke all revolve around the central tension between pursuing what is desirable, just, and/or fair for the individual, on the one hand, and sustaining social authority, on the other hand. Ultimately, Shakespeare prefers the personal injustices brought about by rigid, hierarchical, medieval social conventions and codified laws to the more devastating threats posed by lawless human monsters who indulge their immoral or amoral wills (i.e., Iago in *Othello* and Edmund in *King Lear*). For Shakespeare, *even victims must adhere to the law*.

With some modifications, *Thelma & Louise* centers around similar conflicts and comes to similar conclusions. Like Shakespearean tragedy, *Thelma & Louise* affirms the primacy of the social order over personal justice. In this respect, the worldview of *Thelma & Louise*, like Shakespeare's, is essentially conservative, in the nineteenth-century sense of that word. Because the film upholds the sanctity of a flawed social authority over individual justice, the protagonists must die. Sarandon expresses this notion in a 1998 television interview with James Lipton: "What separates *Thelma & Louise* from a . . . male revenge film is that there was a sense in this character, I believe, that she had to pay the price, and that even when she blew up the truck, or when any of those things happened, she was trying to understand *why?* " (Lipton).

Thus the film generates a rich set of conflicting desires, where our sympathies for the protagonists induce us to hope for their escape, but the film's endorsement of law and order renders unacceptable any ending in which the women survive without paying retribution for their crimes. (Even if killing Harlan may arguably have been defensible, the armed robbery of innocents in the convenience store, the incarceration of the state trooper who was simply performing his job, and the destruction of the gas truck are not.) The final spectacle showing the two women fleeing an army of police cars and helicop-

ters not only establishes the awesome power of the social authority over the individual, it also makes us both thankful and sad about the relative lack of power
the individual has in the face of the social order.

Like Shakespeare, Scott tests the tension that results when an inflexible social authority conflicts with an essentially good and well-intentioned protagonist. Shakespeare creates dramatic situations in which "all events do conspire,"
almost but not entirely, to require the tragic hero to violate the social authority
and thereby initiate the chain of events that will ultimately doom him. In essence, the tragic hero is sacrificed for the preservation of social order and codes
of authority.

The tragic sensibility centers on our recognition that we must subordinate
our sympathies for the heroes to the requirement that they be held accountable for their misdeeds. Thus, for example, Hamlet's demise is necessary because of the guilt he bears for the deaths he caused, even though he was
basically well intentioned and often placed in situations where his deadly actions were among his most viable choices under the circumstances, such as
when he slays Laertes and Claudius. Though we may sympathize with Hamlet's plight, understand how he was driven to kill three men and order the
deaths of two more, and see him to be in a no-win situation, within the morality of Shakespeare's tragic universe his extenuating circumstances do not justify violating human and divine law. To permit the tainted tragic hero to
survive unpunished would be to perpetuate an imbalance within society and
within God's universe. Only through the tainted hero's fall from fortune can
tragedy perform its function of restoring order to a society out of balance
("The time is out of joint. O cursed spite, that ever I was born to set it right"
Hamlet, Act I, Scene 5, lines 189–90).

Thelma & Louise employs a similar tragic tension. The plot generates strong
desires in the audience for a happy ending but simultaneously creates ever-
strengthening expectations for a sad one. The deeper we move into the plot
the more we like the protagonists, admire their growth in self-knowledge, and
approve of the bond they form with each other. At the same time, however, the
evolving plot pushes them into greater and greater conflicts with the social order, as Louise shoots Harlan, Thelma commits armed robbery, and they jointly
threaten and incarcerate a police officer and incinerate a gasoline truck. As in
the case of *Hamlet*, the film's tragic power stems from the interplay between
our desires for the protagonists' success and well-being and our intensifying
expectations that the preservation of law and order will require their demise.

The movie's dual protagonists seem as star crossed as Romeo and Juliet,
fated for doom in spite of their best efforts to survive in a hostile world. Once
Thelma accepts Harlan's overtures at the lounge, their situation moves inexo-
rably from bad to worse despite their best efforts, until it becomes completely
hopeless in their final confrontation with the police. Any momentary hopes are
quickly dashed: when he steals their cash, J.D., the hitchhiker, rapidly
squelches the promise of Thelma's sexual awakening and the women's hope

for freedom. Would-be law-abiding citizens, Thelma and Louise are compelled by circumstances to break the law with increasing frequency.[2] Unlike Butch and Sundance or Bonnie and Clyde, Thelma and Louise are repeatedly pushed into situations in which their criminal behavior becomes their most viable option.

At the same time the audience can never finally approve of their actions; to do so would be to abandon the entire premise of an ordered society governed by law. As in other tragedies, especially Shakespearean tragedy, we feel that the protagonists' deaths are somehow necessary if social order is truly to be maintained. Because they *are* breaking the law, their tragic universe requires retribution from them, *sympathetic as their plight may be*. This requirement represents a very hard-nosed, uncompromising, inflexible view of the universe, but that is why we call it tragedy.

On the other hand, the tragic experience also elevates the protagonists, who grow in stature and self-knowledge through their adventures. Thus, their demise is both sacrificial for the good of the society and uplifting for them personally: it is the price they pay for their enhanced self-knowledge, much as Oedipus's grief and blindness were the price he paid for his insight. The film's final shot captures both the uplift and fall that characterize tragedy, as Thelma and Louise arc above and into the Grand Canyon. The protagonists peak as they plunge to their doom.

As in classical tragedy, increased insight and growth in self-knowledge are what make the fall from fortune worthwhile. Both protagonists learn about love between women, about love with men, and about what does and does not constitute acceptable behavior from their mates and from men in general. Moreover, as Thelma comes into her own sexually, she realizes her identity in other ways too. After she "finally got laid properly," she becomes more assertive and self-confident. When Louise becomes immobilized by despair after J.D. steals their money, Thelma forces her to leave the hotel and in other ways takes charge of the situation. Significantly, Thelma now drives the car. She completes her transformation from passivity to action when she robs the convenience store. Afterward, she no longer requires others to think or act for her, and she reaches a higher level of consciousness. "I feel awake. . . . Wide awake. I don't remember feeling this awake. . . . Everything looks different." Her transformation intensifies throughout the film; when the state trooper pulls them over for speeding, it is Thelma who takes charge, placing the gun to the officer's head, ordering him into the trunk, and commanding Louise to destroy the radio. Prior to her sexual awakening and armed robbery, Thelma has always taken orders from others and emulated others. Afterward she is a more fully realized person, and for the first time in her adult life, she looks forward to the future. "Something's like crossed over in me, and I can't go back. I mean I just couldn't live." With the sort of perverse irony characteristic of a Flannery O'Connor short story, Thelma's criminality, along with her full experience of her sexuality, has enabled her to grow personally and perhaps even spiritually.

Shortly before the final scene Thelma tells Louise, "No matter what happens, I'm glad I came with you."

Although Louise's personal development is not as dramatic as Thelma's—because she begins as a stronger, more independent figure—she too grows from her experience. If her trauma in Texas had caused her to conduct herself in a cautious and guarded fashion, her status as fugitive ironically liberates her. As events progress she becomes freer, less uptight, more cheerful, and more open to life and to the splendor of nature. Her development is evident in her grooming and manner as, after they become fugitives, she lets down her hair, wears more revealing, more casual, less confining clothes, and carries herself in a more relaxed fashion.[3] Whereas Louise had always seemed in a hurry to reach her destination, even when they first set out for the cabin, she later stops the car to enjoy the sunrise over the mountains. After she becomes a fugitive, Louise also becomes clearer about what she wants from her relationship with Jimmy. At the beginning of the film she had hoped to extract a marriage proposal by going away and making him miss her, but after she shoots Harlan and flees, she rejects Jimmy's offer of marriage because she now recognizes that his fear of losing her is not a good enough reason to marry. On the other hand, her adventure also brings out the best and most decent side of Jimmy, and before he departs Louise realizes the depth of their passion for each other, perhaps for the first time. Thus, as with Hamlet, the women's deaths come only after they have reached a degree of personal growth, self-acceptance, and acceptance of their situation: "The readiness is all" (*Hamlet*, Act V, scene 2, line 220).

Thelma & Louise has other characteristics that give it greater affinity to *Romeo and Juliet* than to *Hamlet*. The plot of *Romeo and Juliet* hinges on Romeo's slaying of Tybalt after Tybalt has killed Romeo's best friend, Mercutio. In avenging Mercutio Romeo violates the Prince's command against further feuding among Montagues and Capulets and thereby sets into motion the chain of events that will lead to his banishment and to his and Juliet's eventual deaths. Shakespeare believed that civil order was paramount; thus the "right" thing for Romeo would have been to report Mercutio's death to the Prince and allow him to carry out the threatened death sentence against Tybalt. Had Romeo so acted, his tragedy would not have ensued.

However, while Shakespeare shows us that relying on the enforcement of the law is Romeo's proper response, he simultaneously creates a dramatic situation where Romeo has virtually no option but to take on Tybalt. After all, Romeo's peace-making efforts made Mercutio vulnerable to Tybalt's attack: Tybalt kills Mercutio under Romeo's arm. Moreover, Tybalt taunts Romeo, who would certainly have lost his self-respect and his honor among his friends if he did not seek revenge. Thus, we feel that Romeo is almost compelled to fight Tybalt, even though such a choice flies in the face of the social order and will inevitably prove disastrous for him. Moreover, he must decide in the heat of passion, moments after Mercutio has been slain, when he is reacting from gut instinct instead of from reason. Shakespeare thus creates a wonderful literary moment where doing the wrong thing is virtually, but not entirely, irresistible for Romeo, and doing the right thing is virtually, but not entirely, impossible. Romeo's tragic doom becomes inevitable after he violates the Prince's command.

Thelma & Louise hinges upon a very similar dramatic moment. Like Romeo, Louise sets in motion a dooming chain of events by yielding in a highly emotional moment to an impulse that was virtually impossible for her to resist or for the audience not to sympathize with, but that was also completely incompatible with social authority. However strong and understandable the impulse was, shooting Harlan was not the right thing for Louise to do. Had she killed him while he was attempting to rape Thelma, the murder might have been justified. But just as Shakespeare introduces a critical delay between Tybalt's slaying of Mercutio and Romeo's revenge, Scott has Louise kill Harlan after the rape has been prevented and both parties have separated. Consequently, defense is no longer an issue. Thus, the killing transforms Louise from victim to victimizer and from someone who, in critical moments, governs her life according to reason to someone who is driven by passion. It also makes her apprehension and punishment something necessary for maintaining social order. From a Shakespearean point of view, the proper action would have been for Louise to send for a police officer and charge Harlan with sexual assault, regardless of any external factors.

But as Shakespeare does for Romeo, Scott and writer Khouri create a set of external factors that makes doing the right thing all but impossible. The first is Louise's experience in Texas in which she was presumably sexually assaulted and then demeaned and abused by the justice system. Louise's violent insistence that she will not even discuss what happened in Texas heightens our sense of its traumatic impact upon her. Even without such a past, she is justly enraged by Harlan's verbal abuse just moments after he has physically assaulted Thelma. The audience is sympathetic to Louise's strong, visceral impulse to shoot him, just as it sympathizes with Romeo's attack on Tybalt. However, in both plots the dramatists have carefully introduced crucial time delays between the antagonists' assaults and the protagonists' retaliation, thereby eliminating any claim of self-defense. Thus, in a world where reason is expected to restrain passion even at the most extreme moments, where conformity to law is expected of all citizens regardless of past injustices, both Romeo and Louise bring about their dooms by failing to restrain almost irresistible impulses.

Probably what struck the strongest chord in popular audiences was watching two strong-willed, self-assured women take control of their destinies, largely unassisted and frequently impeded by men. Men are both their tormentors and their victims, and this paradoxical relationship between men's attempts to dominate Thelma and Louise and the women's violent victimization of men lies at the center of much of the film's controversy and its tragic vision.

Shakespeare was not the only earlier author to explore this paradoxical inversion of victim and victimizer. Herman Melville does likewise in "Billy Budd, Sailor" where the sympathetic title character is unjustly accused of disloyalty. Rendered unable to defend himself verbally by a fierce stutter that occurs when he is angry, Billy impulsively strikes and kills his accuser, Claggart. By establishing Billy's stutter earlier in the story, portraying Billy as an extremely good-natured, well-intentioned, "handsome sailor," and depicting Claggart's natural depravity, Melville makes us and Captain Vere extremely sympathetic to Billy's action. Yet we must finally respect Vere all the more because he condemns Billy, in spite of his sympathy and affection for the unjustly accused sailor. For Vere the situation is clear: the odious Claggart has been "struck dead by an angel of God! Yet the angel must hang" (Melville, 101). Even Billy accepts the conclusion that a greater authority requires his punishment, and he goes to his death proclaiming, "God Bless Captain Vere!" (Melville, 123). Like Shakespeare, Melville maintains that even victims must be fully accountable before the law, even in the most extenuating of circumstances, although he makes this slightly more of an open question by casting some doubt as to whether Vere was legally required to pursue the retribution as relentlessly as he did.

Thelma & Louise closes the question more firmly by presenting the police officers as generally positive figures who act professionally. Whatever Thelma's experience with the Texas authorities may have been, the police we see on screen perform their duties responsibly, in a businesslike fashion, and sometimes with compassion. If the agents who take over the case show less sympathy and understanding for the women than Hal does, it is not because Thelma and Louise are women, but rather because these agents have become cynical over the years and regard Louise and Thelma merely as another pair of killers and armed robbers on the loose. But they never use demeaning slang to refer to the women or otherwise act unprofessionally in their pursuit of them. Moreover, even if one anonymous officer reads a girlie magazine during a lull on a stakeout, none of the police ever alludes to Thelma or Louise's sexuality or to Thelma's free-spirited dancing with Harlan. Even the officer who pulls Thelma over for speeding in the desert treats her with formal, if stern, professional courtesy.[4] Although several other men abuse and demean the protagonists, we never see a policeman or policewoman do so. Moreover, we never question the appropriateness of their pursuing the fugitives.

Detective Hal Slocum, one of the officers responsible for enforcing the law, shares Captain Vere's tragic vision. According to Khouri, "Hal represents that part of us all that wants law and order. He represents law and order with a human side. He wants to understand what would lead someone like Louise to kill someone" (Winter, 7). Hal knows of the abuses to Louise in Texas and appreciates how that experience has made her distrust the legal system. He sympathizes with the women's plight and exhibits contempt for the men who have victimized them: Thelma's husband Darryl, Harlan, and J.D. Like the audience, Hal is truly concerned for the protagonists' well-being and wants them to emerge as well as possible from the episode. And like the audience, he becomes increasingly fearful that this will not occur. Nonetheless, Hal must subordinate his sympathy for Thelma and Louise to his duty as a police officer. The law requires that they be held accountable for their deeds, and no acceptable resolution to the problem will allow him to settle for less than that. And so, like Captain Vere, he plays out within his psyche the tragic tension between his desires for the women and his obligations to the social order.

Thelma and Louise share another common feature with Billy Budd. Like Billy, they commit the act that dooms them in part because they cannot communicate effectively. However, where Billy's problem is physical and emotional, the women's difficulty is social. Because of Louise's Texas experience, they are convinced that the justice system will not seriously listen to them, that it will not believe that Harlan had assaulted an unwilling Thelma after she had been seen drinking and dancing with him. Correct or not, their perception that the truth will inevitably be distorted and never properly heard pushes them into more and more desperate actions. Like Billy, they turn to violence when they cannot represent themselves in words. And, as with Billy, we sympathize with them precisely for this reason. But here again our sympathy does not relieve them of their responsibility to conform to the demands of the law; it does, however, intensify our sense of the tragedy.

Another feature *Thelma & Louise* shares with "Billy Budd, Sailor," *Hamlet*, and *Romeo and Juliet* is that someone else's unjust act propels the protagonists into the situations that cause them to behave in the ways that doom them. Had Claggart not falsely accused Billy, had Tybalt not persisted in provoking a fight with Mercutio, had Claudius not killed Old Hamlet, and had Harlan not attacked Thelma, there would have been no tragedies. In Louise's case, an even earlier injustice comes back to haunt her: her traumatic experience in Texas. We have already seen that it induces her to reject the proper course of action because it has created in her too much fear of the justice system. Beyond that, it literally enables the police to trace her phone call and track down the women. When Hal tells Louise that he knows what happened to her in Texas he flusters her, causing her to remain on the line long enough for his agents to fix her location. Hence she continues to be victimized by her Texas trauma, even as her crime spree flourishes. Thus, like Shakespeare and Melville, Scott creates a tragic tension by holding victims accountable for actions that they committed because of their victimization. These actions are double-edged, at once condemning the protagonists to their doom and at the same time allowing them to experience the personal growth necessary for them to confront their fates in a noble and affirmative fashion. By constructing the plot in this fashion, Scott updates to contemporary terms the age-old tragic tensions between individuals and society.

NOTES

1. Portions of this discussion first appeared in slightly different form as Richard A. Schwartz, "The Tragic Vision of *Thelma & Louise*," *Journal of Evolutionary Psychology* 17.1 (March 1996): 101–107.

2. Hal makes this point explicit when he tells J.D. that by stealing all of their money he has forced the women into increasingly desperate acts and thereby severely diminished their chances for survival.

3. I would like to acknowledge my student, Jennifer Edward, for pointing out how Louise's personality changes throughout the film, especially in terms of her mannerisms and dress.

4. The rather absurdist scene where a Rastafarian bicyclist smoking a huge marijuana cigarette encounters this police officer locked in his trunk functions similarly to the grave-digger scene in *Hamlet*. Positioned at the beginning of the final act, these moments of comic relief briefly expand our perspective and alter our point of view before we telescope back onto the final sequence of events that will doom the heroes.

1492: Conquest of Paradise

(1992)

CAST

Columbus	Gérard Depardieu
Sanchez	Armand Assante
Queen Isabel	Sigourney Weaver
Older Fernando	Loren Dean
Beatrix	Angela Molina
Marchena	Fernando Rey
Noxica	Michael Wincott
Pinzon	Tcheky Karyo
Captain Mendez	Kevin Dunn
Santangel	Frank Langella
Francisco Bobadilla	Mark Margolis
Arojaz	Kario Salem
Fernando (age 10)	Billy Sullivan
Brother Buyl	John Hefferman
Guevara	Arnold Vosloo
Bartolome	Steven Waddington
Giacomo	Fernando G. Cuervo

| Alonso | Jose Louis Ferrer |
| Utapan | Bercelio Moya |

PRODUCTION

Director	Ridley Scott
Producers	Ridley Scott and Alain Goldman (a Paramount release of a Percy Main/ Legende/Cyrk production)
Screenplay	Roselyne Bosch
Director of photography	Adrian Biddle
Production designer	Norris Spencer
Supervising art directors	Benjamin Fernandez and Leslie Tomkins
Art direction	Raul Antonio Paton, Kevin Phipps, Martin Hitchcock, and Luke Scott
Set decoration	Ann Mollo
Costume design	Charles Knode and Barbara Rutter
Editors	William Anderson and Françoise Bonnot
Music director	Vangelis

SYNOPSIS

The film *1492: Conquest of Paradise* tells the story of how Christopher Columbus managed to win backing during the Spanish Inquisition for his then-radical, almost heretical plan to sail west across the Atlantic Ocean to Asia; then how he suppressed his mutinous crew when landfall did not come as quickly as anticipated; and finally, after landing in the Caribbean islands, how he settled the New World. It depicts Columbus as a passionate, compassionate, enormously determined dreamer and a foreigner of common birth who both benefits from and is undermined by the Spanish nobility that uses him for its own ends.

The opening credits appear against a red background that features pen and ink drawings of fifteenth-century sailing ships and early illustrations of the New World. The music by Vangelis reflects the Arabic influence of the Moors who inhabited much of Spain until Ferdinand and Isabel drove them from the Iberian peninsula in early 1492. This Arabic-sounding music repeats throughout the film. Following the credits is a written prologue that describes Spain of that time as "a nation gripped by superstition, ruled by the crown and a ruthless Inquisition that persecuted men for daring to dream. One man challenged that power. Driven by his sense of destiny, he crossed the sea of darkness in search of honor, gold, and the greater glory of God."

The written prologue is followed by narrative spoken by Fernando, Columbus's son, who recalls his father's words: "Nothing that results from human progress is achieved with unanimous consent. And those who are enlightened before the others are condemned to pursue that light in spite of others."

The opening scene shows Columbus and the young Fernando on the shore, looking out against a deep red sky at a ship sinking beneath a vast horizon. As Columbus peels an orange, he has Fernando observe the sequence in which the parts of the ship disappear from sight, and then he uses the orange to illustrate how the earth is round, which accounts for why the sails seem to sink into the horizon instead of pitch forward, as they would if it were flat.

The pair then go to the monastery where Fernando's older brother Diego greets them. Brother Buyl gives Columbus good news: the University at Salamanca has agreed to hear his proposal. Buyl asks what he will tell them, and Columbus says he wants to go to Asia by sailing west. He describes Marco Polo's reports of spices and wealth in China and notes that currently only two routes exist for going there. But the sea route around Africa takes a year, and Turks have closed off the land route to Christians. Buyl asserts the ancient belief that the distance to the west is infinite, but Columbus dismisses this as superstition. Instead, he cites the calculations of several of his contemporaries and claims that Asia is 750 leagues west of the Canary Islands. But these men are either Jewish or regarded as heretics by the Inquisition, and Buyl tells him that people are being burned for less: "Already you are a dead man." He adds that Columbus must control his passion if he is to succeed, but Columbus replies that passion cannot be controlled. Buyl characterizes the men behind the Inquisition as having no feelings at all, and he reminds Columbus that he needs their approval to pursue his goal. Columbus bristles and speaks out against medieval superstition. He will not be told what to believe.

That night, as Columbus and Fernando ride through town, they witness the priests overseeing the burning of heretics at the stake. They arrive home where Columbus tells Beatrix of his opportunity. If he succeeds, he may be gone for years. He apologizes for not having given her a better life, but she has no complaints. They seem very much in love.

At Salamanca, the university officials, who are also priests, cite the ancient authority of Aristotle and Ptolemy, who were much revered in the Middle Ages and who believed that the ocean could not be crossed. Columbus replies that he can cross it in six or seven weeks. Sanchez, who is the treasurer for the royal court, and not a priest or member of the university, asks how Spain would benefit from his voyage. Citing Marco Polo, Columbus answers, "trade." When the priests object to his ungodly materialism, he adds that he would also bring the word of God to Asia and make the people there subjects of Castile (King Ferdinand) and Aragon (Queen Isabel). Spain, he maintains, will no longer be just a realm; it will become an empire. When the priests ask sarcastically if he thinks God waited for Columbus to reveal this truth to the world, Columbus retorts that He chose a carpenter's son to reveal Himself. But when a priest asks if Columbus believes himself to be the chosen one, he falls silent before finally declaring, "Asia can be found to the west, and I can prove it."

After the hearing concludes, Sanchez and Arojaz, one of the priests, share a sumptuous meal. Arojaz declares that such independent minds are dangerous and that Columbus is both a heretic and a mercenary. But although Sanchez acknowledges that the decision belongs to the priests at the university, he believes Columbus might be of some use to Spain. When Arojaz demurs, Sanchez begins to fill the man's glass with wine. As he does, he states, "The fascinating thing about power is that what can be given so effortlessly. . . ." Sanchez then stops filling the priest's glass and pours the drink into his own, as he concludes, "can so easily be taken away."

Despite Sanchez's implied threat, when Columbus returns home Father Buyl informs him that his petition has been denied. Columbus goes into a rage in which he assaults the monks and destroys their work. Subsequently, he is forced to maintain a vow of silence as penance for is behavior. But when Pinzon, a shipowner, tracks him down in the monastery and informs him that he has important friends who can arrange an audience with the queen, Columbus breaks his silence and demands to know where he can meet this man.

Columbus and Pinzon ride to Granada just after it has fallen to the Spaniards in early 1492. They watch the Christian cross replace the Muslim crescent above the palace at Alhambra, and Pinzon observes that it is "a tragic victory. . . . We're losing a great culture. But I suppose there's a price to be paid for every victory." Inside the palace, Columbus again meets Sanchez, who gestures for him to proceed to the room where Queen Isabel conducts her business. Isabel tells him that Sanchez has described him as "not completely mad," and Columbus replies, "No more than the woman who said she would take Granada from the Moors." When Isabel notes that "they believe the ocean is uncrossable," Columbus asks, "What did they say about Granada before today?" She smiles and answers, "That it was impregnable." They seem to establish a rapport, and Isabel describes him as someone who "doesn't accept the world as it is." She then tells him she will notify him of her decision.

After Columbus departs, Isabel meets with Sanchez and complains that the expense would be prohibitive, but Sanchez replies that the mission would cost no more than two state dinners. He adds that they have much to gain if Columbus succeeds and little to lose. After Isabel agrees, Sanchez and Columbus negotiate over the terms of the contract. Columbus insists on receiving titles and 10 percent of all the wealth found under his jurisdiction. Eavesdropping on their conversation, Isabel confides to one of her companions that she thought Columbus was an idealist, but the lady replies that idealism and ambition are not incompatible. Sanchez tries to squeeze Columbus by threatening to find someone else who will accept more modest terms. But Columbus answers that if he can find such a person, "I'll become a monk." His retort greatly amuses Isabel, who instructs Sanchez to accept Columbus's terms. Columbus returns home to convey his good news to Beatrix, who remains loving and supportive.

The second part of the film begins at the port of Palos on August 3, 1492, as Columbus prepares to set sail following a religious processional that leads to the sea. Before he leaves, Columbus goes to confession, where he admits to Buyl that he has under-represented the length of the journey in order to win approval. Buyl demands that Columbus report the truth, but he refuses, claiming the men will not follow him if they know the truth. Buyl threatens to tell them himself, but Columbus reminds him that he is bound by an oath not to divulge what is said in the confessional. Then he asks Buyl for absolution.

They set sail as the red sun rises. At night, Columbus uses a sextant to navigate by the stars, as the Moors do when they are out of sight of land. He maintains that he will follow the twenty-eighth parallel until they reach land. After nine weeks they still have not spotted land, and Pinzon, who captains one of the ships, accuses Columbus of having lied to him. He wants to turn back and warns of mutiny, but Columbus says it is too late to turn back. He then inspires the crew with a speech about the importance of overcoming fear and keeping faith with God and themselves. The crew becomes motivated again, and soon afterward Columbus observes bugs attracted to the ship's lights. This suggests land is close by, and the next day, as the fog lifts, a tropical paradise appears before them. He rushes ashore, kneels, regards the splendor around him, and claims the island for Spain in the name of Ferdinand and Isabel. He names the island San Salvador.

Hacking their way through the lush, primeval forest, Columbus and his men see snakes, parrots, and exotic plants and wildlife. When they encounter natives, he insists that his men not fire upon them. Instead, they remain passive while the natives check them out and then lead them to their village, where everyone finds them to be great curiosities. When Columbus meets the chief, the chief laughs, and Columbus laughs back, and they establish feelings of good will. A few days later Columbus writes, "I think we have returned to Eden. This is how the world must have been at the beginning of time." He adds that they will convert the natives by persuasion, not by force: "We come in peace and with honor. They are not savages, and neither will we be." He commands his men to treat them with respect, under threat of severe punishment.

When Columbus notes the natives' silver medallions, he asks where they came from. They answer "Cuba," and Columbus and his men set sail. Soon they are panning for precious metals and sailing from island to island, where the natives mistake them for gods and treat them generously. But apart from the few artifacts the natives have given as tokens of submission, they do not find gold. In December Pinzon becomes extremely ill, and they decide to return to Spain after assigning thirty-nine men to remain behind in a fort on Haiti. Columbus admits that he has not seen anything like what Marco Polo described; nonetheless, he is anxious to return again to the New World. "This is a chance for a new beginning."

They are greeted lavishly at the Spanish royal court, and Beatrix shows how proud she is of her man. At the height of Columbus's triumph a priest leans over to Sanchez and declares, "It won't be easy to get rid of your prophet now." But Sanchez replies, "On the contrary, it seems to me the man is preparing his own cross." At a royal banquet, Columbus introduces tobacco to the court, and Noxica, one of the noblemen, chokes on it. Columbus explains how nature is the natives' god. "It's as if God and nature were one. They see God in everything." When Sanchez asks about the gold, Columbus makes a big show of the gold trinkets he has collected. He also shows off some of the natives who have returned with him, along with some of the wildlife. Sanchez acts unimpressed, but Isabel is enthusiastic, and she approves a much larger, second expedition.

The next day, as Columbus and Sanchez practice their sword play, Sanchez tells him that he defends himself well "for a commoner." Sanchez then introduces Francisco Bobadilla, who seeks an appointment as one of the island governors. But Columbus tells him the positions have been filled. Bobadilla answers that he assumes the new governors will be "men of quality," and after he leaves, Sanchez tells Columbus that he has a talent for making enemies. In fact, against their will and despite their lack of experience, Columbus has selected his brothers Bartolome and Giacomo to govern with him, as he feels he can trust no one else.

The much larger second expedition arrives in the West Indies in November 1493, with numerous provisions including oxen and horses, the first to appear in the New World. Mounted on a beautiful white horse, Noxica is among the party. They present a formidable military presence, and Columbus fires the cannons to announce his arrival. When no one comes to greet them, they investigate and find the skulls of the men they had left behind from the first voyage. The natives they encounter are fascinated by Noxica's horse, and their chief maintains that warriors who came from the sea killed the Spaniards. Noxica does not believe the chief and urges Columbus to kill all of the "monkeys," as he refers to the natives. But Columbus assures the chief they will not harm his people, even though they can. Instead, Columbus enlists their aid in building a European-style settlement, complete with church and a cast iron bell that they raise with great difficulty. Initially, Noxica refuses to allow them to use his horse for this heavy labor, and there is an overly polite confrontation in which Columbus insists. Noxica submits, but a rift becomes apparent. Subsequently, Columbus explains that he intends to build an ideal city and is using plans drawn up by Leonardo da Vinci. Soon they will be able to make bread from meal they have processed on the island.

They establish a gold mine in which the natives toil, while Noxica and the other nobles rest and make fun of Columbus, whom they demean because he is a commoner. However, when Noxica accuses one of the natives of hiding gold and cuts off the man's hand as a lesson, he undoes the good will Columbus has created with the natives. Columbus imprisons Noxica, who remains defiant and accuses Columbus of failing to produce either gold or an earthly paradise. The next day Columbus discovers some of the Spaniards crucified in the mines. When he orders one of the natives to find the perpetrators, the man answers, "You did the same to your God."

The Spaniards attack the Indian village but are met by an intense counterattack. Meanwhile, Noxica's sympathizers kill his guards and liberate him. He torches Columbus's quarters and then leads an ambush against Columbus and his men. Assisted by a sympathetic native, Columbus chases Noxica into the forest. Seeing that he is trapped, Noxica removes his sword, defiantly tells Columbus, "You know what will be said about you in Spain," and calls him a "nothing whose bastards will never inherit the title." Noxica then jumps from a cliff to his death.

Columbus executes the other mutineers and then resumes the work of the colony. The priest objects, saying that he does not understand what Columbus hopes to gain by treating the natives as equal of the nobles. Columbus replies, "a new world," but the priest rejoins, "No one wants one, only you." Columbus points to the other men who have remained and says that they want one too. He then gives the priest permission to return to Spain but adds that his leaving will not help Columbus make the place more godly. Subsequently, Columbus tells his brother, "Paradise and hell can be earthly. We carry them with us wherever we go."

A hurricane rips through the settlement, and as we view the devastation, we hear Sanchez detailing Columbus's failings to Isabel. After these are confirmed by the priest, Sanchez recommends that Bobadilla replace Columbus.

Bobadilla arrives at the settlement and informs Columbus that he is now in command. Columbus accepts the change, declaring that he will at last be free to search for the mainland. But Bobadilla tells him that Amerigo Vespucci has already discovered it. It is only about a week's sail away. Columbus claims that he is not disappointed, Vespucci's discovery validates his theory and vindicates him. But then Bobadilla informs Columbus that he is being sent back to Spain, where he will be imprisoned for his malfeasance.

Columbus's sons Diego and Fernando visit him in prison and assure him that they are arranging his release. Columbus says he cannot wait to return to the New World, and Fernando is anxious to go with him. Diego says that it is madness for him to go in his condition, but Fernando sticks up for his father. Subsequently, Columbus meets with Isabel, who says that she has tried, but she cannot find a reason to allow him to return. He tells her he wants to explore the land of his dreams before he dies, and she finally permits another voyage, but he must not take his brothers and he may not return to Santo Domingo or the other colonies. "The New World," she says, "is a disaster." In return, Columbus questions if the Old World is any better. As Columbus leaves, he encounters Sanchez, who accuses him of being a dreamer. Columbus asks Sanchez to look out at the city and describe what he sees. Sanchez sees palaces, steeples, spires that reach to the sky—civilization. To this, Columbus replies, "All of them created by people like me. No matter how long you live, Sanchez, there is something that will never change between us. I did it. You didn't."

Back home, there is a brief expression of affection between Columbus and Beatrix. Then, in a public ceremony, Arojaz, the priest from the university who rejected Columbus's initial request, now proclaims that the university has always defended the existence of new territories to the west, and he celebrates Vespucci as the discoverer of a new continent. When Arojaz spots Columbus he tells Sanchez, "What a waste of a life." But Sanchez answers that if he and Arojaz will ever be remembered, it will be because of Columbus.

The film ends as Fernando reads aloud Diego's letter from the colonies, while Columbus looks out to sea. Fernando asks his father to tell him everything he remembers, so he can write it down. When Columbus hesitates, Fernando asks for the first thing he remembers, and Columbus recalls his first view of the lush New World peeking through the fog.

A written statement adds that in 1502, Columbus and Fernando sailed to the New World, where natives showed them the Pacific Ocean, and that Fernando's biography restored Columbus's name to its rightful place in history. In 1992, his descendant, Christopher Columbus, was an admiral in the Royal Spanish Navy. A concluding epigram reiterates Columbus's words: "Life has more imagination than we carry in our dreams."

RECEPTION

The film *1492: Conquest of Paradise* did not fare well either at the box office or among the critics. Budgeted at $47 million, the film grossed only $7.2 million in the United States. It proved more popular abroad and managed to recover its production costs by grossing $52 million overseas (Sammon, *Ridley Scott*, 112–15). Some 25 percent longer than typical Hollywood films, the two-and-a-half-hour movie was criticized for lack of a cohesive plot and shallow character development. In addition, many viewers found Depardieu's English difficult to understand in places. Although Vincent Canby of the *New York Times* was impressed by the scenery and other production qualities, he panned the movie, declaring that it "is not a terrible film. Yet because it is without any guiding point of view, it is a lot less interesting than the elaborate physical production that has been given to it" (Canby, Review of *1492*). The *New York Times*'s Janet Maslin also criticized it, calling the film "unnaturally still and talky" (Maslin, Review of *1492*). *Variety*'s Todd McCarthy expressed similar criticisms. In addition, he complained about the lack of depth in the relationships among the characters, the movie's "ponderous pacing," and the "overbearing wall-to-wall score" by Vangelis. On the other hand, he too praised the visual aspects of the production, especially the cinematography, production design, and costuming (Sammon, *Ridley Scott*, 145–47).

DISCUSSION

Made to commemorate the 500th anniversary of Christopher Columbus's arrival in the New World, *1492* celebrates the explorer as a strong-willed independent spirit who is willing to overcome all obstacles to manifest his dream. However, because the story is based on historical accounts, it lacks the tight plot structure found in original scripts that center around the development and resolution of a particular conflict or related set of conflicts. (*White Squall*, which is also based on a historical account, suffers from the same problem.) This absence of specific conflicts accounts for why many critics found the story ponderous. On the other hand, *1492* is beautifully filmed, and the lush shots of the pristine tropical forests communicate how the New World must indeed have seemed Edenic to the Spaniards who arrived from parched Iberia. In this respect, the photography alone conveys Scott's point that the New World represents for Columbus a second chance for humanity, a place where the human race can start anew and strive to create an earthly paradise.

In addition, the film presents several significant themes. Paul M. Sammon notes that, like *White Squall* and *G.I. Jane*, *1492* depicts "the high personal costs paid by outsiders willing to challenge the dominant social order. . . . Columbus overcomes aristocratic arrogance and religious ignorance to prove the existence of a New World; his reward is scorn, imprisonment, and disgrace (Sammon, *Ridley Scott*, 111). The film *1492* also raises other issues that Scott has introduced elsewhere. In particular, it addresses the need to temper passion with rational restraint, a theme first introduced in *The Duellists*; the value of constructive imagination, which appears in *Legend* and *Gladiator*; the problem of containing evil, depicted in *Alien* and *Legend*; intolerance fostered by differences in social class, addressed in *Someone to Watch over Me* and, to a lesser extent, *White Squall*; the problems that arise when self-serving individuals in positions of power thwart the sincere efforts of those who do not enjoy power, a theme found in *Alien*, *Blade Runner*, *Gladiator*, and *Hannibal*; of strong women who know their own minds, shown in *Alien*, *Thelma & Louise*, *G.I. Jane* and *Hannibal*.

The film expresses greater approval of strong passion than Scott's earlier work, although it still recognizes the need to temper it with reason. Columbus is almost as driven as Feraud from *The Duellists*, but even though he insists in his exchange with Buyl that passion cannot be controlled, he typically channels his passion more productively than Feraud. Apart from the scene where he becomes infuriated and attacks the monks after his petition is denied, Columbus manages to contain himself enough to stay out of trouble. When the priests at Salamanca try to trap Columbus into committing heresy by comparing himself to Christ, he holds his tongue and then changes the subject. In Haiti, he avoids divisive confrontation with the insubordinate Noxica by politely insisting on the use of Noxica's horse and thanking him afterward, and he controls his outrage when dealing with the natives after learning of the slaughter of the men he had left behind. In fact, as an administrator he routinely exercises restraint and self-control; these become part of his vision for the ideal New World he wants to create. And though the nobility criticizes Columbus for them, his temperate policies win the viewers' approval.

Nonetheless, along with Jordan O'Neil from *G.I. Jane* and Maximus from *Gladiator*, Columbus stands out among Scott's protagonists as someone who is driven by a quest. Unlike the propagators of the Inquisition, who are described as cold men without any feelings, Columbus is fueled by his intense desire to realize his dream. Without such intensity, he could not prevail.

At the same time, however, Columbus emerges as the voice of reason. He suppresses the nascent mutiny at sea by convincing his crew not to allow themselves to be governed by fear, and he rejects the fearful, medieval superstition that makes possible the cruelty of the Inquisition and restricts the human imagination. Instead, like other harbingers of the Renaissance, Columbus advocates a rational view of the cosmos instead of the theological one promulgated by the university's medieval scholastics. Thus, when the priests dismiss the calculations of the contemporaries Columbus cites because they are Jewish or heretics, and when they endorse instead the theories of Aristotle and Ptolemy because they are ancient authorities, they appear guilty to Columbus and to us of such logical fallacies as argument *ad hominem* and argument by authority. Columbus's rational empiricism seems compelling by contrast.

At the same time, he is not bound too strictly by an empirical approach to a world he can apprehend only incompletely with his senses. Only because Columbus allows himself to imagine the possibility of new lands across the ocean is he able to pursue it through rational and other means. In this respect he is like Maximus in *Gladiator*, who tells his men that if they can imagine their victory, it will happen. As the film's final quote insists, "Life has more imagination than we carry in our dreams," and Scott, through his depiction of Columbus, suggests that, by enabling us to move beyond the limits of our empirically known world, leaps of imagination are what advance civilization. Scott thereby insists on the necessity of granting everyone the freedom to make such imaginative leaps, especially as the breakthroughs can come from anyone, of any social class or gender.

Although the evil in *1492* is not as pure as in *Legend* or as insidious as in *Alien* or *Blade Runner*, Columbus must overcome its manifestations if he is to succeed. The perpetrators of the Inquisition are power crazed and, like the Company in *Alien*, capable of dispassionately ordering acts of great cruelty. Columbus overcomes them by forging a powerful alliance with Sanchez, but Sanchez is motivated by power and wealth too, and his friendship proves to be a double-edged sword. Noxica is more sinister, and, because the story is based on fact instead of fiction, Columbus ultimately fails to find a way to deal appropriately with him. Although Noxica dies, his selfish, arrogant acts of insubordination undermine Columbus's efforts to maintain peaceful relations with the natives and, finally, to retain his position as viceroy.

The question of class difference is raised repeatedly throughout the film. Although he consorts with nobility, Columbus is a sailor of common birth. In the highly structured medieval society of fifteenth-century Spain, in which royalty and nobility were regarded as signs of divinely given favor, the aristocrats naturally regard Columbus as their inferior. Thus Sanchez tells him that he defends himself well "for a commoner," and Noxica goes to his death deriding Columbus as a "nothing whose bastards will never inherit the title." In fact, it is Noxica's sense of being inherently superior that provokes him to his treacherous acts of insubordination. Given Scott's egalitarian, left-wing sensibilities, he treats such notions as both ridiculous and harmful. Sanchez's acknowledgment at the end that he and his cohorts will be remembered only because of Columbus repudiates once and for all the notion that people from privileged social classes are inherently superior.

Aligned with Scott's rejection of hierarchies of social class is his belief that sincerely motivated people who try to achieve important deeds are often inhibited, if not outright thwarted, by self-centered people in positions of authority. The Company undermines the crew of the *Nostromo* in *Alien*; top navy officials and Senator DeHaven oppose O'Neil in *G.I. Jane*; and Commodus undercuts Maximus in *Gladiator*. In *1492*, Sanchez regards Columbus simply as a tool to be exploited, and he plots against the explorer as readily as he assists him. For Sanchez, wielding power is an end in itself, and not just a means to facilitate a better life for all. And his actions toward Columbus illustrate the threat he implies to Arojaz: "The fascinating thing about power is that what can be given so effortlessly, can so easily be taken away."

Isabel, on the other hand, appears sincerely motivated, and, as depicted in this film, she represents another in the line of strong-willed, assertive, self-confident women that Scott likes to portray. Although her role is small, she not only supports Columbus, but she also respects him and shares important qualities with him. Notably, they are both willing to dream and to attempt things that conventional wisdom says are impossible. When she tells Columbus that "they believe the ocean is uncrossable," he asks, "What did they say about Granada before today?" Her reply, "That it was impregnable," not only makes Columbus's point about defying conventional thought; it also underscores their common sensibilities.

A much more minor figure, Beatrix, the only other female character in the film, comes across more conventionally as the loving, supporting mate. But even she is shown to exercise choice. She stays with Columbus not because she depends on him for sustenance or the conventions of the time require her to remain, but because she wants to. When Columbus returns from his travels, he makes this point explicit by pointing out that she must have had many opportunities with other men. And she replies that she remained because she has chosen him.

Columbus's own motivations appear more problematic. Clearly, he is most forcefully driven by his quest to explore unknown realms and prove his belief that the world is different than commonly believed. He also claims that he wants to bring the word of the Christian God to new lands and to expand the power and influence of Spain, although he may mostly be giving lip service in order to satisfy the authorities whose support he requires. On the other hand, his desire for wealth and position also motivate him. He is willing to risk the mission for which he has striven so hard only if he receives his share of power and wealth and a title that would elevate him from the class of commoners. When Isabel seems surprised by his adamant stand, as she thought Columbus was an idealist, her companion gives what seems to be Scott's reply: idealism and ambition are not incompatible.

Nonetheless, as happens frequently in literary and cinematic representations of historical figures, Scott seems to have remade Columbus, if not in his own image, at least in an image that projects Scott's notion of the ideal man. At a time when Columbus's achievement has fallen under attack from leftist revisionist historians, Scott presents a politically correct representation of the explorer. Whereas most historical accounts have typically depicted Columbus as vain, ambitious, greedy, and ruthless, Scott depicts him as a loving father and mate, an inspirational leader, and a compassionate ruler who respects indigenous cultures. Although Columbus lived in an era when notions of being a good parent and spouse were markedly different from the liberal beliefs of the 1990s, the film's opening sequence shows Columbus as a good father in today's terms. Patiently explaining to his young son how a round earth accounts for the way ships disappear over the horizon, he appears as a loving teacher who spends quality time with Fernando and gives him necessary guidance. Similarly, in all of the scenes with Beatrix he acts tenderly and shows concern for her feelings and well-being. Scott does not devote many scenes to showing Columbus as a leader of men, but Columbus does manage to quell a potential mutiny by inspiring them with the forcefulness of his personality and his own belief in his mission. His speech plays off Franklin Roosevelt's famous radio address that declared, "The only thing to fear is fear itself," and, as Canby notes, Henry V's speech before the battle on St. Crispin's Day: "gentlemen in England now a-bed/ Shall think themselves accurs'd they were not here" (William Shakespeare, *Henry V*, Act IV, scene 3, lines 62–63).

Finally, Scott's Columbus is a compassionate governor who seeks to live in harmony with the natives. When Pinzon notes at Granada that the eradication of the Moorish civilization is tragic, "We're losing a great culture. But I suppose there's a price to be paid for every victory," his observation seems intended to apply to the natives as well. (The Arabic-sounding music that permeates the film persistently reminds us of the cultural loss.) Yet, it is not Columbus's intention to harm the natives or destroy their culture. "We come in peace and with honor," he declares. "They are not savages, and neither will we be." Although Columbus asserts his military superiority, he restrains his men's impulse to attack and he befriends the indigenous people instead. Indeed, his respectful treatment of the natives becomes one of the reasons he is later imprisoned. All cruelty is deflected onto the nobleman Noxica; so Scott's Columbus bears no direct responsibility for the devastation the Spaniards wreck upon the natives.

Moreover, although Columbus says he wants to convert the natives to Christianity, this claim does not seem deeply felt. We never see his missionary zeal on screen; on the other hand, we do watch him describe approvingly how nature is the natives' religion and how they see God in everything. This sentiment conforms to popular contemporary views of religion embraced by certain feminists, environmentalists, and practitioners of "New Age" culture (as well as by such earlier figures as Ralph Waldo Emerson, Baruch Spinoza, and Albert Einstein). Released at a time when revisionist historians emphasized the overwhelming cruelty and destruction characteristic of the European conquest of the New World, while overlooking the immense historical significance of Columbus's achievement, *1492* presents Columbus in a sympathetic, politically correct fashion that allows Scott to share with the revisionists his dismay over the exploitation and murder of the natives, without diminishing the enormity of Columbus's achievement or the greatness of the man who changed the course of history, for better and for worse.

White Squall

(1996)

CAST

Captain Sheldon ("Skipper")	Jeff Bridges
Dr. Alice Sheldon	Caroline Goodall
McCrea	John Savage
Chuck Gieg	Scott Wolf
Frank Beaumont	Jeremy Sisto
Gil Martin	Ryan Phillippe
Robert March	David Lascher
Dean Preston	Eric Michael Cole
Shay Jennings	Jason Marsden
Francis Beaumont	David Selby
Girard Pascal	Julio Mechoso
Sanders	Zeljko Ivanek
Tod Johnstone	Balthazar Getty
Tracy Lapchick	Ethan Embry

PRODUCTION

Director	Ridley Scott
Producers	Mimi Polk Gitlin and Rocky Lang (a Scott Free production distributed by Buena Vista Pictures in association with Largo Entertainment)
Screenplay	Todd Robinson
Director of photography	Hugh Johnson
Art director	Joseph P. Lucky
Set decoration	Rand Sagers
Costumer	Judianna Makovsky
Production designers	Peter J. Hampton and Leslie Tomkins
Editor	Gerry Hambling
Music director	Jeff Rona

SYNOPSIS

Based on a real event from 1961, *White Squall* is set in 1962, a year highlighted by the Cuban missile crisis and early space exploration. It tells how a tough, demanding, but compassionate sea captain builds character, instills values, and forges a sense of community among a group of troubled teenage boys from wealthy families. The film then shows the fate of the captain and crew when a fierce storm, a "white squall," suddenly arises and sinks the ship.

The boys study aboard the *Albatross*, on which they also serve as crew, and the rigors of the sea compel them to accept the discipline that Captain Sheldon imposes. As a result of their maritime experiences, they finally bond as a cohesive unit and accept both personal responsibility and responsibility for the well-being of their shipmates. Told from the viewpoint of one of the boys, Chuck Gieg, the story has three basic sections: the voyage out that culminates as the teens complete their various rites of passage and come together as a true community; the voyage back that culminates when the tempest sinks the *Albatross*; and Sheldon's trial.

The voyage out shows how the boys bond and learn to assist in each other's personal growth. Sheldon and the sea are the other agents that facilitate their transformations from troubled, fearful, insecure, lonely souls to responsible, self-confident crewmates. The film begins as Chuck tries to convince his skeptical father that going on this voyage will be more valuable to him than an Ivy League education. We then follow Chuck to a Caribbean island where the boat is docked and see his initial, aloof interaction with the other boys. Subsequent events not only reveal conflicts among the boys and eventual resolutions, they also provide insights into the specific demons that plague each young man.

Most of their problems result in one way or another from bad parenting. Gil is obsessed with his brother who died accidentally while trying to escape his parents' bitter quarrel; Chuck, himself, feels his father does not know him well and has no appreciation for his aspirations; and Frank Beaumont feels hopelessly inadequate because nothing he does is good enough for his arrogant, overbearing dad. On the other hand, Dean is hostile and defiant because he thinks he is stupid and is ashamed of it.

Filmed against a stunning, lush tropical background, the voyage out concludes on a high note. The section resolves or ameliorates most of the boys' problems and shows their transformation into young men. It also reveals and resolves Sheldon's conflicts with his wife, Alice, who is also doctor and biology teacher, and with the cook, Girard, an exile from Castro's communist regime in Cuba. These conflicts question the appropriateness of Sheldon's "tough love" and his insistence on always remaining in control of himself and of every situation.

The boys facilitate each other's growth, but this can only come about in the communal environment that Sheldon deliberately creates. Chuck teaches Gil how to deal with his nightmares about his dead brother; a group of boys tutors Dean so he can pass a critical exam; and Chuck becomes more confident of his abilities, better attuned to who he is, and more willing to assert himself socially. For several, the passage into manhood includes sexual initiation by island prostitutes or by girls from a Dutch school. Frank, too, becomes more friendly and learns to interact better with others, until his domineering parents appear unexpectedly at a port of call. During the visit his father humiliates him when he tries to assert himself, and Frank regresses. His friends save Frank from a self-destructive, drunken binge, but the damage has been done, and soon after Sheldon expels him from the ship for wantonly killing a dolphin. But even Frank's expulsion provokes a spirit of unity among the other boys, who protest the punishment as too severe. Though Sheldon remains firm in his decision to expel the boy, he encourages the others to vocalize their support to him. Their subsequent expression of unity ultimately gives Frank the courage to defy his father at Sheldon's trial and make the critical gesture that leads to the captain's acquittal.

Other character-building episodes on the voyage out include a sixteen-hour storm at sea and a confrontation with a Cuban military vessel that first fires at and then boards the *Albatross*, either during or shortly after the Cuban missile crisis. When the leader of the boarding party threatens to remove a boy who had forgotten his passport, Sheldon declares that none of his crew is leaving; he offers himself instead. But a U.S. fleet appears suddenly on the horizon, and the Cubans depart. Following this encounter, the boys complete their final rite of passage by passing their academic exams.

Now truly a unified crew of young men who are no longer boys, they reach their destination, a beautiful volcanic island on the other side of the equator. Carrying bows and arrows and dressed as Indians, they hike up the mountain to the crater lake and inscribe their names in a book that documents their visit. Back aboard ship, Sheldon and Alice are alone for the first time, and it becomes evident that they have smoothed over their differences and love each other deeply. Sheldon's rift with Girard, the opinionated, anti-Castro exile, also presumably heals after Sheldon stands tall against the Cuban navy.

During the voyage out, McCrea, the ebullient English teacher, repeatedly quotes from Shakespeare's *The Tempest* and Samuel Taylor Coleridge's "The Rime of the Ancient Mariner." This practice ironically foreshadows the disaster that dominates the second part of the film. The voyage back begins happily. With a gorgeous sunset in the background, the boys celebrate the news that they have all passed their exams, including Dean. They acknowledge among themselves the personal growth they have gained at sea. The next scene, however, shows the first effects of a fast-approaching storm. The crew scrambles to batten down the hatches as the boat careens in the rough seas. In the background the radio broadcasts the flight of Mercury 1, America's first manned space shot.

As the storm strikes in its full fury, Sheldon looks up at an approaching wall of water and declares, "white squall." Alice is knocked unconscious below deck, while Sheldon struggles to save the ship above. To avoid lightning strikes he has ordered the boys out of the rigging, but this has precluded him from stabilizing the ship by trimming its sails. Fearful that the vessel might capsize, he orders the helmsman to perform a risky maneuver, but the helmsman twice refuses. The mast breaks and the ship rolls over. As the crew scrambles for the life boats, Gil goes below deck to retrieve a photograph of his brother and becomes trapped. Unable to open the door to free his friend, Chuck says a final goodbye to Gil and then, with Dean urging him on, he escapes before the ship goes down. Similarly, Sheldon watches in anguish as his wife, suddenly revived, looks up helplessly through a portal from the water-filled room in which she is trapped. He wails in agony and then kisses her through the window before swimming to his life boat. Girard and Dean become entangled in the ship's debris and drown along with Alice and Gil.

That night, after the storm has passed, the survivors look up from their life boats and watch a bright speck move across the sky; it is Alan Shepard passing overhead in Mercury 1. The next day they are rescued by a passing ship.

The final section centers on a Coast Guard hearing that will determine whether Sheldon should lose his license. Convinced that Sheldon handled the situation as well as he could have and that the charges against him are trumped up, the boys first conclude that the Coast Guard is trying to make Sheldon a scapegoat and then that the hearing is really an act of revenge orchestrated by Frank's father, who was humiliated when Sheldon expelled Frank. Chuck confronts Frank, who refuses to help. Chuck hands him the ship's bell, which Gil had rung in a farewell salute when Frank departed, and he tells Frank to do what he has to do.

At the trial, the prosecution depicts Sheldon as lax and out of control. The fifteen-year-old helmsman tries to assume responsibility for the loss of the ship, because he disobeyed Sheldon's order, but Sheldon refuses to let him. Instead, he claims full responsibility and offers to surrender his license: "I can't bring your sons back. If you want my ticket, if that will ease your pain, that's the least I can do."

Chuck confronts Sheldon as he tries to leave the room, but Sheldon acknowledges that he lost control and people died. When Sheldon refuses to allow the boys to share responsibility, Chuck accuses him of making a sham of everything he had taught them about unity and collective responsibility. Sheldon continues to refuse, but then, in open defiance of his father, Frank rings the bell. Sheldon embraces Frank and Chuck, and the other boys then cluster around in a solid display of support. The film concludes with a shot of Sheldon leaving the courthouse. In a voice-over Chuck says that Sheldon was acquitted but will probably never return to sea. Then Chuck adds, "Today he joined the circle he created by allowing us to share his burden, the burden of sea captains and fathers. The burden of men." Chuck concludes by quoting one of Sheldon's character-building maxim's, "You can't run from the wind. You face the music; you trim your sails, and keep going."

RECEPTION

Like other Scott films, *White Squall* was praised for its beautiful photography and visual effects, but criticized for defects in the storyline and character development. The review by *Variety*'s Brian Lowry is representative. He suggested renaming the movie *Floating Poets Society* or *Dead Sailors Society*, in reference to Peter Weir's *Dead Poets Society* (1989), a movie that likewise shows how an inspiring teacher creates unity and builds character among a group of disaffected prep school boys who have problems with their parents. In that movie, too, the inspiring father figure is held accountable for an ill fate that befalls one of his students. Lowry complained that *White Squall* coasts "aimlessly at times before suddenly leaping to a more intense dramatic plane" and suggested that it will be best remembered as the film debut of Scott Wolf, star of the then-current television show for teenagers, *Party of Five*. Lowry pointed to structural problems in the plot, called the final section anticlimactic, and criticized the "rather facile, anachronistic 'Oprah-esque' approach toward the boys' feelings about their families and the Skipper's role as a 'tough love'-minded surrogate father." On the other hand, Lowry acknowledged that "Scott remains a gifted visual stylist and cinematographer Hugh Johnson beautifully captures the open seas as well as confined spaces." Lowry extended special praise to the "staggering, if at times confusing," storm sequence and the other episodes featuring turbulent seas (Sammon, *Ridley Scott*, 147–49). Audiences mirrored the critics' lukewarm endorsements. The film earned only

$10.3 million in North America and $40 million worldwide (Sammon, *Ridley Scott*, 120).

DISCUSSION

The story is based on an actual 1961 maritime disaster in which a freak storm, called a "white squall," sank the *Albatross*, a square-rigged brigantine sailing ship that housed the Ocean Academy, a "floating prep school" for troubled boys from wealthy families. Four of the thirteen students aboard were killed, along with two faculty members. One of the surviving students was Chuck Gieg, Jr., who, along with Captain Sheldon, is the central character in Scott's recreation of the doomed voyage. (The real Gieg and Sheldon served as technical directors on the film.) The movie was filmed primarily in the Caribbean islands of St. Lucia, St. Vincent, and Grenada, but additional scenes were shot in Georgia, South Carolina, the Bahamas, and even a spot off the coast of the Cape of Good Hope, at the southern tip of Africa, where the production team could be assured of the requisite high seas.

Scott's intentions were to present an honest, earnest, unsentimental rite-of-passage story and to offer an emotional catharsis for the actual survivors of the *Albatross* (Sammon, *Ridley Scott*, 117, 122). His inability to reconcile these goals accounts for the structural problems in the story that reviewers have noted. On the one hand, Scott wanted to give the actual survivors "the chance to see their story told properly." This presumably culminates with the storm and the prosecution of Sheldon. On the other hand, as described in the synopsis above, the boys' personal problems and their rites of passage are introduced and resolved during the first section. Though the boys' ability or inability to overcome their personal problems might have been shown to be factors in either the ship's sinking or the saving of lives, Scott's interest in remaining faithful to the actual incident renders them largely irrelevant in the crucial storm scene. Perhaps Scott could have shown lapses in personal responsibility to be responsible for the sinking, or shown boys overcoming specific phobias to save their crewmates. But his interest in remaining faithful to the facts required him to depict the tragedy as an act of nature and not a failure of self-discipline or personal responsibility. As a result, the seemingly climactic storm sequence actually has little connection to the boys' successful rites of passage. This structural problem becomes especially apparent when we consider that the film opens with Chuck's expression of his need to find his own path in life, but it closes by focusing not on Chuck or the other boys but on Sheldon, whose acquittal vindicates the actual captain of the *Albatross*.[1]

Elsewhere, Scott embellishes the narration with literary allusions that provide ironic foreshadowing. McCrea, the colorful English teacher, welcomes the boys to the boat by quoting from the first scene of Shakespeare's *The Tempest* in which Gonzalo's ship has sunk in a storm and he offers to trade "a thousand furlongs of sea for an acre of barren ground. I would fain die a dry death."

Later McCrea quotes John Donne, "Ask not for whom the bell tolls. It tolls for thee." More significantly, shortly before Frank shoots the dolphin, an act that leads to his expulsion, which in turn results in Sheldon's trial, McCrea quotes from Samuel Taylor Coleridge's "The Rime of the Ancient Mariner." In that poem, a sailor dooms his shipmates by killing an albatross, a creature, like the dolphin, that sailors traditionally associate with good luck. By making this and other connections to Coleridge's poem (Sheldon's ship is the *Albatross*), Scott identifies Frank with the ancient mariner and suggests that Frank's shooting the dolphin will have similarly disastrous results. He also leaves open the possibility that Frank, like the ancient mariner, may eventually expiate his sin and be redeemed. But Scott fails to develop the theme further. Certainly, there is no sense that Frank's act is in any way responsible for the storm that kills his shipmates. He does emerge stronger and somewhat redeemed after he defies his father and supports Sheldon at the trial, but this is spontaneous; it lacks the prolonged penance and suffering that are so central to Coleridge's poem. Moreover, to read *White Squall* in terms of "The Rime of the Ancient Mariner" would necessarily make Frank a more central figure than he is, and it would make the white squall seem like divine punishment instead of a random act of nature, as Scott prefers to represent it. So, though thought provoking, the comparisons to the "Ancient Mariner" ultimately do little more than foreshadow the maritime disaster suggested by the movie's title.

In spite of the narrative problems, Scott continues his practices of making beautiful, visually exciting movies and asserting the need for personal responsibility, individual integrity, self-control, communal bonding, and social order. These themes are played out not only through the boys' passage from childhood to manhood, but also through the characterization of Sheldon. And although the final act fails to unify the storyline adequately, it does bring together these thematic concerns.

Scott has always insisted on personal responsibility, individual integrity, self-control, and respect for social order. His first film, *The Duellists*, depicts an officer who possesses these very qualities and his triumph over a hot-headed, disingenuous, disrespectful foe. And most of his protagonists either exhibit these traits from the beginning, or they develop them as they move toward their destinies.

In *White Squall* the boys acquire these neoclassical virtues by confronting their personal phobias, as Sheldon predicts they must. By contrast, Sheldon himself embodies these attributes from the start. Consequently, the film develops two parallel points of interest. In the first, which focuses on the boys' personal evolutions, the characters are dynamic. Their personalities change over time, and that change is the locus of our interest. Sheldon is our second point of interest. However, we watch not to see how he will change, but how he will remain the same. Scott places Sheldon in a series of increasingly difficult and painful situations in order to demonstrate how exercising integrity, self-control, and respect for social order yields the best outcome in most circumstances. On the other hand, nature is a powerful, untamed, unpredictable force that can thwart even the most virtuous and courageous figures, and we must be humble before it.

Although Sheldon occasionally intervenes to direct the boys' growth, he mostly relies upon the demands of sailing to compel them to unite as a crew and to assume personal responsibility and respect for social order. The boys quickly learn that the sea is unforgiving, even of the slightest lapses, and it cannot be argued with or complained to. This presumably underlies the philosophy of the Ocean Academy and other similar ship-based programs designed to socialize troubled and/or undisciplined children. And Scott dedicates numerous shots to showing how the boys learn to recognize and accept their responsibilities and appreciate the value of a functioning society. As Sheldon tells them on their first meeting, "If we don't have order, we have nothing."

An early example of how Sheldon actively teaches the need for responsibility comes when Chuck falls from the rigging and becomes entangled in the ropes. Sheldon orders Gil, the closest boy, to climb up and save him, but Gil freezes—his brother had died in a fall and he is afraid to climb. After Sheldon frees Chuck, himself, he forces Gil up the rigging, even though Gil is so terrified and traumatized that he wets his pants. Although Alice and Girard subsequently criticize Sheldon for being too rough on the boy, the episode emphatically demonstrates Sheldon's point to the crew and the audience: Gil's inability to perform his duty was unacceptable, as it nearly cost another boy his life. In a different situation, it could sink the ship. By extension, any failure in personal responsibility endangers everyone; so it is literally a matter of life and death that everyone be capable of fulfilling his duties. As Sheldon later tells his outraged cook, "We're as strong as our weakest link. I don't want to find that out the hard way. We'll challenge them . . . and they'll come together. And I don't care if they like me or not."

Sheldon also demands that Shay, his first mate, explain why he did not inform Sheldon of Gil's phobia. He says it is Shay's responsibility to know about each crewmate's limitations. By making this point, Sheldon displaces the blame from Gil, solely, to everyone. Thus, he uses the near-disaster to impress upon the crew that everyone is responsible for one another. He uses it further to underscore how a failure in communication can lead to tragedy. Elsewhere, Sheldon demands that all orders be repeated. Besides serving the practical purpose of avoiding misunderstandings, this cultivation of enhanced communication also makes the crew more aware of their mutual dependency. The repetition of orders compels active interaction among them and thereby makes them function as a unit. In this respect, these exercises in literal vocalization—including Sheldon's insistence that they sing together—require the boys at once to assert themselves through their speech and help them recognize that they exist within a social environment and that they require social order in order to survive.

Sheldon lectures the boys from time to time and sometimes becomes involved directly in their development, such as when he gives Chuck the helm, despite Chuck's apparent doubts about his ability to handle the job. Since Chuck's personal demons center mostly on his self-doubts and proclivity for receding anonymously into the background, the decision to make Chuck one of the helmsmen demonstrates Sheldon's sensitivity to Chuck's needs. It further suggests that he is likewise attuned to the specific problems and needs of the other boys as well.

But Sheldon's greatest contribution to their development comes from his willingness to let the ocean do its work, while he remains an aloof role model. At their first meeting he tells the boys that confrontation with the elements builds character, "such as it is developed only on battlefields, mountaintops, and deserts." An early example of this comes when, during their first encounter with rough seas, Dean falls overboard while trying to fix the jib. The crew responds to Sheldon's orders, thereby enabling Alice finally to rescue him. Initially, Dean had been the most defiant boy, with the worst attitude. In fact, at their first meeting Sheldon specifically tells him he lacks character. But after falling overboard and experiencing the helplessness of being lost at sea and the joy of being rescued, Dean begins to change his view and facilitate his transformation. As he comes back aboard, Sheldon tells him, "Now you have something to write home about."

Otherwise, Sheldon serves as a role model for the young men he is molding. Like a Hemingway hero, he exhibits grace under pressure. When they encounter their first severe storm, he tells them that they cannot run from the wind; they can only make their best preparations and persevere. Sheldon then puts his words into action. While the boys vomit and retreat below deck, he remains at the helm for sixteen consecutive hours until the waters subside, loving every moment. Chuck's subsequent diary entry demonstrates how the event has solidified Sheldon as his role model: "Skipper is tough, but you want to please him. I wonder if we'll ever live up to his expectations."

If Sheldon's behavior during the first storm shows the boys what it means to exercise courage and personal responsibility under adverse circumstances, his defiance of the Cuban navy either during or immediately following the Cuban missile crisis further demonstrates what it means to show communal loyalty during times of crisis.[2] When the Cuban military vessel first approaches, Sheldon immediately takes command of the situation. He respects the Cubans' power, but is not intimidated by it. He acts calmly but forcefully, ordering the American flag to be flown and telling his crew not to be heroes. He calms Girard, a Cuban national who fears he will be abducted, and keeps the situation from becoming explosive. But he steadfastly insists that he will not tolerate the removal of any of his crew. If the Cubans insist on taking someone, he offers himself. Both Sheldon's personal courage and his refusal to allow even one member of his community to be taken show once again how Sheldon puts his deepest beliefs into practice. At the same time, by identifying the boys as his crew, he communicates that he has fully accepted them, that they have indeed met his expectations. This acknowledgment, in turn, represents the culmination of the boys' development, and the ship proceeds directly from the encounter with the Cubans to the volcanic island, where the boys enact a ritual rite of passage by hiking to the crater lake, dressed as Indians.

If Sheldon and the sea create a conducive environment, the boys play more direct roles in facilitating each other's maturation. Their mutual assistance in overcoming their personal demons both spurs individual growth and solidifies the community they create among themselves. Unfortunately, the representations of their personal crises are facile and clichéd. Most of the boys' problems appear to result from either neglectful or overbearing parenting. Because Gil's parents ignored their children while they argued between themselves, Gil and his brother sought sanctuary on a nearby hill, where his brother eventually fell from a tree and died. The parents did not even discover he was gone until the following day. Though less culpable, Chuck's father, according to Chuck, also fails to see his son for who he is. Instead, he wants Chuck to conform to his own preconceived notions. His mother, like Frank's mother, shows more sympathy for him, but seems largely ineffectual before her assertive husband. If Gil's father was inattentive and Chuck's is insensitive, Frank's is arrogant, overbearing, and unyielding. He carries an unexplained chip on his shoulder and is preoccupied with demonstrating to the world at large, and his son in particular, that he is wealthier, more powerful, and altogether superior. None of the fathers has taught his son the value of personal responsibility or communal loyalty, and they therefore stand as foils to Sheldon. Moreover, the film suggests that their failures have crippled their sons emotionally and necessitated their participation on the voyage.[3]

The traumas of bad parenting, then, are the demons that these boys must overcome. In addition, Dean must overcome the feelings of inferiority and inadequacy that have been provoked by his poor academic skills and for which he tries to compensate with belligerent, antisocial, and reckless behavior. The boys' personal growth is thus defined by how fully they succeed in resolving these problems.

In each case, their success, whether complete or limited, requires assistance from the others. Thus, communal bonding becomes identified with individual achievement. A group of boys makes Dean confess that he must cheat on his tests to pass—thereby making him consciously acknowledge his problem. They then convince him that he is not stupid; he merely needs help. And they form a secret study group to ensure that he will be able to pass honestly. His success prompts the boys' last and most clear-cut expression of unity before the disaster. Significantly, Dean dies during the storm because he puts communal loyalty before personal safety. He drowns after waiting for Chuck, while Chuck tries to free Gil.

Although Gil's character is not deeply explored, he seems to blossom under the guidance of Chuck, who may serve as a surrogate brother for him. Chuck reassures Gil and even teaches him how to wake himself up from a night-mare—"the only good advice [my father] ever gave me." That Gil foolishly elects to go below the deck of a sinking ship to retrieve his brother's photo shows that his emotional rehabilitation was incomplete. He remains the weak link because, by giving in to his emotional impulse instead of following orders, he causes his own death and, indirectly, Dean's. Nonetheless, Gil has clearly benefited from the camaraderies. He dies a stronger, happier person than he was at the outset, and it seems to mean something that he dies not alone, as he had been, but comforted by a loving friend.

Chuck, himself, gains from the community a level of self-confidence he had lacked. Initially unsure of himself and aloof, he steps up as a leader among the crew members, becoming "the glue that holds us together," as Dean calls him. His personal growth and newfound sense of belonging become most evident in the final scene, when Chuck stands up for his beliefs by confronting Sheldon and the court and demanding that the crew be permitted to share responsibility for the tragedy.

Frank's personal growth, too, occurs only after he learns to accept personal responsibility as a member of the community. Initially, he makes progress along these lines, but despite initial gestures of solidarity, he regresses after his father pays a surprise visit and separates him from the crew and then humiliates him at dinner. Frank subsequently becomes self-destructive and loses self-control. Even so, the other boys remain loyal to him, and their loyalty pays off in the long run. When Sheldon expels Frank for killing the dolphin, Chuck and some others meet with Sheldon and try to change his mind. Instead, Sheldon encourages them to tell him of their support for him, and he reminds Frank that they never gave up on him, as he escorts him from the ship. Then, despite his fear of climbing, Gil ascends the rigging and rings the ship's bell as a gesture of solidarity.

This is the bell that Chuck hands Frank before the trial, telling him to do what he has to do. On it is inscribed, "Where we go one, we go all." By ringing the bell at the climactic moment in the trial Frank not only asserts his independence from his father and identifies himself with the crew, he also resurrects the seemingly defunct community that had become splintered—not by the storm but by the return to land and to the authority of parents and the government. Not only does communal solidarity enable Frank to overcome his personal demon—his father's dominance—but in return Frank resuscitates the community. After Frank rings the bell, Sheldon embraces Frank and Chuck, and then the other boys who ring around him in defense. The camera pointedly turns to Chuck and Frank's fathers, who look on in distress. Frank has chosen sides, and both he and his friends are the better for it.

An unspoken protagonist in the film is nature, itself. The stunning tropical sunsets and lush, romantic Caribbean islands, on the one hand, and raging seas, on the other, convey nature's expansive range, power, and grandeur. In many scenes the vast skies and expansive ocean fill the frames and diminish the physical presence of the people and the ship. Part of Sheldon's appeal is that he appreciates nature's entire spectrum and remains humble before it. "Behold the power of the wind," he joyously tells his crew as the ship sets sail. Even violent storms have his respect and admiration.

The presence of the large, unpredictable forces that Sheldon so admires introduces an element of uncertainty into the rational, responsible, efficiently ordered society he tries to create. As a sea captain, he believes he is personally responsible for the well-being of everyone aboard his ship, and that it is imperative to remain in control at all times. To this end, he promotes and lives by the neoclassical virtues discussed above. He expels Frank because he believes the boy was coming apart and had "lost control." By this point in the story, the necessity of maintaining self-control on a sea-going vessel seems obvious, but Alice asks accusingly, "What's so important about being in control?" Sheldon asks if she's talking about Frank, but she says she's talking about him, Sheldon. Clearly her remark suggests that he has too controlling a personality, but the matter is never further developed. Sheldon, who realizes he must remain in control of his ship if he is to act responsibly, merely lets the matter drop.

But the tempest that kills Alice and three others revives the issue, and Sheldon's accusers raise the possibility that the tragedy might have resulted because Sheldon lost control of the ship. From the storm scene and trial testimony, we know that Sheldon did not trim his sails because he feared someone might be struck by lightning. Though this decision makes the ship less stable, it appears prudent and responsible. We also know that the helmsman disobeyed his direct order twice just before the ship went over. The prosecution suggests this failure to maintain control over his crew resulted in the tragedy. Sheldon, himself, confesses as much, stating that he lost control, "maybe for an instant, maybe all along. . . . [I]t got away from me, the whole thing, and people died."

We admire Sheldon's integrity and exercise of personal responsibility when he refuses to let the young helmsman assume blame, and we admire his subsequent resistance to Chuck's insistence that they share the responsibility, as he had taught them to. His responses are consistent both with his personal values and his acceptance of ultimate responsibility as the captain of the ship.

But the visuals from the storm sequence contradict Sheldon's insistence on personal responsibility for events that appear clearly beyond his control. Even if the sails had been trimmed or the helmsman had complied, the storm is filmed to appear so intense that it seems unlikely that the *Albatross* could survive, regardless of what Sheldon, or anyone else, might have done. The real Captain Sheldon has described the white squall in just that manner, comparing it to being struck by a gigantic downdraft. "It just sprang out of nowhere, hit the water, and created a kind of strange flattening effect. . . . Then it hit the *Albatross*. Its sails immediately filled out and—bang!—the wind took the ship right over" (Sammon, *Ridley Scott*, 119).

As Chuck tells the court, some things are beyond human control. "Why do we need to blame it on someone?" he demands. This seems to be the general conclusion of the movie: By doing everything we can to maintain order and retain control of each situation we enhance our chances of survival and success. Moreover, we improve the quality of our lives. But in the long run, no one is in complete control; no one is impervious to the random acts of the universe. As Scott's photography reminds us visually throughout the entire film, nature is larger, grander, and more powerful than all of us. In Sheldon's words, the best we can do is "face the music . . . trim your sails, and keep going."

NOTES

1. Chuck endangers his life trying to save Gil, and Dean loses his waiting for Chuck, but loyalty was not particularly a lesson Chuck needed to learn, so his futile efforts on Gil's behalf do little to advance his character development or connect his action during the storm to his rite of passage. Dean's death comes closer to fusing Scott's twin goals, but his role in the scene is too limited to have strong impact. Nothing in the way the scene is shot directs our attention to the fact that Dean, the former loner, is risking his life for his shipmates. After he drowns, no one mentions him again, except in the catalog of the dead.

Similarly, during the trial, the boys exercise the courage, responsibility, loyalty, and sense of unity they learned on the voyage out, and showing this was clearly a big part of Scott's intention. But at the trial the focus shifts from them to Sheldon, and their display of personal growth is obscured by Scott's interest in doing justice to the actual Sheldon. So, when Chuck addresses the court and Frank rings the bell, our focus is not on recognizing how much they have grown to be able to make these gestures, but on whether Sheldon will be cleared. But Sheldon's acquittal appears fundamentally anticlimactic: it does not resolve any compelling issues that were driving the story.

2. Although the actual voyage of the *Albatross* occurred in 1961, the opening shot sets the film in 1962. Scott presumably changed the dates to capitalize on the dramatic tension spawned by the Cuban missile crisis, which occurred from October 14 to 28, 1962. However, apart from superimposing President Kennedy's radio broadcast upon a shot of Frank pretending to shoot a shipmate, Scott does little with the event. It is unclear how much time passes between Kennedy's broadcast and the encounter with the Cuban navy, but it seems to be more than two weeks. In any case, Scott fails to link the encounter to the crisis. For although the *Albatross* is boarded on Fidel Castro's personal orders and is rescued by the American fleet, the rescuing fleet is not engaged in the naval quarantine that Kennedy imposed during the crisis. Instead, Chuck tells us they are en route to the Bay of Pigs. But the Bay of Pigs invasion occurred in April 1961. (It is interesting to imagine how the outcome of the missile crisis might have differed if Castro and Khrushchev had acquired a shipload of American students as hostages.)

Similarly, Scott overlaps the storm that sinks the *Albatross* with the launch of Alan Shepard in the Mercury 1 spaceship. But that flight occurred on May 5, 1961, about three weeks after the Bay of Pigs invasion. Presumably, both the invasion and Mercury 1 flight occurred while the real *Albatross* was at sea in 1961, and Scott was trying to do justice to the actual history by inserting them. Treated differently, the historical intrusions might have intensified the drama or created suggestive parallels between the voyage into outer space and the one at sea. But as presented, the anachronisms merely confuse viewers who lived during these times.

3. Interestingly, although the film's depiction of parental ineptitude is heavy-handed, Sheldon does not seem to accept this as an explanation for the boys' problems. When his friends try to blame Frank's father for Frank's aberrant behavior, Sheldon rejects their argument. "There are ground rules in a family," he says, "just like on a ship." However, the film never develops this viewpoint further and instead shows how Frank's vindictive father, in particular, causes not only Frank's emotional breakdown but also Sheldon's trial.

G.I. Jane

(1997)

CAST

Lt. Jordan O'Neil	Demi Moore
Master Chief John Urgayle	Viggo Mortensen
Senator Lillian DeHaven	Anne Bancroft
Theodore Hayes	Daniel von Bargen
Captain Salem	Scott Wilson
Royce	Jason Beghe
Cortez	David Vadim
Blondell	Lucinda Jenny
McCool	Morris Chestnut
Flea	Josh Hopkins
Slovnik	James Caviezel
Newberry	Angel David
Wickwire	Boyd Kestner
Instructor Pyro	Kevin Cage
Instructor Johns	David Warshofsky
Chief of Staff	John Michael Higgins
Stamm	Steven Ramsey

Miller   Gregg Bello

PRODUCTION

Director	Ridley Scott
Producers	Roger Birnbaum, Demi Moore, Suzanne Todd, and Ridley Scott (released by Buena Vista Pictures)
Screenplay	Danielle Alexandra and David Twohy, based on a story by Alexandra
Director of photography	Hugh Johnson
Production designer	Arthur Max
Supervising art director	Bill Hiney
Art director	Richard Johnson
Set design	Thomas Minton
Set decoration	Cindy Carr
Editor	Pietro Scalia
Costume designer	Marilyn Vance
Music director	Trevor Jones
Military technical advisor	Harry Humphries

SYNOPSIS

G.I. Jane tells the story of a female navy officer who is selected as a test case for full integration of women into all aspects of the military. As part of a deal made between the navy and a powerful female senator, Lt. Jordan O'Neil enters the navy SEALs' CRT training, "the most intensive military training known to man." If she can pass the program, the navy has agreed to allow women to participate in every aspect of its operations, including combat. A triathlon athlete and topographic analyst with naval intelligence, O'Neil agrees to undergo the training not because she wants to make a political statement, but because she knows that her career can advance only if she has the operational experience that is currently unavailable to women. Demanding that she be given no special treatment, she completes the training, overcomes last minute political attempts to sabotage her efforts, and helps lead her team in a difficult, secret military mission. In the process, O'Neil gains the respect of the men who had tried to keep her down.

The film opens with an airborne shot of the Potomac River, with the Washington Monument in the background. In a committee room inside the Capitol building, Senator Lillian DeHaven criticizes Theodore Hayes, a top navy official, for a report about the crash of an F-14 jet that had been piloted by a woman. Unlike analogous documents in which male pilots were involved, the report discusses the woman's personal life, sexual behavior, and other irrelevant matters, and Senator DeHaven threatens to vote against Hayes's confirmation as secretary of the navy. Soon afterward, the Department of Defense arranges a meeting with her in which they strike a deal. She will support Hayes's nomination and the navy will allow a test case to see if women can compete equally with men. If the female candidate succeeds, the navy will permit full integration of women into all of its operations within three years. After the deal has been struck, Hayes selects the toughest program possible for the test case to ensure that the woman fails. The CRT program, which prepares special operatives for behind-the-lines enemy reconnaissance, has a 60 percent drop-out rate, even among the highly trained men from the SEALs, Army Delta, and marine reconnaissance units who apply for it.

The scene cuts to the Naval Intelligence Center where Lt. O'Neil is monitoring a SEAL unit with whom they have lost contact during a mission. Even though her specialty is topographical and not operations analysis, she anticipates how the SEALs will respond to their predicament and convinces her superiors to choose her recommendation over others. At the last minute, she is proven correct, and contact with the lost SEALs is established.

Back in Washington, DeHaven has insisted on approving the final candidate for the test. Concerned about how the candidate will appear in the media, she rejects one woman because she looks too much like a man and another simply because she is ugly. Instead, she chooses O'Neil, who was not only a triathlon Olympic contender but is also smart and good looking. O'Neil subsequently meets with the senator in her office and learns that the test case can change national policy forbidding women in combat. O'Neil reveals that she had wanted to serve during the Persian Gulf War but was turned down for an opening as an intelligence officer on a submarine because there were no separate bathroom facilities aboard the ship. When DeHaven asks how she felt about this, O'Neil admits that she was pissed off. DeHaven responds, "I like pissed off." Finally, DeHaven asks about O'Neil's sexual orientation to avoid the possibility of an embarrassing incident that might undermine the test, and O'Neil assures the senator that she is not a lesbian.

Back home, O'Neil shares a candle-lit bath with Royce, the man in her life, and tells him about the new opportunity for her career. She assures him that she can take care of herself; after all, she survived jump school and dive school, but that she does not want to become "some poster girl for women's rights." Royce, a navy officer who served in the Persian Gulf War, warns her that the SEALs will be hostile because she is a woman, and he asks why she wants operational experience anyway. O'Neil points out that military experience is the key to advancement and that women cannot get it. Royce tells her to go ahead and do it—she always does what she wants anyway, but because he cares for her, he is reluctant for her to leave him for a prolonged period. When she demands to know if he will wait for her if she succeeds and takes a military assignment for three years, Royce becomes upset and declares that he was not prepared to decide the rest of his life when he entered the bath. He adds that he does not know what he will feel in three years—and neither does she. O'Neil responds that until he said that, she thought he did.

The scene shifts to Cataland Naval Base, Florida, where O'Neil arrives in a Humvee and reports to Captain Salem, her commanding officer. He treats her with considerable deference, offering her a beverage, allowing to keep her hair long if she wears it above the collar, and telling her about arrangements for her to have a separate dormitory and bathroom. When she says that she is not seeking special treatment, he replies, "We're not trying to change your sex." He also insists that he be notified immediately if she is harassed, so he can address the problem immediately. When O'Neil tries to reassure him that she is not trying to make a statement and that she only wants operational experience like everyone else, Captain Salem answers that if she were like everyone else, "we wouldn't be making statements about not making statements."

O'Neil leaves her gear in her barracks, which she has to herself, and then enters the mess, where the other trainees are complaining about her. One man resents that it took two years for his application to be accepted and now that he finally has his chance, his achievement will be diluted because a woman has been admitted. Another brags that he could "set her straight" in one night alone with her. Finally, someone tells them to "stow it," as they know the policy about harassment.

The trainees assemble outside where Salem addresses them. He tells them they are about to begin the most intense military training known to man and points out that even though they come from specialized units where they have already proven themselves, 60 percent will fail. He then introduces Master Chief John Urgayle, who examines them like a drill sergeant inspecting new recruits. When Urgayle tells them that he "never saw a wild thing feel sorry for itself. A bird will fall dead from a bough without ever having felt sorry for itself," one of the trainees snickers and Urgayle confronts him. He asserts his authority and then orders them to begin a series of strenuous activities, declaring that the first day will not end until someone quits. Instructors then taunt the trainees as they push heavy barrels up hills, do push-ups in the water, and perform other arduous tasks. After an exhausting day of physical activities and meals grabbed from garbage cans, they are commanded to stay awake while writing essays and listening to opera. As they do this, we see Urgayle reading a book of literature in his barracks.

The next day the trainees break into groups and are ordered to run in the rain through an obstacle course filled with gunfire and exploding objects. When O'Neil is told to use special steps to assist her, she objects. But her objections are ignored. However, when they reach the wall, she overturns the ladder and bends over so her teammates can step up on her back to climb over the obstacle. However, as Urgayle watches them through the telescopic gunsight on his rifle, the last teammate, Cortez, releases her hand while pulling her up, and O'Neil must struggle alone over the wall. Then she trips a wire and is held responsible for "killing" the entire class in the simulation. Subsequently, Urgayle confronts Cortez for abandoning her.

After the troops are dismissed, O'Neil goes to see Urgayle and demands to know why she passed and Cortez did not, even though he finished ahead of her. He informs her that she received a thirty-second deduction from her time for "gender norming." When O'Neil objects, she is rebuffed. She then goes to Captain Salem and complains that the special treatment makes her an outsider. She learns that he resents how politicians have turned his base into a social experiment, but he agrees to eliminate the double standard he had established for her. O'Neil then goes to the barber shop and shaves her head, just like the other trainees. Then she brings her gear into the men's barracks and declares that she will stay there. This makes some of the men nervous, but Urgayle simply orders that a schedule be drawn up to rotate the shower facility.

The scene changes to Washington, where a party is being held to celebrate Hayes's appointment as secretary of the navy. Royce is present, and he sees that Hayes is upset about publicity covering O'Neil's training, especially an article that describes her as "G.I. Jane." Hayes is even more upset that O'Neil has made it through "hell week," and he orders Royce to provide detailed updates about her progress. Elsewhere, DeHaven learns of the media coverage and demands that all subsequent publicity be coordinated by her office. But independent photographers and reporters swarm around the entrance to the base, and when DeHaven calls to complain of their access, Salem, who also dislikes their presence, reminds her that he cannot bar them from public areas without violating the Constitution.

The trainees undergo further rigorous exercises, and O'Neil has a physical exam that reveals she has acquired jungle rot, tendinitis, and abrasions. When Nurse Blondell, who has quietly supported O'Neil, asks her why she is doing this, O'Neil inquires if she asks the same thing of the men. Blondell says that she does; they say they like to "blow shit up." O'Neil answers, "Well, there you go," implying that she does too.

During an exercise at sea O'Neil has difficulty reentering the boat and is left behind. But when one of her teammates gloats, Urgayle orders the entire team back in the water, asserting that they do not leave their own behind. As the entire team is left to swim back to shore, a black team member recounts how, during World War II, his grandfather was barred from combat duty simply because of his race. He expresses sympathy for O'Neil, whom he calls "the new nigger on the block."

Later, Urgayle confronts O'Neil as she showers alone. He expresses his concern that men will feel a special need to protect their female comrades and will unduly endanger themselves and their missions as a result. After he acknowledges that he won his Navy Cross for carrying a large, wounded man from a burning tank, she answers, "So, when a man tries to rescue another man, he's a hero. But when he tries to rescue a woman, he's gone soft." In turn, Urgayle questions whether O'Neil, who had been unable to pull herself into the raft earlier that day, would be physically capable of such a feat. O'Neil then requests permission to dry off, and Urgayle stares briefly, without expression, at her body. He then informs her that he is naming her commander of one of the boats because, with the departure of one of the other trainees, she is most senior. He adds that there are no bad crews, only bad leaders.

In Washington, the navy officials are concerned that O'Neil might pass the test and, unaware of her connection to Royce, they ask him to dig up background information on her. He asks if he is being requested to provide ammunition against her, and although they put a different spin on it, this is clearly their intention. After Royce leaves, the officials concoct a plan to pressure DeHaven to halt the test by closing several navy bases in her state. This would undermine her political viability shortly before she runs for reelection. Meanwhile, Royce phones O'Neil at the base to warn her of subterfuge, but she takes it the wrong way and becomes resentful, as though he too wants her to fail. He admits that he does not want to lose her, but he does not want her to wash out. She does not seem to understand and remains angry and defiant. Nonetheless, he closes the conversation by telling her to watch out for herself.

O'Neil's team is sent on a training exercise in which they are to gather intelligence in enemy territory. She proves adept at command, but Cortez's insubordination causes the team to be captured. They are severely beaten, and Urgayle singles out O'Neil for especially brutal treatment. But she wins the respect of her teammates by insisting that they not give up any information on her behalf, even when it appears Urgayle is about to rape her. O'Neil fights back, bloodying his nose and kicking him in the body and groin before he knocks her temporarily senseless. While she lies on the ground, Urgayle tells her crewmates that he is doing them a favor by eliminating her from the program, so they will not have to see her tortured in a real situation and risk succumbing to the desire to save her. When O'Neil revives, Urgayle tells her to "seek life elsewhere," to which she replies, "Suck my dick!" Her words inspire her teammates, who chant the phrase and begin to riot. As Urgayle walks away, he gives her a look that acknowledges her toughness. Then, while he washes the blood from his face, he confides to his subordinates that she is not the problem, "We are."

Back in Washington DeHaven recognizes that threatening to close the bases is the navy's way of signaling they want to deal with her. Meanwhile, Urgayle watches as O'Neil tells Nurse Blondell that she is going for a drink with her teammates, but that she will join Blondell and some other women at the beach later. At the bar her teammates drink to O'Neil; even Cortez makes up to her. Then she goes to the beach where a photographer secretly snaps pictures of her with Blondell.

Later, O'Neil is called out from training and told to report to Captain Salem, who relays anonymous accusations that she has engaged in lesbian acts. He emphasizes that he is not allowed to ask if she is gay, but that they must investigate the charge. She will be assigned to a desk job pending the outcome of the investigation and, if she is cleared, she will be allowed to go through the training again. O'Neil vehemently denies the charge and, seeing Blondell in the waiting room on her way out, she tells the nurse that it is she, O'Neil, they are after, not her. O'Neil then angrily quits the program and returns home.

Royce admits that there was a time when he wanted her to fail so he could have her to himself, but this is no longer the case. They kiss, and the next day he shows her documents revealing that DeHaven was behind the false accusation. Royce and O'Neil go to the Capitol, where a hearing reveals that DeHaven has made a deal to prevent the closing of the bases in her state. When O'Neil confronts DeHaven and threatens to go to the media, DeHaven talks about political survival. She assures O'Neil that the charges will be dropped, and her career will go forward, "albeit in Washington." Then she adds, "Don't tell me you wanted that kind of life." O'Neil retorts, "I wanted the choice. That's how it's supposed to be." But DeHaven insists that Americans are not yet ready to see women come home in body bags. O'Neil refuses to accept this explanation, or the implication that women's lives are more valuable than men's or that their deaths are more painful to the survivors. DeHaven admits that she never expected O'Neil to succeed; the entire test was simply a ploy for getting votes. "It was never going to happen." But O'Neil insists that she will not stand by idly while anyone besmirches her good name. The she demands that the charges against her be dropped so she can finish her training. Otherwise, she will go to the press. DeHaven succumbs, and O'Neil returns to her team.

While aboard ship in the Mediterranean for a final training exercise, the team is called into action for real. A U.S. satellite carrying power cells with weapons-grade plutonium has crashed to earth in Libya, and a team of Rangers has been sent in to recover the cells. O'Neil's team is being sent to extract the Rangers and the plutonium from Libya and return them to the ship.

As Arabic music plays in the background, the team comes ashore on rubber rafts and occupies an abandoned clay building. Going off to reconnoiter, O'Neil and Urgayle spot a Libyan military patrol. One of the soldiers approaches the spot where O'Neil is hidden, and Urgayle, who watches through his telescopic gunsight, advises her of his movements and tells her to prepare to kill him with her knife, as it is important to avoid noise. As O'Neil prepares to strike, however, the soldier becomes suspicious, and Urgayle shoots him. He dies instantly, but the gunfire draws the attention of other soldiers who pursue Urgayle. O'Neil returns to the team, and they are forced to make new arrangements for extracting the Rangers. Most of the team goes to rendezvous with the Rangers, but O'Neil's crew remains behind to save Urgayle. As with the lost SEALs at the beginning of the film, she anticipates how he will run and her crew moves to intercept him. In the process, she recognizes a position that is ideal for ambushing his pursuers. The ambush is set, but Urgayle falls wounded in the "kill zone." O'Neil runs out to carry him back, and when they have cleared the danger area, her crew mates launch the ambush. Ultimately, both the Rangers and O'Neil's team return safely to the ship. Afterward, one of O'Neil's teammates says that he would go to war with her any day.

The film concludes on graduation day, as Urgayle presents the team with medals that signify that they have passed the training. When O'Neil goes to clear out her locker, she finds a book of poems by D. H. Lawrence that Urgayle has left for her. He has marked a page with the poem he recited on their first day about how wild things never feel sorry for themselves. Urgayle watches as she reads; they exchange knowing glances, and then he walks away.

RECEPTION

Although it was not as financially successful as Scott had hoped, *G.I. Jane* did well both at the box office and among the critics. It had an especially strong showing during the first week of its release, and the film, which cost $50 million to produce, grossed $80 million worldwide. Television's Siskel and Ebert gave it two "thumbs up"; Steve Arvin of UPI Radio called it "the most powerful motion picture of the summer", and Jeffrey Lyons of WNBC-TV declared that "Demi Moore gives the performance of her career" (Delaney, 218). In his review, *Variety*'s Todd McCarthy praised the film's "accumulation of highly charged challenges and confrontations, authentic-seeming details, tart dialogue, vibrant performances and credible emotions," and he singled out for commendation Scott's "visceral cinema" in his handling of the military scenes, Mortensen's portrayal of the tough but sensitive Urgayle, and Moore's fierce determination and dedication in her depiction of O'Neil (Sammon, *Ridley Scott*, 149–51). Although critical of the script, Janet Maslin of the *New York Times* was also impressed by Scott's depiction of the arduous training program and by Moore's convincing portrayal of stubbornness, which Maslin described as "perversely spectacular." She added that "military training has looked tough before, but not precisely this nightmarish" (Maslin, Review of *G.I. Jane*). To make the film, Moore got into the best physical shape of her life, and she impressed several reviewers with her prowess, especially the one-handed push-ups she performed on-screen. Although the film addressed a topical political controversy—whether women should be allowed to fight in combat—it did not generate a lot of debate about the topic. Bill Delaney, however, asked if the public was "being insidiously conditioned to accept the idea of drafting women should the U.S. become involved in another really big war" (Delaney, 220). The American-Arab Anti-Discrimination Committee raised a different political issue when they objected to "a gratuitous end sequence with star Demi Moore and her Navy SEAL chums on a rampage killing Arabs" (Sammon, *Ridley Scott*, 127).

DISCUSSION

Just as *Thelma & Louise* and *Alien* project feminist values by employing a well-known genre (the road outlaw film and the horror film, respectively) and substituting a woman for a man as the protagonist, *G.I. Jane* plays off of such well-known war films as Allan Dwan's *Sands of Iwo Jima* (1949, starring John Wayne), Raoul Walsh's *Battle Cry* (1955), and Stanley Kubrick's *Full Metal Jacket* (1987). In all of these, as in *G.I. Jane*, a tough drill instructor whips his charges into shape and then watches them rise to the occasion in battle.

G.I. Jane's central point, which O'Neil expresses during her confrontation with Senator DeHaven, is that women should be able to decide for themselves what they can or cannot attempt. If O'Neil had washed out of the program because she was unable to compete equally, even she would have agreed that she should not have passed. This is why it is so important to her, and to the values of the film, that she be held to the same standard as the men. She has no use for "gender norming." But conversely, given her ability to perform at the same high level as the men who complete the training, she believes—and the film endorses the notion—that she should have the choice of participating in all activities conducted by her unit, including active combat.

Apart from the notion, which O'Neil disproves, that no woman is physically able to perform at the same levels as men in wartime situations, the film takes on other reasons that have been given for excluding women from combat. O'Neil dispatches the problem of finding separate showers and sleeping accommodations by moving into the men's barracks. No sexual tension arises among the grimy, sweaty, exhausted trainees, and O'Neil and her teammates overcome their modesty. Significantly, even when Urgayle confronts her in the shower, she does not try to cover herself or otherwise show embarrassment. And just as significantly, apart from briefly and blankly staring at her body at the conclusion of their conversation, he does not leer at O'Neil in this or any other scene, or otherwise respond to her in a sexual fashion, except when he threatens to rape her in order to drive her from the program. Thus the film suggests that mature men and women can live in close proximity with one another without responding sexually even when they are, of necessity, occasionally naked. (Of course, the navy's Tailgate scandal and other high profile incidents of sexual harassment by ranking officers cast doubt as to how realistic Urgayle's restrained behavior might be.)

DeHaven introduces another standard objection to allowing women in combat: Americans are not yet ready to see women come home in body bags. O'Neil counters that argument by asking if women's lives are more valuable than men's, or their deaths more painful. Her implication is that, if they are not, then Americans should be as readily prepared to have their daughters die for their country as their sons.

Along with the question of whether women can handle the physical demands of combat, the argument most central to the plot is the claim that women inherently endanger their male comrades because the men will instinctively feel compelled to protect them. This instinct, Urgayle maintains, will cause men to recklessly expose themselves to danger or, when captured, to reveal secret information in order to prevent their female comrades from being tortured or sexually molested. This, in fact, is Urgayle's greatest fear about himself, and it motivates much of his behavior toward O'Neil. When he expresses it during the shower scene, O'Neil counters by pointing out that he received his medal for risking his life to save a male soldier, thereby implying that soldiers often face extraordinary risks out of loyalty for their comrades, regardless of gender. Urgayle has no answer for this. He does, however, question whether O'Neil would be physically capable of carrying a full-grown man to safety. She resolves that issue at the climax of the movie when she risks her life to carry the wounded Urgayle to safety during battle.

The film's most dramatic moment also centers around Urgayle's fear of his own instinct to protect women. When he brutally tortures O'Neil after her team has been captured, and even threatens to rape her, he tells her teammates that he is doing it so they will not have to confront their protective impulses for the first time in actual battle. But his true motivation is to drive O'Neil from the program, so the possibility of him, or any other man, witnessing a female comrade under torture never will arise. But O'Neil subverts his intention by refusing to succumb to his brutality, and the scene closes with Urgayle acknowledging to his underlings that the women are not the problem, "We are."

Indeed, when he is put to the test in actual combat, Urgayle succumbs to his protective instinct. The final sequence in which the SEAL team combats the Libyans has been criticized as superfluous; however, it shows not only how O'Neil rises to the occasion in a real military situation, but also how Urgayle gives in to his need to protect her. When O'Neil is alone in the outpost and the Libyan soldier approaches the spot where she is hiding, Urgayle initially commands her to use her knife, as they need to avoid noise that would alert the rest of the patrol. However, just as she is prepared to strike, Urgayle undermines his own tactic and fires on the soldier instead. He saves O'Neil from the Libyan, but in the process he almost scuttles the mission. His gunshot, indeed, sparks a response from the Libyans, who for the first time become aware of an enemy presence nearby. Consequently, the SEAL team must hastily arrange for a new rendezvous point to extract the Rangers and their plutonium, much to the disgust of the Rangers. And O'Neil and several others must risk their lives to save Urgayle, who now has drawn the enemy fire. Not incidentally, several more Libyans are killed on their own soil as the SEALs fight to rescue their comrade. Had Urgayle treated O'Neil as he would have treated one of his male teammates, he would have allowed her to attack the soldier with her knife. Because he was telling her over the radio of the Libyan's exact movements and location, and because O'Neil presumably passed the part of her training involving hand-to-hand combat, there is every reason to believe O'Neil would have succeeded. Had that been the case, the mission may well have proceeded smoothly, with less risk that the plutonium and the Rangers might be captured, less risk to the SEALs, and fewer dead Libyans. Thus Urgayle's action illustrates the acute dangers that arise when male soldiers succumb to their impulse to protect their female counterparts at all costs.

In addition to the movie's overriding concern with women's equality, *G.I. Jane* also stresses another theme that Scott has developed in his more recent films: the importance of loyalty and teamwork. *White Squall* and *Gladiator* address this theme most directly, but it also appears in *1492*, *Black Rain*, and *Thelma & Louise*. Moreover, its absence figures strongly in such early films as *Alien*, in which the crew members lack any strong bond or sense of loyalty to one another and consequently die off one by one, and *Blade Runner*, in which only the androids function as a team. One of Urgayle's greatest concerns is that a woman's presence will undermine the cohesiveness of the SEAL crews, and his fear is initially borne out by Cortez, whose disregard for O'Neil prompts him to disobey her orders and thereby causes their team to be captured during the training exercise. By contrast, much of O'Neil's effort is spent trying to be accepted as an equal member of her team. For this reason she complains to Captain Salem about her special treatment, and she moves into the men's barracks and shaves off her hair. She finally wins acceptance from her teammates, even Cortez, after she withstands Urgayle's brutal torture and defiantly shouts back, "Suck my dick!" That declaration not only provokes cheers from her teammates, it also asserts her sense of being fully equal to men in every respect.[1] Finally, her ability to function smoothly and effectively as a team member in the Libyan sequence vindicates her presence in a combat role.

By contrast to O'Neil and the other SEALs, the politicians and bureaucrats demonstrate a woeful lack of team spirit or loyalty. The navy brass at the Pentagon work to undermine O'Neil, who is one of their own; earlier they presented a report that vilifies the female pilot whose plane crashed. They even decide which bases to close not on the basis of their performance or usefulness, but for the political leverage they offer. Senator DeHaven is no better. She chooses the test candidates on the basis of how they will appear in the media, sets up O'Neil for failure right from the start, and then sabotages O'Neil when she fails to fail. Like the Company in *Alien*, Tyrell and Bryant in *Blade Runner*, the royal court officials in *1492*, and Commodus in *Gladiator*, Scott depicts a world in which rank-and-file workers who actually make the extraordinary achievements from which their societies benefit are routinely undermined by the careerism and personal ambition of individuals in high places.

For a movie otherwise concerned with political matters, *G.I. Jane* remains strangely silent on the repercussions of the botched mission in which many Libyan soldiers were killed and wounded while protecting their homeland against armed American intruders. The film's happy ending shows O'Neil's graduation and final acceptance by Urgayle and the other men, but it does not even hint at the political fallout from their raid, and it does not consider the propriety of clandestine operations that violate the sovereignty of other countries. Given Scott's leftist proclivities, his apparent acceptance of such nationalist behavior is puzzling. In spite of Moammar al-Qaddafi's past misdeeds, in this scenario Libya emerges as a passive victim. After all, it did nothing to divert the plutonium cells to its soil. At the very least, the U.S. would have had to contend with protests from the other Arab nations, and perhaps even suffer U.N. condemnation for its action. Thus the suggestion that it is acceptable for Americans to enter other sovereign nations and kill their soldiers without provocation introduces a jingoistic element that contradicts the other liberal values projected by the movie.

NOTE

1. Janet Maslin observes that in *The Long Kiss Goodnight* (1996) Geena Davis was the first woman to exclaim these words in cinema. Moreover, in *Thelma & Louise*, which stars Geena Davis as Thelma, Louise shoots Thelma's would-be rapist after he tells Louise to "suck my cock."

Gladiator

(2000)

CAST

Maximus	Russell Crowe
Commodus	Joaquin Phoenix
Lucilla	Connie Nielsen
Proximo	Oliver Reed
Marcus Aurelius	Richard Harris
Gracchus	Derek Jacobi
Juba	Djimon Hounsou
Falco	David Schofield
Gaius	John Shrapnel
Quintus	Tomas Arana
Hagen	Ralph Moeller
Lucius	Spencer Treat Clark
Cassius	David Hemmings
Maximus's wife	Giannina Facio
Maximus's son	Giorgio Cantarini
German leader	Chick Allen

PRODUCTION

Director	Ridley Scott
Producers	David H. Franzoni, Branko Lustig, and Douglas Wick (released by Dreamworks Pictures in conjunction with Universal Pictures)
Screenplay	David H. Franzoni, John Logan, and William Nicholson
Director of photography	John Mathieson
Production designer	Arthur Max
Art directors	David Allday, Benjamín Fernández, John King, and Keith Pain
Set design	Jille Azis, Elli Griff, Sonja Klaus, and Crispian Sallis
Editor	Pietro Scalia
Costumer	Janty Yates
Original music	Hans Zimmer (additional music by Lisa Gerrard and Klaus Badelt)

SYNOPSIS

Set in the year A.D. 180 and loosely based on historical figures, *Gladiator* tells the story of how Maximus, a Roman general loyal to the good Emperor Marcus Aurelius, falls afoul of Marcus's evil son and successor Commodus, suffers enslavement, becomes a gladiator, and ultimately gains revenge. The opening sequence establishes Maximus as an able, courageous, and well-respected general who engineers Rome's victory over the last of the barbarian armies in Germania. In contrast to the passionate but disorganized barbarians, the Romans are organized, efficient, and cooperative. Before the battle Maximus encourages his troops and advises them that if they can imagine their victory, it will happen. He fights bravely and viciously during the battle and wins the congratulations of Marcus, who knows he is dying and asks Maximus to serve as Protector of Rome until the republic can be restored and the Roman senate can assume full power.

Desiring only to return to his farm where his wife and son await him, Marcus is reluctant to accept the appointment, but he consents after praying to his ancestors for guidance. However, before the transfer of power is announced, Commodus arrives on the scene with his sister Lucilla and privately kills his father after he learns that Marcus will not appoint him successor. Commodus then announces his father's death and his own claim to the throne. When Maximus declines to support Commodus, Commodus orders him killed. But Maximus manages to overpower his would-be executioners and escape.

Wounded, he returns home to find his farm destroyed and his wife and son burnt and crucified. He passes out and awakens to find himself abducted by a slave trader who takes him to Zucchabar, a remote Roman province in the desert. The trader sells him and Juba, a black African hunter, to Proximo, a former gladiator whom Marcus Aurelius had freed years earlier and who now earns his living by furnishing gladiators for public fights. Juba and Maximus, now known simply as "the Spaniard" because of his military service in the provinces, befriend one another and delight local audiences with their heroics within the gladiator ring. Impressed by Maximus's talent, Proximo recounts how he won his freedom by pleasing the crowds in Rome and suggests that Maximus might one day also gain the emperor's pardon if he can do likewise. Proximo also says that Commodus is inaugurating new gladiator games in the Roman Colosseum, ostensibly to mourn his father, who ironically had closed the games years earlier, but actually to celebrate himself and win favor among the Roman people. Proximo will be taking his gladiators to Rome to participate. Maximus replies that he wants to stand before the emperor and vows to give the crowds something they have never before witnessed.

Prior to Maximus's first fight in Rome, Lucius, son of Lucilla and nephew of Commodus, visits the gladiators and talks with Maximus, who displays affection for the child whose identity he does not initially know. As the gladiators enter the ring to play the role of the enemy in a reenactment of Rome's great victory over Carthage, Maximus asserts himself as leader and tells his cohorts they will have a better chance to survive if they work together. He then leads his men to a surprise victory over better armed soldiers who are playing the part of the early Romans.

Impressed by the performance, Commodus enters the ring to congratulate the victorious gladiators. Maximus picks up an arrow head and prepares to kill the emperor before the crowd, but he refrains after Lucius runs up and stands between the men. Commodus asks Maximus his name, but Maximus, who is masked, merely replies that his name is Gladiator. He then turns his back to the emperor and walks away. Outraged by the insult, Commodus demands to know his name, and the gladiator declares his identity: Maximus, general of the Roman army, loyal to Marcus Aurelius, father of a murdered son, and husband to a murdered wife. He then tells Commodus that he will have his revenge in this life or the next. The cheering crowd compels Commodus to save Maximus's life, and Lucilla, who had been romantically involved with Maximus years earlier, before both married other partners, looks on admiringly.

Back in his palace Commodus, who has incestuous desires for his sister, expresses his anger that Maximus had not been executed as he commanded, and he asserts that he did what was necessary to keep the empire together. Lucilla assures her brother that she feels no desire for Maximus. When Commodus reminds her how Maximus hurt her, she replies that her injury was no worse than what she inflicted on him. Commodus then asserts that he seeks respect as a means to gain the people's love.

Pretending to be a wealthy woman desiring sex with the gladiator hero—apparently a common practice in Rome—Lucilla then secretly visits Maximus where he remains imprisoned between fights. Maximus tells her how his wife and son were killed, and she replies that she mourned them. She adds that she now lives in fear of her brother, who keeps her a virtual prisoner, and that she too has a son whom she loves and wants to protect. She says that today she saw a slave become more powerful than the emperor. When Maximus answers that he is mere entertainment for the people, Lucilla replies that this is power. She asks Maximus to meet with Gracchus, a senator who supports the interests of the common people against the emperor, but Maximus sends her away.

Following some comic relief in which a fellow gladiator tests Maximus's food for him and pretends to die, Juba tells Maximus that he has a great name and that Commodus must destroy his name before he can kill Maximus. Commodus plots to eliminate Maximus by bringing Rome's only undefeated gladiator out of retirement. In addition to fighting this giant, Maximus must also contend against chained tigers. But Maximus prevails in the contest, and again publically insults Commodus by refusing to kill his opponent, even though the emperor has ordered him to do so. As Commodus enters the ring to face Maximus once more, the crowd shows its overwhelming approval of the gladiator, chanting "Maximus the Merciful." Telling Maximus they are not so different—they both take life when they must—Commodus then further provokes the gladiator, saying that Maximus's son squealed like a girl when they crucified him and that his wife moaned like a whore when the soldiers raped her repeatedly. But Maximus does not respond to the taunt. Instead, he exits the Colosseum to the loud cheers of the crowd.

A friend from Maximus's former command slips him a bag containing small votive statues of his ancestors, and Maximus prays to them and speaks to his dead wife and son. Commodus, on the other hand, is distraught because the people now love Maximus even more for his mercy. But he rejects an advisor's counsel to have him killed, as he does not want to make Maximus a martyr. Instead, he decides to wait for Maximus and his friends to make a mistake and orders his henchmen to follow every senator.

After his friend assures Maximus that the army remains loyal to him despite new leadership, he agrees to meet with Gracchus. Lucilla arranges the meeting, and after Maximus assures the senator that he will not merely substitute one dictatorship for another, they agree on a plan for Gracchus to purchase Maximus's freedom and return him to his troops. Subsequently, Proximo warns that Commodus already knows too much. He adds that although Maximus is willing to die for honor, Rome, and his ancestors, he, Proximo, is simply an entertainer. But Maximus wins his support when he replies that Commodus killed Marcus Aurelius, the man who gave Proximo his freedom.

Commodus persists in his efforts to seduce his sister, but she manages to deflect his advances. Lucilla then returns to warn Maximus that Gracchus has been arrested, and she confesses that she has much to pay for. But he assures her that she has been strong for her son. Lucilla replies that Commodus hates Maximus because she and Marcus loved him, and that the only time in her life she has not felt alone was when they were together. They kiss and then she leaves.

As Lucius pretends to play gladiator in the palace, Commodus overhears the boy calling himself Maximus, Savior of Rome. When Commodus learns that Lucilla had used that phrase, Commodus threatens to kill Lucius if Lucilla does not cooperate fully with him and inform on everyone who is plotting against him. Then he has the implicated senators arrested or assassinated and sends soldiers for Maximus. But with the assistance of the other gladiators and Proximo, who dies for his efforts, Maximus escapes and proceeds to a prearranged rendezvous, where he falls into a trap and is arrested.

Commodus visits Maximus in prison. Saying they are brothers because they both loved Marcus, Commodus embraces Maximus. But as he wraps his arms around the gladiator, the emperor stabs him in the back. Then he orders his soldiers to hide the wound with armor and insists that Maximus face him in the Colosseum in single combat. However, in the contest that follows Maximus knocks the sword from Commodus's hand, and Quintus, who was formerly Maximus's second-in-command and now commands the soldiers monitoring the fight, refuses to rearm the emperor. Maximus drops his sword too. Then he turns Commodus's dagger against him and kills him. Following an out-of-body experience in which he returns to his farm, Maximus orders Quintus to free Gracchus, the imprisoned gladiators, and the other senators, and, as Marcus had desired, he orders the transfer of power to Gracchus and the Roman senate. Following another out-of-body experience, he falls to the ground. Lucilla runs up to him, and Maximus assures her that Lucius is now safe. She tells him to go to his family, and she cries as he leaves his body and greets his wife and son in the next world. As Lucius watches, Lucilla closes the dead gladiator's eyes, and soldiers bear Maximus's body from the Colosseum. Commodus's corpse remains ignobly behind. The movie ends as Juba buries the votive statues of Maximus's ancestors, and the final shot shows the sun setting over the Colosseum.

RECEPTION

Gladiator was one of the top-earning movies in 2000. Budgeted at $103 million, it earned $34.82 million during its opening weekend, when it appeared on 2,938 screens nationwide. Within two weeks it had grossed some

$103.14 million in the United States. In addition, it was also a huge, popular success in Europe and throughout the world.

The initial critical reception was more mixed. However, the film gathered more acclaim over time and *Gladiator* won Academy Awards for best film, best actor (Russell Crowe), costume design, sound and visual effects. Scott was nominated for best director and Joaquin Phoenix for best supporting actor. The movie was also nominated for best screenplay, original score, art direction, cinematography, editing, and sound. Prior to the Academy Awards, *Gladiator* received the BAFTA award in England for best film, and Russell Crowe was nominated as best actor.

Elvis Mitchell of the *New York Times* called the film "silly," "pandering," and "detached." He added, "It's like a handsomely designed weapon: you can't take your eyes off it even though you may be repelled by its purpose." Mitchell also noted that Maximus's effort to maintain his dignity in the face of humiliation is a trait shared by characters "in most of Mr. Scott's films, from Harvey Keitel's in *The Duellists* to Demi Moore's in *G.I. Jane*" (Mitchell). As with other films directed by Scott, critics praised *Gladiator* for its lavish costumes, sets, and camera work and criticized it for its characters, script, and violation of historical accuracy. The combat scenes also received praise, along with the computer-generated sets and special effects that led some critics to deem it one of the best "sword-and-sandal" epics ever produced in Hollywood. Russell Crowe, Joaquin Phoenix, and Oliver Reed, who died during the filming, were also lauded for their acting. (The film is dedicated to Reed, and some of his scenes were completed with computer simulations.) Rene Rodriquez of the *Miami Herald* added that the "film's neatest, most subversive trick is the way it allows the viewer to share the blood lust of the crowds at the Colosseum, cheering the gladiators on as they hack away at each other with maces and war hammers. When Maximus . . . asks the stunned crowd, 'Are you not entertained? Is this not why you are here?' he might as well be speaking to the audience in the movie theater."

DISCUSSION

Apparently speaking for Scott, Proximo tells Maximus that he is an entertainer, not an activist, and *Gladiator* works best when viewed in this light. Above all else, it is entertainment, and it thrills viewers with spectacular special effects, fast-paced action, lavish costumes, exotic animals, impressive real and computer-generated sets that accurately recreate what we know of second-century Rome, a massive cast, and a plot that pits uncompromising good against unscrupulous evil. Apart from two or three brief, gory shots, the movie does not rely on excessive bloodshed for its impact.

On the other hand, as Lucilla observes, entertainment is a form of real power, and even Proximo dies serving the cause of justice. So, although the movie's greatest achievement is its use of spectacle, the film also asserts values common to Scott's earlier films and to early Rome, itself. Scott promotes these values to criticize not only Rome's subsequent decadence under the leadership of successive, self-important, self- serving emperors, but also to critique contemporary Western society's obsession with fame and self-indulgence at the expense of personal integrity.

Ancient chroniclers often celebrated the early Romans and attributed the fledgling city's survival in and domination of its hostile surroundings to their courage, patriotism, stoicism, piousness, and dedication to family. Virgil's *Aeneid* (30–19 B.C.), which traces the founding of Rome to the heroic Trojans who survived the wrath of vengeful Greeks in the Trojan War, asserts these values most forcefully. However, these virtues also appear in speeches by Cato the Elder (234–149 B.C.) and Cicero (106–43 B.C.); in Julius Caesar's chronicles of his Gallic wars (circa 51 B.C.); the satires of Horace (65–8 B.C.), Petronius (circa A.D. 65), and Juvenal (circa A.D. 100); and other works from the late republic and early empire. Scott promotes similar values in *Gladiator* by contrasting them to the licentiousness of the later empire under Commodus (A.D. 180–192), who is said to have inaugurated Rome's final decline.

Maximus, whose name in Latin means the "greatest," embodies all of the virtues of the early Romans. He is strong, courageous, and accomplished in the martial arts; he seems indifferent to wealth and material comforts; and he disdains power for its own sake but will assume the mantle of leadership to serve his homeland. Like Aeneas, he piously worships his dead ancestors and is deeply concerned with his son's success and well-being. However, unlike Aeneas, who abandons his lover Dido and later enters into a political marriage, Maximus also demonstrates profound love for his wife and a general appreciation of women. In this respect, Maximus mirrors other Scott protagonists who show deep respect for women. And although he is personally accomplished, he repeatedly asserts the importance of teamwork, a theme that appears in such films as *White Squall* and *G.I. Jane*. Moreover, Maximus recognizes the importance of positive thinking, as he tells his followers that they can achieve whatever they can imagine. Finally, Maximus hails from the countryside and has never experienced the corrupting influences of the big city which, according to Marcus and other respected figures in the film, has lost touch with the values that made Rome great. The action of the movie shows how Maximus triumphs over Commodus and his corrupted cohorts by adhering to the basic values he retains from the heartland.

Throughout the film various positive characters comment that Rome has deviated from the virtues that made it great. The masses are easily distracted by spectacles and other forms of entertainment, while the leaders concern themselves only with self-gratification and the accumulation of power. Among the leaders, personal integrity has yielded to political expediency, stoicism to indulgence, courage to cowardice, and ancestor worship to patricide. Power is acquired not through courage and ability but through betrayal and deceit; love of family has degenerated into perverted incest; and children, once cherished, now are prisoners to be manipulated or even executed for cynical purposes.

Scott highlights the contrast in values by showing Maximus to be a paragon of Roman (and Scott-endorsed) virtues and Commodus a figure of pure wickedness. Although these heavy-handed characterizations undermine the story's realism and provide the basis for some of the criticism of the film, they also enable Scott to focus squarely on a theme that pervades his work: the problem of how best to confront evil. Unlike *The Duellists, Alien, Blade Runner*, and *Legend*, where the evil figures are powerful and self-assured in addition to being deceptive and manipulative, in *Gladiator* evil is the product of weakness and poor self-esteem.

Commodus's weakness and cowardice are the first things we learn about him, as he arrives in Germania in a splendidly furnished carriage only after the final battle has been waged. Then he pretends to be sorry he has missed the combat. When he learns that Marcus does not intend to appoint him emperor, Commodus first behaves like a whiny, spoiled child before killing his father while pretending to embrace him. Even Lucilla, a much stronger figure, later asks if he is still afraid of the dark, and Commodus, like the historical emperor on whom Scott's character is based, uses threats, intrigue, and assassination to maintain power. Of course, his most egregious act of cowardice comes when he literally stabs Maximus in the back before their contest in the Colosseum.

Moreover, Commodus is mean-spirited, and Scott suggests that the absence of nurturing love in his youth is a major cause of his psychological deformity. Marcus acknowledges that he was a poor father who neglected his son in order to fight the barbarians, and most of Commodus's pernicious behavior is motivated by a misplaced desire to be loved. As Lucilla observes, his cruelty toward Maximus stems from his jealousy that Marcus loved his courageous general more than his cowardly son, and from jealousy of Lucilla's affection for Maximus. But instead of trying to win love by making himself lovable—by acting with courage, compassion, and integrity—Commodus tries either to buy it, as he does when he hosts the gladiator games to gain the love of the masses, or to compel it through domination, as he does with Lucilla. By contrast, Maximus has earned the love and respect of his troops through his courage and confidence, and he shares the love of his family because of the affection he shows them.

The evil in *Gladiator*, then, results when a weak, insecure, egocentric person achieves a position of power. Throughout his career Scott has consistently shown a bias in favor of the working class and against the wealthy, and Commodus continues this line of venial, arrogant, self-absorbed, and morally corrupt, powerful men who appear in Scott's other movies, such as Tyrell in *Blade Runner*, Francis Beaumont in *White Squall*, and Neil and Win in *Someone to Watch over Me*. By contrast, Maximus, a farmer by choice, possesses the traditional working-class traits that Scott celebrates in such figures as Deckard in *Blade Runner*, Ripley in *Alien*, Sheldon in *White Squall*, and Mike and Ellie Keegan in *Someone to Watch over Me*. Implied in these contrasts is a critique of contemporary Western society that, in Scott's eyes, is dominated by morally

deformed, rich men who have achieved power through privilege and not because of their own virtues and accomplishments. At the same time, the ease with which someone like Commodus can retain power by appealing to spectacle and cheap emotions also suggests a critique of a contemporary society in which entertainment has, indeed, become a form of real power. After all, the plebeians in Rome, unlike the soldiers on the frontier, support Maximus not because of his personal virtues but because of his ability to show them something they have not seen before.[1]

To add power and ostensible credibility to this study in values, Scott draws on both ancient history and more recent movies and television shows. His depiction of Commodus seems generally accurate. The young emperor was indeed said to crave public attention; however, his compulsive thirst for his father's love in the movie appears to derive mostly from pop psychology. (In this respect, Commodus is like the teenage boys in *White Squall*.) Scott's unlikely representation of an emperor fighting an enslaved gladiator before a mass audience in the Colosseum is also rooted in the emperor's actual behavior, as the real Commodus scandalized Rome with his appearances in the public arena. He even planned to dress as a gladiator when he was to be appointed consul, but a wrestler working at the behest of his advisors assassinated him the night before. Commodus's incestuous desires for his sister in the film appear to be based on the earlier, notorious emperor Caligula, whose excesses were featured both in the popular television mini-series *I, Claudius* and the 1980 film *Caligula* that was directed by Tinto Brass and produced by the publisher of *Penthouse* magazine. The brothers Gracchus were indeed Roman reformers interested in redistributing the wealth and addressing the needs of the people. But they, along with Cicero, a staunch defender of the republic, are anachronisms in *Gladiator*, as they lived hundreds of years before Commodus. In casting Derek Jacobi as Gracchus, Scott also alludes to the Emperor Claudius (A.D. 41–54), Caligula's more beneficent successor whom Jacobi portrayed in *I, Claudius* and to whom Commodus alludes in the film. Similarly, by having Richard Harris play Marcus Aurelius, Scott evokes positive associations to King Arthur, whom Harris played in *Camelot* (1969). His representation of Marcus's long campaigns against the Germanic barbarians and of his humanitarian concern for the well-being of his subjects is more or less accurate, although there is no indication that Marcus ever repudiated his son or intended to restore the republic, which, in any case, mostly served the aristocracy and was never the egalitarian democracy Scott implies. Nor was the republic resuscitated after Commodus's death. Thus, like Shakespeare in his history plays, Scotts reconfigures historical events to serve his dramatic and thematic needs.[2]

NOTES

1. As Harvey Greenberg observes in his critique of *Alien*, *Gladiator* literally profits from the practices it attacks. Scott and the producers have not only become wealthy (or more wealthy) as a result of *Gladiator*'s success, but they have achieved that suc-

cess by appealing to the same sense of spectacle and bloodlust that Commodus appeals to in his efforts to win the masses.

2. Founded around 750 B.C., Rome was a kingdom until around 500 B.C., when the Tarquin kings were supplanted by a republic that gave power both to the aristocracy (patricians) and the masses (plebeians). However, power was mostly concentrated among the patricians who dominated the Roman senate. Tiberius and Caius Gracchus tried to introduce reforms to reduce the power of the senate and increase that of the general populace, but they were assassinated in 133 and 121 B.C., respectively. As the city expanded and its power and influence spread, power gravitated to the consuls, who functioned as the executive branch of the government. The senate's influence diminished as first Marius, then Sulla, then Pompey, and finally Julius Caesar assumed increasingly greater powers as consul. As reported in Plutarch's *Parallel Lives* (circa A.D. 100) and dramatized by Shakespeare in 1599, Caesar was assassinated by factions who feared he would dissolve the republic after he was named dictator for life in 44 B.C. A civil war then ensued in which Caesar's nephew Octavian finally prevailed over Marc Antony at the battle of Actium in 31 B.C. Subsequently Octavian assumed the title Augustus Caesar and became Rome's first emperor. Although Rome prospered greatly under his rule, his accession to power terminated its republican form of government. The empire was then ruled by a succession of Caesars, including such figures as Caligula (A.D. 37–41) and Nero (A.D. 54–68), whose cruelty, perversion, and decadence have become legendary.

Antoninus Pius (A.D. 138–161) and Marcus Aurelius (A.D. 161–180) presided over what is often called the Golden Age of the empire. Admired for his Stoic writings, Marcus spent much of his time campaigning against barbarians in the west. However, he improved living conditions for poor Romans, especially poor children, and he reduced the brutality of the gladiator shows.

The only major criticism historians have levied against Marcus is his selection of his licentious son Commodus to succeed him (A.D. 180–192). Commodus, who craved attention and is believed to have gone insane, is credited with initiating the final, prolonged demise of the empire. Commodus reinvigorated the gladiator games and even participated in hunting and fighting exhibitions in the public arena, although such activities were reserved for lower-class individuals such as criminals, condemned prisoners of war, and professional gladiators. After discovering plots against him, Commodus instituted a reign of terror. He would sometimes pay people to make false accusations of treason against powerful senators, whom he then sentenced to death. Commodus would confiscate the dead man's property and reward the accuser from the profits. When his wife Crispina and his sister Lucilla were accused of plotting against him, Commodus banished them and later had them killed. A group of senators was also implicated in the plot. Finally, at the behest of advisors who had earlier tried and failed to poison him, Commodus was strangled to death by a wrestler on New Year's Eve, A.D. 192, the day before he was to be named consul. He had planned to accept the honor dressed as a gladiator. Pertinax succeeded him.

In A.D. 284 the army made Diocletian emperor, and he divided the realm into eastern and western empires. In 313, his successor, Constantine I, issued the Edict of Milan, which for the first time permitted the practice of Christianity within the empire. (He did not, as commonly believed, make Christianity the official religion of Rome, but Constantine believed he would prevail over his foes by embracing Christianity.) He moved the capital of the eastern empire to Byzantium (modern-day Istanbul), dedicated it to the Virgin Mary, and renamed it Constantinople. The western portion of the Roman empire dissolved in A.D. 476 after Goths from modern-day Germany successfully invaded the city and deposed Emperor Romulus Augustulus. Constantinople fell temporarily to the army of the Fourth Crusade in 1261 and finally to the Ottomans in 1453.

Hannibal

(2001)

CAST

Hannibal Lecter	Anthony Hopkins
Clarice Starling	Julianne Moore
Mason Verger	Gary Oldman
Inspector Rinaldo Pazzi	Giancarlo Giannini
Paul Krendler	Ray Liotta
Barney	Frankie R. Faison
Allegra Pazzi	Francesca Neri
Dr. Cordell Doemling	Zeljko Ivanek
Evelda Drumgo	Hazelle Goodman
F.B.I. Agent Pearsall	David Andrews
F.B.I. Director Noonan	Francis Guinan
Gnocco, the pickpocket	Enrico Lo Verso
Perfume expert	Mark Margolis
Carlo	Ivano Marescotti
Matteo	Fabrizio Gifuni
Tomasso	Marco Greco
Ricci	Ennio Coltorti

Young boy in airplane   Ian Iwataki

PRODUCTION

Director	Ridley Scott
Producers	Dino De Laurentiis, Martha De Laurentiis and Ridley Scott; released by Metro-Goldwyn-Mayer Pictures and Universal Pictures in association with Dino De Laurentiis
Screenplay	David Mamet and Steven Zaillian, based on the novel by Thomas Harris
Director of photography	John Mathieson
Music director	Hans Zimmer; additional original music by Patrick Cassidy ("Vide Cur Meum")
Production designer	Norris Spencer
Art director	David Crank
Set design	Crispian Sallis
Editor	Pietro Scalia
Costume designer	Janty Yates
Special effects	Kevin Harris and Tim Burke
Make-up	Fabrizio Sforza, Alessandra Sampaolo, Brian Sipe (prosthetics), and Wesley Wofford (prosthetics)

SYNOPSIS

Hannibal is the sequel to *Silence of the Lambs* (1991), the critically acclaimed, highly popular suspense thriller directed by Jonathan Demme and starring Anthony Hopkins and Jodie Foster. Demme, Foster, and Hopkins all received Academy Awards for their work, and the film won Best Picture. *Silence of the Lambs*, in turn, is the sequel to Michael Mann's less successful but critically acclaimed *Manhunter* (1986), which first introduced the character of Dr. Hannibal Lecter, a brilliant, exquisitely cultured psychopath who eats his victims. All three movies were adapted from novels by Thomas Harris. In *Manhunter* Brian Cox plays Lecter; *Silence of the Lambs* first features Hopkins in that role, which he reprises in *Hannibal*. It also introduces Foster as Clarice Starling, an FBI agent-in-training who has been assigned to interview him in order to obtain information on another murderer who is nicknamed "Buffalo Bill," because he flays his female victims alive. In bits and pieces, Lecter trades the information Starling seeks for revelations about her personal life and her relationship to her impoverished, rural parents. He degrades her family as "poor white trash" and provokes Starling's feelings of inferiority due to her background, but he also acquires respect for her as she retains her professionalism throughout their interviews and exhibits strength of character and a dedication to her purpose that he admires. Although she never succumbs to the temptation to compromise her duty, Starling comes to know "Hannibal the Cannibal" more fully than is revealed in the media or his FBI file, and she finds much to admire in his depth of understanding, in addition to being repulsed by his capacity for dispassionate cruelty. At the end of the film, she succeeds in gaining the information necessary for capturing Buffalo Bill. But although Buffalo Bill is stopped before he can murder a senator's daughter, Hannibal escapes—with no assistance from Starling.

Set ten years later, *Hannibal* tells the story of Mason Verger's failed attempt to exact revenge on Lecter, who had convinced Verger, his sixth victim, to cut off all the skin from his face and feed it to his own dogs while under the influence of a potent drug Lecter had given him. (The event is shown in flashback, as the "Blue Danube Waltz" plays on the soundtrack.) *Hannibal* further develops the relationship of attraction and repulsion between Lecter and Starling. It concludes as Lecter exacts revenge for himself, by arranging Verger's gruesome death, and for Starling, by arranging the death of her superior at the FBI, an unimaginative, mean-spirited, male chauvinist who has vindictively destroyed her career.

Hannibal opens and closes in darkness. The opening establishes Lecter as a figure of interest, makes us aware of a special connection between him and Starling, and shows Verger to be grossly deformed. Before the credits roll, a voice discusses Lecter over a dark screen. It asserts that Dr. Lecter does not regard psychology as a science and adds that Lecter is especially offended by bad manners and prefers to eat rude people, whom he calls "free-range rude." Another voice asks about Starling and Lecter. Then the credits appear against the darkened portion of a split screen, whose opposite side reveals a large, expensively furnished room in a palatial dwelling. Barney, a large black man, sits in a chair. Sitting apart from him and interrogating him are Verger and Cordell, Verger's private physician. A close-up shot showcases Verger's deformed face, and the dialogue reveals Lecter's fondness for Starling. Barney, who had attended Lecter when he was incarcerated, admires him at some level, has apparently won Lecter's good will, and has clearly been influenced by him. For a large sum, he sells Verger a medieval-looking mask that prison guards would place over Lecter's face to prevent him from biting guards, visitors, and other prisoners. Following a jump cut to a panoramic photograph of Florence, now in full screen, the credits continue over a series of black and white shots of the city that concludes with a flock of pigeons feeding on the ground of a public square. For a brief moment, their formation suggests the form of Lecter's face. Then the birds scatter. Playing over the credits is pianist Glenn Gould's perfor-

mance of "Aria da capo" from J.S. Bach's "Goldberg Variations." In addition
to establishing a cultured tone for *Hannibal*, the music also joins the film to *Silence of the Lambs*, as Lecter listens to the "Goldberg Variations" prior to his escape at the end of that movie.

Verger has posted a large reward for proof of the whereabouts of Lecter,
who has been missing since his escape ten years earlier at the end of the first
film. Rinaldo Pazzi, a Florentine police inspector, recognizes Lecter as the
would-be successor to the curator of the library at the Palazzo Capponi, who
has mysteriously disappeared. Desperate for money to satisfy the expensive
tastes of his young wife, Pazzi defies police protocol and tries to claim the
bounty. He compels a gypsy pickpocket to accost Lecter, so he can secure a fingerprint that will prove to Verger that Lecter is in Florence. Lecter quietly
grabs the pickpocket by the polished silver bracelet that Pazzi has placed on his
wrist and efficiently stabs the man, who bleeds to death as Lecter calmly walks
on. But Pazzi ignores the homicide and carefully removes the bracelet, the
prints on which earn him an advance of several hundred thousand dollars from
Verger. Pazzi later unexpectedly encounters Lecter at an opera based on
Dante's *La Vita Nuova*, where Danielle De Niese and Bruno Lazzaretti sing
Patrick Cassidy's "Vide Cor Meum" and where Lecter charms and is charmed
by Pazzi's wife. Afterward, Pazzi coordinates with Verger's men to arrange
Lecter's abduction. They plan to kidnap Lecter following his scholarly lecture
about avarice in Dante's *Inferno* and then to feed him to wild boars so Verger
can watch him suffer. But Lecter captures Pazzi first, tapes his mouth, and
binds him to a handcart. By blinking his eyes, Pazzi answers Lecter's questions
about his pursuers. In return, Lecter promises not to eat Pazzi's wife, whom
Lecter approvingly smelled at the opera. He then pushes the cart off the balcony. It falls until a cord abruptly halts it in midair. In the process, Pazzi is disemboweled and hung from the Palazzo Vecchio, where one of his ancestors
was also ignominiously hung after trying to kill Lorenzo de' Medici during the
Italian Renaissance. Lecter subsequently thwarts the attempted abduction by
Verger's agents, killing one of his would-be captors and escaping safely back to
America.

Meanwhile, due partly to bureaucratic over-reaction to negative publicity
and partly to malicious interference by Paul Krendler, an envious ranking
agent whose sexual advances Starling once spurned, Starling has been reassigned from active duty following a botched raid in which she killed five criminals. Among the dead was their ringleader, a woman who was carrying a baby
as she shot at Starling. Although Starling clearly acted bravely and professionally, the Bureau prepares to sacrifice her as a scapegoat to the adverse publicity
surrounding a rash of high-profile arrests that have resulted in civilian deaths.
Her career is spared at the last moment when a phone call from the politically
connected Verger abruptly terminates the administrative hearing and puts her
back on Lecter's case. Known to Krendler, who receives payments from Verger

for his assistance, but not to Starling, Verger plans to use Starling as bait to lure Lecter so he can capture and then torture him.

A grotesquely disfigured man with power, wealth, and influence, Verger is driven by his keen passion for revenge. He believes that Lecter appears to his victims in the guise of a mentor but that he is excited by distress, and his greatest satisfaction comes from humiliating people. Verger believes Lecter will be drawn to Starling in her fallen state—not to save her but to humiliate her. When the rabbit is wounded, Verger tells his cohorts, the fox comes running, but not to help.

Verger has a forged letter from Lecter sent to Starling. The card features a reproduction of William Blake's grotesque painting entitled "The Ghost of a Flea." When Starling is suspended from duty for not reporting the correspondence, which she never received, and is required to surrender her badge and pistol, she accurately accuses Krendler of colluding with Verger, but her protests are ignored. Meanwhile, as Krendler goes biking, Lecter enters his house, examines his mail, and intimidates his watch dog. Then Lecter goes shopping for fine dinnerware and steals a saw and other equipment from the autopsy lab in a hospital, as a rich, lyrical duet plays on the soundtrack. Next, he drives to a house and enters. This is followed by a match cut showing Starling entering the same house. Before falling asleep, she listens to a tape from ten years earlier in which Lecter compares her to a kind of pigeon, a "deep roller." Lecter notes that if two deep rollers mate, their offspring will roll all the way down, crash, and die, and adds that we must hope that one of her parents was not a deep roller.

After Starling falls asleep, Lecter enters her room, stands over her, touches her hair, and then leaves. She wakens to a phone call from him and sees a picture he has left showing her hanging. He instructs her to drive, and he follows, still conversing on the phone. He tries to humiliate her by discussing her situation at the FBI, but she will not be engaged in that discussion. Lecter tells her that the FBI officials resent her because, "You serve the idea of order, they don't. They are weak and unruly and believe in nothing." Starling answers by informing Lecter that Verger wants to kill him, but Lecter answers that Verger just wants him to suffer. He then continues humiliating her, taunting her about her lower class background and wondering how her parents would react to her disgrace at the FBI. But Starling only points out that they are being followed.

Lecter has Starling go to the lobby of Washington's Union Station, and as she searches for him, he offers to make the FBI officials scream, but she rejects him. Riding on a merry-go-round horse, he reaches out and, unbeknownst to her, touches her hair—an action several reviewers cite as the scariest moment in the movie. Then he departs, leaving a pair of Gucci shoes for her, presumably a gift he brought back from Florence. Outside in the parking lot, Lecter is struck in the back by a tranquilizer dart fired by Carlo, who had led the failed abduction plot in Florence, where Lecter killed his brother. Starling witnesses the kidnapping, notifies the authorities, and accuses Verger. But an inspection of Verger's house fails to reveal Lecter. After the officers leave, however, Carlo and his accomplices bring Lecter to Verger, wheeling him in on a handcart while the "Blue Danube Waltz" again plays on the soundtrack. Verger enters in an electric wheelchair and describes how he intends to keep Lecter alive as wild boars devour his feet for an appetizer, before returning to finish him off the next day. When Verger asks if Lecter is sorry that he did not kill him in the first place, Lecter answers dispassionately that he prefers Verger alive, as he is, rather than dead. Verger then tells Cordell that he expects him to witness the torture. When Cordell demurs, Verger humiliates him before Lecter.

Meanwhile, Starling has driven to Verger's mansion (shot at the Biltmore estate in Asheville, Tennessee), and as she prowls through the grounds Lecter is wheeled into the barn. As Carlo puts on a tape of a screaming man to excite the hogs, Lecter, bathed in golden light with his arms outstretched and secured, as though he were being prepared for a crucifixion, taunts Carlo with his brother's death and says that Matteo must smell as bad now as Carlo does.

Starling enters the barn, and even though she has been relieved of duty, she identifies herself as an FBI agent and demands that Carlo and his men surrender. When they try to shoot her instead, she kills Carlo and one of his accomplices, and tries to free Lecter. Pressed for time, she gives him a knife to so he can unbind himself, but assures him that she will kill him if he tries to escape. However, a third accomplice shoots her and she passes out just as the boars break out from their pen. Lecter picks her up and stands still as the boars swarm around them before devouring Carlo. Verger and Cordell then appear at their viewing station in the loft. Verger orders Cordell to kill Hannibal, but Cordell refuses. As Lecter exits, he suggests to Cordell that he push Verger onto the barn floor and blame him, Lecter. Cordell does this and Verger is consumed by the boars, as Lecter carries Starling to safety in a shot reminiscent of the Phantom carrying Christine in *The Phantom of the Opera*.

Lecter brings Starling to Krendler's empty vacation house on the lake, injects her with morphine, and tends to her wounds. When Krendler arrives for the Fourth of July, Lecter sneaks up behind him and renders him unconscious, as Starling sleeps upstairs. When she awakens, she finds herself wearing a black, low-cut evening gown. Still under the influence of the drug, she staggers downstairs in a fog. As the sounds of a saw cutting emanate from off-screen, Starling tries to use the telephone, but the line is cut. A second phone, however, works, but then the scene shifts to Lecter in the kitchen, who observes, as he prepares dinner, that she is using it. The camera shows a close-up of the autopsy saw and then another of Krendler in the dining room, with an especially stupid look on his face.

As a column of police cars races down a highway, their lights flashing and sirens sounding, Lecter and Starling join Krendler at the table. Lecter asks Krendler to say grace, which he does. But he adds gratuitous insults about Starling, whom he calls "white trash." Lecter admonishes him, first pointing out that the apostle Paul also hated women and then, after Krendler insults her further, Lecter accuses him of being rude. "I hate rude people," he adds, reminding us of Barney's opening remark about his preference for eating "free-range rude."

When Krendler complains about the soup, Lecter assures them that the next course "is to die for." He then removes the top of Krendler's skull and reveals his brain, a portion of which he slices and sautés at the table. As he does, Lecter points out that the brain has no nerve endings and Krendler feels no pain. Starling tries to save Krendler by offering to tell Lecter how to escape, but Lecter ignores her. Krendler, who becomes progressively stupider, thinks the cooking brain smells great, and he eats it with gusto, as Starling gags. (The progressive deterioration of Krendler's mental capacity as he loses more and more of his brain evokes the breakdown of the supercomputer HAL, as its memory chips are systematically removed in Stanley Kubrick's 1968 film, *2001*.)

Taunting her about her betrayal by the FBI, Lecter wheels Krendler into the kitchen as the police cars approach over the causeway. Starling tries to sneak up on Lecter and knock him out, but he catches her and presses her against the refrigerator. "I came half way around the world to watch you run," he tells her. "Let me run." Then he asks her to say that she loves him, but Starling retorts, "Not in a thousand years." He forces a kiss upon her, and a tear passes briefly down her face before she handcuffs herself to him.

Lecter admits that being handcuffed interferes with his plans and that he hasn't much time. He threatens to chop off her hand if she will not unlock him, but Starling refuses. He raises a meat clever and as he brings it down the camera cuts to flashing red and blue lights of the police cars around the lake. As rich, classical-sounding music plays in the background, Starling, standing on the shore, holds up both hands and identifies herself as an FBI agent. She points ineffectually to a boat that is pulling away. As she watches him disappear, Fourth of July fireworks explode over the lake, and Starling stifles her tears. (The filming of the fireworks display recalls the scene from Alfred Hitchcock's *To Catch a Thief* [1955], where Grace Kelly first kisses Cary Grant, whom she believes to be a criminal.)

The movie concludes with Lecter sitting in an airplane cabin, his arm in a sling. He rejects the airplane fare and produces his own gourmet food, which includes the leftovers from Krendler's brain. A little boy sitting beside him says he can't eat the airplane food, and Lecter assures him that he shouldn't try. Telling the child that "It's import always to try new things," Lecter offers him a piece of Krendler's brain. A narrowing iris shot closes on Lecter's blue eye and closes, leaving the screen in darkness.

RECEPTION

The critical reception was lukewarm. Some reviewers, like the *Miami Herald*'s Rene Rodriguez and *Time*'s Richard Corliss praised the sequel, even though

Hannibal projects a different tone and sensibility from *Silence of the Lambs.* Rodriguez described the "wickedly, malevolently funny" film as a "full-blown love story—a one-sided love story, perhaps, and an exceedingly twisted one. But still a romance." And he praised Scott for "his grand, sumptuous stagings" (Rodriguez, Review of *Hannibal*). Corliss also applauded Scott's "corrosive and haunting film version" of Harris's novel (Corliss, Review of *Hannibal*), and *Entertainment Weekly*'s Owen Gleiberman rated the film "B+," singling out Hopkins's performance for special praise.

On the other hand, *People Magazine*'s Leah Rozen called *Hannibal* "a rancid, blood-soaked disappointment." But she conceded that Hopkins "is all seductive evil, using his velvet voice like a caress [and that] Moore, successfully supplanting memories of Foster, is compelling as a hard-driving professional determined to nab her man-eating man. In the end, one leaves *Hannibal* conflicted: there's lasting queasiness at its many stomach-turning moments but admiration for Hopkins and Moore for managing to be as credible as they are amid this exploitative silliness" (Rozen, Review of *Hannibal*). Gary Susman of the *Boston Phoenix* was even more severe. Objecting to the gruesome violence, which he found gratuitous, Susman called *Hannibal* "the most cynical and expensive exploitation movie yet made" (Susman, Review of *Hannibal*). *USA Today*'s Mike Clark complained, "Hopkins' Hannibal is no longer mysterious, Clarice is no longer vulnerable, and the overextended Florence scenes dash any hopes of early momentum, even if Giancarlo Giannini is perfect as the cop." The *New Yorker*'s Anthony Lane, who maintained that Scott understands Lecter better than he does Starling, also panned the movie. "You can feel Scott, like Harris before him, cranking up the weird and the wicked until they hit the level of the laughable" (Lane, 88). The *New York Times*'s Elvis Mitchell dismissed the film as "a silly though handsomely staged adaptation of the Thomas Harris novel . . . meant for the whole family—the Manson family." Mitchell described the story as "mournfully beautiful" and suggested that the beauty provides a "soothing contrast to the arterial sprays of crimson that occasionally flood the screen." Although Mitchell accused Scott of being cold blooded—he described *Alien* as "an achievement in gore"—he credited the director for filming "some of the most sumptuous backgrounds ever seen in a B-picture." In particular, he claimed that some of the shots composed by cinematographer John Mathieson "are so superb that you want the movie to stop so you can take them in, as when Lecter is crossing a street in the rain and a white car shimmers in the light like a ghostly stallion." Mitchell also praised the operatic staging, which "rivals any sequence Mr. Scott has ever made; it lives and breathes in a cat-and-mouse gambit between Lecter and Pazzi" (Mitchell, Review of *Hannibal*).

But if the critics were lukewarm or cold, the movie-going public was enthusiastic. *Hannibal*, which is rated "R," was an instant box office hit. On its opening weekend it grossed a record $58 million, which was more than the next 15 movies combined. It was the top-grossing film for the first three weeks of its release, earning $128.5 million in its first 17 days. It was finally displaced on its fourth weekend, but was still a top money-earner that grossed an additional $10.1 million that weekend, and it remains in theaters as of this writing.

DISCUSSION

Following the success of *Silence of the Lambs*, Universal Studios contracted with De Laurentiis to produce the sequel, and when Harris finally wrote the novel *Hannibal* (1999), he sold the rights for an unprecedented $10 million. But the fate of the project quickly fell into doubt. Demme would not direct the sequel because he felt the script was too violent. Scott, who was filming *Gladiator* when he read the book, was signed to replace him, after he received a lucrative contract entitling him to a percentage of the profits. Subsequently, Foster declined to reprise her role because she was uncomfortable with the violence and did not want to compromise the character of Starling, which she believed the novel does by undermining Starling's integrity. Hopkins was noncommital about his willingness to play Lecter again, especially without having first seen a completed screenplay. Consequently, there was initial uncertainty whether *Hannibal* would actually be made, especially after Universal rejected the initial screenplay by David Mamet. However, Steven Zaillian was brought in to rewrite the script, and that revived the project, which ultimately cost $80 million to produce. Julianne Moore, who had worked with Hopkins in James Ivory's *Surviving Picasso* (1996), was signed to play Starling.

Scott's treatment of the story is more beautiful than horrifying, although he plays the beauty and the horror against each other to intensify one another. As he does in *Alien*, another horror film that relies on gruesome special effects to terrify viewers, Scott shows violence and bloodshed sparingly and usually only for short duration. Their restricted use heightens the dramatic effect of the violent moments and renders them more vivid and powerful. But overall, *Hannibal* is more elegant than grotesque; it is arguably Scott's most exquisitely filmed and scored movie.

Scott contrasts the beautifully lit, elegant shots of Florence and the deep, rich operatic arias, on the one hand, with the moral turpitude of the characters on the other, to mirror Lecter's double-edged personality. A man of great learning, refined tastes, and incredible self-control, Lecter is also a wild beast who lives by instinct and is capable of committing monstrous acts. Ironically for such a beast, bad manners—especially rudeness—offend him deeply, but he has no reservations at all about flushing out and devouring his prey, like a vicious predator. With the sensitivity, dexterity, and acute hearing of a well trained classical musician, Lecter performs masterfully at the piano and deeply appreciates an outstanding vocal performance. With the finely nuanced smell of a wolf, he detects danger, fear, and vulnerability.

The contradiction between the exquisite sights and sounds and the degraded human motivations and behaviors they contain also intensifies our appreciation of Starling's ambivalent feelings for Lecter. Both Barney and Starling have grown from their earlier encounters with him. Barney has developed his intellectual curiosity, critical thinking skills, and ability to express himself, and Starling has presumably gained self-confidence. She tells Barney that she thinks of Lecter for at least thirty seconds each day. Although she never articulates why Lecter so fascinates her, the attraction apparently stems from both his exceptional sensitivity and understanding on the one hand and his cold-hearted cruelty on the other.

Starling feels better understood and, at times, more respected and even more loved by Lecter than by anyone else she knows. Yet she also fears the harm he can inflict upon her and others because he is as an out-of-control murderer. And so, the sympathy she feels for the man who best knows her and most accepts and admires her is balanced by her revulsion for his crimes and her obligations as a law enforcement officer dedicated to preserving public safety, much as the beauty of the Piazza della Signoria at night (where shadows of the famous statues flicker magnificently against the ancient Palazzo Vecchio) is offset by the horror of Pazzi's disembowelment; and the grandeur of Verger's mansion is balanced by the savagery of the wild boars who rip him to pieces in its barn.

The essential need for maintaining social order by distinguishing right from wrong and consistently choosing right action recurs throughout Scott's work and persists in *Hannibal*. Ironically, Lecter also appreciates the same value. He tells Starling that her superiors at the FBI resent her because, "You serve the idea of order, they don't. They are weak and unruly and believe in nothing." Scott both preserves his heroine's integrity and reiterates the necessity of maintaining social order by changing the ending of Harris's novel, in which a disillusioned Starling runs off to South America with Lecter. The decision to alter the book's conclusion was one of the more controversial aspects of the film, but it is entirely consistent with the values Scott has expressed throughout his career. In Scott's ending, Starling subordinates her feelings for Lecter to the greater cause of public safety, and she risks losing her hand in a frighteningly painful fashion rather than abet his escape. Thus, despite the FBI's alarming shortcomings, of which Starling has been made painfully aware, she retains her affiliation with the Bureau, whose mission to protect the public and maintain an orderly society she still values. Her disillusionment falls short of the nihilistic cynicism Lecter attributes to her superiors, and, significantly, her final act in the movie is to identify herself as an FBI agent.

Lecter mirrors Starling in that, in his psychopathic way of thinking, he too believes he is creating a better, more orderly society. All of Lecter's victims are morally flawed and he dedicates himself to purging undesirable elements from the population. Verger is a vindictive, arrogant, child abuser; Pazzi is avaricious and cold-hearted; and Krendler is chauvinistic, lust-driven, greedy, and disloyal. As Lecter maintained after killing a musician whose poor play offended his aesthetic sensibilities, he thinks he is doing society a service by eliminating these people, as well those who are rude or unappreciative. Krendler's grue-some death may also be a gesture of love to Starling, whom Krendler had tor-mented.

But Starling's utter incorruptibility and her dedication to upholding law and preserving order fascinates Lecter, and her refusal to turn cynical despite her disillusionment compels him to respond differently to his own disillu-sioned view of humanity. Lecter's attraction to Starling leads him to test her first by humiliating and endangering her, and then by tempting her. As Starling passes each progressively more difficult test, he comes to admire her more, and even love her. He first tests her dedication to saving the public from himself by having her risk her life by driving to the crowded terminal where he touches her hair from the merry-go-round. On the drive to the station, he taunts her about her suspension from duty. But instead of being vindictive, Starling warns Lecter that they are being followed. We sense that just as Verger has been using Starling to get to Lecter, Lecter has been using her to get to Verger, and that Lecter has deliberately allowed himself to be captured so he can confront Verger. But Starling does not know this. She knows only that she wants to pre-vent yet another murder, even if Lecter is a deserving victim, because murder, itself, is always unacceptable to her.

Starling's second test comes when she risks her life, her career, and even ar-rest—as she has officially been relieved of duty—in order to spare Lecter's life and bring him back to jail. In self-defense, she kills Carlo and his accomplice while rescuing Lecter, and, in dire circumstances, she trusts Lecter with a knife to free himself. But Starling's focus on her duty never wavers, and she makes it clear that, even after risking her life to save him, she will kill Lecter if he tries to escape, because she will not risk the public's safety by permitting him to go free.

If Starling's first tests involve overcoming fear, her last two require her to re-nounce temptation. Lecter tempts Starling with revenge by torturing Krendler, the man who has destroyed her career and humiliated her at every possible opportunity, both professionally and sexually. But not only does Star-ling feel revulsion instead of glee over what Lecter does to Krendler, she even offers to help Lecter escape if he will spare Krendler's life. In other words, she refuses to abandon her principles and insists on treating Krendler like any other hostage, regardless of what he has done to her personally. The preservation of his life remains her first priority, transcending even the capture of Lecter, which would bring her glory and revive her career, as well as complete her mission.

The last temptation of Starling is love. Her defiant rejection of his request for her to say she loves him evidences her unwillingness to compromise her val-ues, despite the mixed emotions suggested by the tear that trickles down her cheek when he kisses her. Had Starling acceded to his request, it is likely Lecter would have chopped off her hand instead of his, because the admission of love under those circumstances would have been unprofessional and would thereby have undermined her heroic values and reduced Starling in Lecter's eyes.

However, Lecter is prompted to act altruistically, perhaps for the only time in his life, because Starling always remains absolutely clear about what is right and what is wrong, and she never allows his taunts, the danger to her career, fear for her life, allure of revenge, or attraction of love to sway her from doing what she knows is right. The morally degraded state of the general population seems to have so appalled Lecter that he became a mass murderer. In fact, in Harris's novel Lecter's depravity is shown to emanate from atrocities committed by barbaric Nazis during World War II. But Starling's heroism and integrity compel him to reassess his disillusionment. In Starling, Lecter finds some hope of redemption for the human species, and perhaps for himself. His willingness to remove his own hand instead of hers is an expression of that hope and a repudiation of the cynicism that has marked his criminal career.

Like Ripley from *Alien*, Jordan O'Neil from *G.I. Jane*, and other strong, self-assured women Scott frequently presents, Starling possesses clarity of vision and steadfastness of purpose that reflect the classical ideals expressed by the ancient literature and fine art Lecter admires. Thus, unlike Demme's *Silence of the Lambs*, which was criticized by some viewers for being hostile toward women and for seeming to equate an ambiguous sexual identity with a disposition toward sexual sadism, Scott's sequel celebrates strong women, both by showing Starling as an ideal and by revealing the pernicious nature of male chauvinism. Like *Silence of the Lambs, Hannibal* shows how Lecter is motivated by the pleasure he takes in humiliating Starling and others, such as Pazzi, whose demotion and disgraced family lineage he quickly points out. But in *Hannibal*, Lecter's sadistic passion for demeaning others is mirrored by Verger and Krendler, who are indeed the least likeable characters in the story. They are also the only characters shown to be sexually perverse and/or perverted. Appropriately, the worst fates in the story befall Verger and Krendler, the two men who misappropriate their considerable power and use it to harm women and children and demean other people.

Verger is an avowed child molester, and by contrast to Starling, whose life he endangers and whose career he trashes without scruple, he employs his immense resources solely to indulge his passions for sexual gratification, power, and revenge. Ultimately, these passions lead to his destruction. His predilection for sexually abusing children made him an appropriate choice as Lecter's victim in the first place. His thirst for revenge brings Lecter back into his life, when otherwise Lecter would have remained in Florence, harmless to Verger if not to the Florentines. And his need to flaunt his power by degrading his underlings brings on his death, for it is only after he humiliates Cordell that the physician accepts Lecter's suggestion and feeds Verger to the boars.

Krendler is a married misogynist who seems obsessed with destroying Starling ever since she rejected his inappropriate sexual advances years earlier. He enjoys demeaning Starling whenever possible, and like Lecter, he does this by mocking her poor rural background. Unlike Lecter, though, Krendler mergers the insult to her family with a crass sexual insult, dismissing Starling as "cornpone country pussy." In fact, Lecter admonishes Krendler for his speech, accusing him of being rude and reminding him that the Apostle Paul hated women too. Given Lecter's preference for "free-range rude," Krendler's lack of basic respect for women in general, and for Starling in particular, make him an attractive choice for dinner.

If not necessarily homophobic, Krendler is also at least guilty of stereotyping homosexuals, and Scott uses this trait to ridicule him when he tells Starling that he always assumed Lecter was gay because he liked the arts and high culture. As depicted under Scott's direction, the remark makes Krendler appear foolish and unprofessional, especially as the conversation takes place in Starling's work area, where she has been painstakingly trying to derive a detailed, psychologically responsible analysis of the criminal's personality. Indeed, she answers Krendler's broad stereotype with a very specific discussion of Lecter's personal tastes and habits.

Pazzi too acts unprofessionally and dies for it. Instead of notifying his coworkers and obtaining the cooperation of the FBI, he acts independently in order to secure the reward. He also fails to exhibit any compassion when the pickpocket he compelled to work for him is killed. But unlike Krendler, Pazzi's greatest flaw is avarice, not arrogance or misogyny; he adores his wife and facilitates Lecter's escape to save her. Consequently, he dies a quick death after suffering humiliation.

Scott's *Hannibal*, then, is ultimately a combination of a medieval morality play and a beauty-and-the-beast tale. As in the morality plays, antagonists such as Verger, Krendler, and Pazzi are strongly identified with one or more of the seven deadly sins, and they suffer their fall from fortune because of these failings. With their downfall comes a feeling that order has to some extent been restored and justice served. Lecter, who begins the story as an antagonist, concludes it more like a beast who has been tamed by his love for a woman pure of mind, body, and spirit. In addition to meting out just desserts to the antagonists, Lecter also learns to suppress the egocentrism that has informed all of his previous behavior, and he becomes a more complete human being by committing an altruistic act of self-sacrifice. Had Lecter escaped "scott-free," viewers might be disappointed at the unequivocal triumph of the psychopath and at Starling's failure to bring him to justice. But although his serving Krendler's brains to the little boy on the airplane indicates that Lecter's passion for perversion has not been extinguished, the fact that his arm is in a sling shows both that he is capable of transcending his narcissism and becoming a better person than he was, and that Starling has made him pay a significant, if not fully adequate, price for his escape. Thus, if Starling's mission was unsuccessful, at least it was not a total failure. The most pernicious characters have been eliminated, Lecter has been punished and driven back underground, and social order has been restored, albeit imperfectly.

Bibliography

GENERAL DISCUSSION OF SCOTT'S WORK

Sammon, Paul M. *Ridley Scott Close Up: The Making of His Movies.* New York: Thunder's Mouth Press, 1999.

ALIEN

Ambrogio, Anthony. "Alien: In Space, No One Can Hear Your Primal Scream." *In Eros in the Mind's Eye*, edited by Donald Palumbo. New York: Greenwood Press, 1986. 169–179.

Bell-Metereau, Rebecca. "Woman: The Other Alien in *Alien.*" *In Women Worldwalkers: New Dimensions of Science Fiction and Fantasy*, edited by Jane Weedman. Lubbock: Texas Tech Press, 1985. 9–24.

Belling, Catherine. "'Where Meaning Collapses': Alien and the Outlawing of the Female Hero." *Literator: Tydskrif vir Besondere en Vergelykende Taal-en Literatuurstudie/Journal of Literary Criticism, Comparative Linguistics and Literary Studies* 13.3 (November 1992): 35–49.

Billy, Ted. "A Curious Case of Influence: *Nostromo* and *Alien*(s)." *Conradiana: A Journal of Joseph Conrad Studies* 21.2 (Summer 1989): 147–57.

Byars, Jackie. "Introduction to Some Ideological Readings of *Alien.*" In "Symposium on *Alien*," edited by Charles Elkins. *Science-Fiction Studies* 7 (1980): 278–82.

Byers, Thomas B. "Commodity Futures: Corporate State and Personal Style in Three Recent Science-Fiction Movies." *Science-Fiction Studies* 14.3 (November 1987): 326–339.

Canby, Vincent. Review of *Alien. New York Times* (May 25, 1979).

Carducci, Mark, and Glenn Lovell. "Making *Alien*: Behind the Scenes." *Cinefantastique* 9.1 (Fall 1979): 10–39.

Cobbs, John L. "Alien as an Abortion Parable." *Literature/ Film Quarterly* 18.3 (1990): 198–201.

Colwell, C. Carter. "Primitivism in the Movies of Ridley Scott: *Alien* and *Blade Runner*." In *Retrofitting* Blade Runner: *Issues in Ridley Scott's* Blade Runner *and Philip K. Dick's* Do Androids Dream of Electric Sheep? edited by Judith B. Kerman. Bowling Green, OH: Popular Press, 1991. 124–31.

Conrad, Joseph. *Nostromo*. 1904. Reprint. London: Penguin Group, 1990.

Creed, Barbara. "Horror and the Monstrous Feminine: An Imaginary Abjection." *Screen* 27 (1986): 44–70.

Davis, Lyn, and Tom Gennelli. "*Alien*: A Myth of Survival." *Film/Psychology Review* 4.2 (1980): 235–42.

Delson, James. "Interview with Ridley Scott, Part 1." *Fantastic Films* 11 (October 1979): 8–21, 24–35.

———. "Interview with Ridley Scott, Part 2." *Fantastic Films* 12 (November 1979): 22–30+.

Eisenstein, Alex. "*Alien* Dissected." *Fantastic Films* 13 (January 1980): 51–63.

Elkins, Charles, ed. "Symposium on *Alien*." *Science-Fiction Studies* 7 (1980): 278–304.

Fitting, Peter. "The Second Alien." In "Symposium on *Alien*," edited by Charles Elkins. *Science-Fiction Studies* 7 (1980): 285–93.

Foster, Alan Dean. *Alien*. New York: Warner Books, 1979.

Gabbard, Krin, and Glen. O. Gabbard. "The Science Fiction Film and Psychoanalysis: *Alien* and Melanie Klein's *Night Music*." *In Psychoanalytic Approaches to Literature and Film*, edited by Maurice Charney and Joseph Reppen. Rutherford, NJ: Fairleigh Dickinson University Press, 1987. 171–79.

Gould, Jeff. "The Destruction of the Social by the Organic in *Alien*." In "Symposium on *Alien*," edited by Charles Elkins. *Science-Fiction Studies* 7 (1980): 282–85.

Greenberg, Harvey R. "Fembo: *Alien*'s Intentions." *Journal of Popular Film and Television* 15.4 (Winter 1988): 165–71.

———. "The Fractures of Desire: Psychoanalytic Notes on *Alien* and the Contemporary 'Cruel' Horror Film." *Psychoanalytic Review* 70.2 (1983): 241–67.

Herman, Chad. "*'Some Horrible Dream about (S)mothering'*: Sexuality, Gender, and Family in the Alien Trilogy." *Post Script: Essays in Film and the Humanities* 16.3 (Summer 1997): 36–50.

Jeffords, Susan. "*'The Battle of the Big Mamas'*: Feminism and the Alienation of Women.*" Journal of American Culture* 10.3 (Fall 1987): 73–84.

Jennings, Ros. "Desire and Design: Ripley Undressed." In *Immortal, Invisible: Lesbians and the Moving Image*, edited by Tamsin Wilton. London: Routledge, 1995. 193–206.

Kaufman, Stanley. Review of *Alien*. *New Yorker* (June 11, 1979): 54.

Kroll, Jack. Review of *Alien*. *Newsweek* (May 28, 1979): 105.

Lee, Clayton. "Cognitive Approaches to *Alien*." In "Symposium on *Alien*," edited by Charles Elkins. *Science-Fiction Studies* 7 (1980): 299–30.

Lev, Peter. "Whose Future? *Star Wars*, *Alien*, and *Blade Runner*.*" Literature/Film Quarterly* 26.1 (1998): 30–37.

Matheson, T. J. "Triumphant Technology and Minimal Man: The Technological Society, Science Fiction Films, and Ridley Scott's *Alien*." *Extrapolation: A
Journal of Science Fiction and Fantasy* 33.3 (Fall 1992): 215–29.

Newton, Judith. "Feminism and Anxiety in *Alien*." In "Symposium on *Alien*," edited
by Charles Elkins. *Science-Fiction Studies* 7 (1980): 293–97.

Robertson, Robbie. "The Narrative Sources of Ridley Scott's *Alien*". In *Cinema and
Fiction: New Modes of Adapting, 1950–90*, edited by John Orr and Colin
Nicholson. Edinburgh University Press, 1992. 171–79.

Schlesinger, Arthur. Review of *Alien*. *Saturday Review* (August 4, 1979): 51.

Stafford, Tony. "Alien/Alienation." In "Symposium on *Alien*," edited by Charles
Elkins. *Science-Fiction Studies* 7 (1980): 297–99.

Sulski, Jim. "An Interview with Gordon Carroll and David Giler, Producers of
Alien." *Fantastic Films* 12 (November 1979): 38–39+.

———. "An Interview with Sigourney Weaver." *Fantastic Films* 12 (November
1979): 33–35.

———. "An Interview with Tom Skerritt." *Fantastic Films* 12 (November 1979):
36–37.

———. "An Interview with Veronica Cartwright." *Fantastic Films* 12 (November
1979): 37–39.

Taubin, Amy. "The *Alien* Trilogy: From Feminism to AIDS." *Sight and Sound 2.3*
(July 1992). Reprint of *Women and Film: A Sight and Sound Reader*, edited
by Pam Cook and Philip Dodd. Philadelphia: Temple University Press,
1993. 93–100.

Torry, Robert. "Awakening to the Other: Feminism and the Ego-Ideal in *Alien*."
Women's Studies: An Interdisciplinary Journal 23. 4 (1994): 343–63.

Vertlieb, Steve. "In Search of *Alien*." *Cinemacabre* 1.2 (Fall 1979): 25–29.

Wood, Robin. "The Return of the Repressed." *Film Comment* (August 1978):
25–32.

BLADE RUNNER

Barr, Marleen. "Speciesism and Sexism in *Blade Runner*." In *Retrofitting* Blade Run-
ner: *Issues in Ridley Scott's* Blade Runner *and Philip K. Dick's* Do Androids
Dream of Electric Sheep? edited by Judith B. Kerman. Bowling Green, OH:
Popular Press, 1991. 25–31.

Carper, Steve. "Subverting the Disaffected City: Cityscape in *Blade Runner*." In *Ret-
rofitting* Blade Runner: *Issues in Ridley Scott's* Blade Runner *and Philip K.
Dick's* Do Androids Dream of Electric Sheep? edited by Judith B. Kerman.
Bowling Green, OH: Popular Press, 1991. 185–96.

Carr, Brian. "At the Thresholds of the 'Human': Race, Psychoanalysis, and the Repli-
cation of Imperial Memory." *Cultural Critique* 39 (Spring 1998): 119–50.

Colwell, C. Carter. "Primitivism in the Movies of Ridley Scott: *Alien* and *Blade Runner*." In *Retrofitting* Blade Runner: *Issues in Ridley Scott's* Blade Runner
and Philip K. Dick's Do Androids Dream of Electric Sheep? edited by Judith
B. Kerman. Bowling Green, OH: Popular Press, 1991. 124–31.

Desser, David. "*Blade Runner*: Science Fiction and Transcendence." *Literature/Film
Quarterly* 13.3 (1985): 172–79.

———. "The New Eve: The Influence of *Paradise Lost* and *Frankenstein* on *Blade Runner*. In *Retrofitting* Blade Runner: *Issues in Ridley Scott's* Blade Runner *and Philip K. Dick's* Do Androids Dream of Electric Sheep? edited by Judith B. Kerman. Bowling Green, OH: Popular Press, 1991. 53–65.

———. "Space, Race, and Class: The Politics of the SF Film from *Metropolis* to *Blade Runner*. In *Retrofitting* Blade Runner: *Issues in Ridley Scott's* Blade Runner *and Philip K. Dick's* Do Androids Dream of Electric Sheep? edited by Judith B. Kerman. Bowling Green, OH: Popular Press, 1991. 110–23.

Dick, Philip K. *Do Androids Dream of Electric Sheep?* Garden City, NY: Doubleday, 1968.

Doll, Susan, and Greg Faller. "*Blade Runner* and Genre: Film Noir and Science Fiction." *Literature/Film Quarterly* 14.2 (1986): 89–100.

Francavilla, Joseph. "The Android as *Doppelgänger*." In *Retrofitting* Blade Runner: *Issues in Ridley Scott's* Blade Runner *and Philip K. Dick's* Do Androids Dream of Electric Sheep? edited by Judith B. Kerman. Bowling Green, OH: Popular Press, 1991. 4–25.

Gravett, Sharon L. "The Sacred and the Profane: Examining the Religious Subtext of Ridley Scott's *Blade Runner*." *Literature/Film Quarterly* 26.1 (1998): 38–45.

Gray, W. Russel. "Entropy, Energy, Empathy: *Blade Runner* and Detective Fiction." In *Retrofitting* Blade Runner: *Issues in Ridley Scott's* Blade Runner *and Philip K. Dick's* Do Androids Dream of Electric Sheep? edited by Judith B. Kerman. Bowling Green, OH: Popular Press, 1991. 66–75.

Gwaltney, Marilyn. "Androids as a Device for Reflection on Personhood." In *Retrofitting* Blade Runner: *Issues in Ridley Scott's* Blade Runner *and Philip K. Dick's* Do Androids Dream of Electric Sheep? edited by Judith B. Kerman. Bowling Green, OH: Popular Press, 1991. 32–39.

Jung, Carl. "Aion: Phenomenology of the Self (The Ego, the Shadow, the *Syzgy*: Animal/Animus)." In *The Portable Carl Jung*, edited by Joseph Campbell. New York: Viking, 1971. 139–62.

Kaveny, Philip E. "From Pessimism to Sentimentality: *Do Androids Dream of Electric Sheep?* Becomes *Blade Runner*." In *Patterns of the Fantastic II*, edited by Donald M. Hassler. Mercer Island, WA: Starmont House, 1985. 77–80.

Kerman, Judith B. ed. *Retrofitting* Blade Runner: *Issues in Ridley Scott's* Blade Runner *and Philip K. Dick's* Do Androids Dream of Electric Sheep? Bowling Green, OH: Popular Press, 1991.

———. "Technology and Politics in the *Blade Runner* Dystopia." In *Retrofitting* Blade Runner: *Issues in Ridley Scott's* Blade Runner *and Philip K. Dick's* Do Androids Dream of Electric Sheep? edited by Judith B. Kerman. Bowling Green, OH: Popular Press, 1991. 16–24.

Kolb, William, M. "Bibliography" and "Bibliography Addendum." In *Retrofitting* Blade Runner: *Issues in Ridley Scott's* Blade Runner *and Philip K. Dick's* Do Androids Dream of Electric Sheep? edited by Judith B. Kerman. Bowling Green, OH: Popular Press, 1991. 229–93.

———. "*Blade Runner* Film Notes." In *Retrofitting* Blade Runner: *Issues in Ridley Scott's* Blade Runner *and Philip K. Dick's* Do Androids Dream of Electric Sheep? edited by Judith B. Kerman. Bowling Green, OH: Popular Press, 1991. 154–77.

———. "Reconstructing the Director's Cut." In *Retrofitting* Blade Runner: *Issues in Ridley Scott's* Blade Runner *and Philip K. Dick's* Do Androids Dream of Electric Sheep? edited by Judith B. Kerman. Bowling Green, OH: Popular Press, 1991. 294–302.

———. "Script to Screen: *Blade Runner* in Perspective." In *Retrofitting* Blade Runner: *Issues in Ridley Scott's* Blade Runner *and Philip K. Dick's* Do Androids Dream of Electric Sheep? edited by Judith B. Kerman. Bowling Green, OH: Popular Press, 1991. 132–53.

Landon, Brooks. " 'There's Some of Me in You': *Blade Runner* and the Adaptation of Science Fiction Literature into Film." In *Retrofitting* Blade Runner: *Issues in Ridley Scott's* Blade Runner *and Philip K. Dick's* Do Androids Dream of Electric Sheep? edited by Judith B. Kerman. Bowling Green, OH: Popular Press, 1991. 90–102.

Lev, Peter. "Whose Future? *Star Wars, Alien,* and *Blade Runner.*" *Literature/Film Quarterly* 26.1 (1998): 30–37.

Marder, Elissa. "*Blade Runner*'s Moving Still." *Camera Obscura: A Journal of Feminism, Culture, and Media Studies* 27 (September 1991): 77–87.

Maslin, Janet. Review of *Blade Runner. New York Times* (June 25, 1982).

Neumann, Dietrich, "*Blade Runner.*" In *Film Architecture: Set Designs from* Metropolis *to* Blade Runner, edited by Dietrich Neumann. New York: Prestel, 1999. 148–159.

Rickman, Gregg. "Philip K. Dick on *Blade Runner.* 'They Did Sight Stimulation on My Brain.' " In *Retrofitting* Blade Runner: *Issues in Ridley Scott's* Blade Runner *and Philip K. Dick's* Do Androids Dream of Electric Sheep? edited by Judith B. Kerman. Bowling Green, OH: Popular Press, 1991. 103–109.

Romero, Rolando J. "The Postmodern Hybrid: Do Aliens Dream of Alien Sheep?" *Post Script: Essays in Film and the Humanities* 16.1 (Fall 1996): 41–52.

Sammon, Paul M. *Future Noir: The Making of* Blade Runner. New York: HarperPrism, 1996.

Shapiro, Michael J. " 'Manning' the Frontiers: The Politics of (Human) Nature in *Blade Runner.*" In *In the Nature of Things: Language, Politics, and the Environment*, edited by Jane Bennett and William Chaloupka. Minneapolis: University of Minnesota Press, 1993. 65–84.

Silverman, Kaja. "Back to the Future." *Camera Obscura: A Journal of Feminism, Culture, and Media Studies* 27 (September 1991): 109–32.

Slade, Joseph W. "Romanticizing Cybernetics in Ridley Scott's *Blade Runner.*" *Literature/Film Quarterly* 18.1 (1990): 11–18.

Stiller, Andrew. "The Music in *Blade Runner.*" In *Retrofitting* Blade Runner: *Issues in Ridley Scott's* Blade Runner *and Philip K. Dick's* Do Androids Dream of Electric Sheep? edited by Judith B. Kerman. Bowling Green, OH: Popular Press, 1991. 196–200.

LEGEND

Benair, Jonathan, and Randall D. Larson. "The Music for *Legend.*" *Cinemascore* 15 (Summer 1987): 38–45, 147.

Biodrowski, Steve. "*Legend* Makeup." *Cinefantastique* 15.5 (January 1986): 25–26, 57.

Bouzereau, Laurent. *The Cutting Room Floor: Movies Scenes Which Never Made It to the Screen*. Secaucus, NJ: Citadel Press, 1994. 79–80.

Canby, Vincent. Review of *Legend*. *New York Times* (April 18, 1986).

Comuzio, E. "Legend Review." *Cineforum* 25.250 (December 1985): 69.

Francillon, Vincent Jacquet. "Interview with Jerry Goldsmith." *The Cue Sheet* 10.3/4 (1993–1994).

Hjortsberg, William. *Symbiography*. Fremont: Sumac Press, 1973.

Jones, Alan. "*Legend*." *Cinefantastique* 15.4 (October 1985): 9, 53.

———. "*Legend*." *Cinefantastique* 15.5 (January 1986): 22, 24, 27.

Larson, Randall D. "The Score/Tangerine Dream, in the Shadow of a Legend." *Cinefantastique* 16.3 (1986): 42, 61.

Maclean, Paul Andrew. "From a Legend to a Dream." *Cinemascore* 15 (Summer 1987): 42–45.

Magid, Ron. "Labyrinth and Legend, Big Screen Fairy Tales," *American Cinematographer* 67 (August 1986): 65–70.

Scapperotti, Dan. "Hjortsberg on Legend." *Cinefantastique* 17.3/4 (1987): 122.

Tolkien, J.R. *The Lord of the Rings*. 2nd ed. London: Allen & Unwin, 1966.

Web site on *Legend*. *www.figmentfly.com/legend/index.shtml* (updated 10/00).

THELMA & LOUISE

Abrams, Janet. "*Thelma & Louise*." *Sight and Sound* 1.3 (July 1991): 55–56.

Boozer, Jack. "Seduction and Betrayal in the Heartland: *Thelma & Louise*." *Literature/ Film Quarterly* 23.3 (1995): 188–96.

Braudy, Leo. "Satire into Myth. " *Film Quarterly* 45.2 (Winter 1991–92): 28–29.

Braudy, Leo, Peter N. Chumo II, Carol J. Clover, Harvey R. Greenberg, Brian Henderson, Albert Johnson, Marsha Kinder, and Linda Williams. "The Many Faces of *Thelma & Louise*." *Film Quarterly* 45.2 (Winter 1991–92): 20–31.

Carlson, Margaret. "Is This What Feminism Is All About?" *Time* 137 (June 24, 1991): 57.

Chumo, Peter N., II. "At the Generic Crossroads with *Thelma & Louise*." *Post Script: Essays in Film and the Humanities* 13.2 (Winter-Spring 1994): 3–13.

Dargis, Manohla. "*Thelma & Louise* and the Tradition of the Male Road Movie." *Sight and Sound* 1.2 (July 1991). Reprint of *Women and Film: A Sight and Sound Reader*, edited by Pam Cook and Philip Dodd. Philadelphia: Temple University Press, 1993. 86–92.

Frost, Linda. "The Decentered Subject of Feminism: Postfeminism and *Thelma & Louise*." In *Rhetoric in an Antifoundational World: Language, Culture, and Pedagogy*, edited by Michael Bernard-Donals and Richard R. Glejzer. New Haven: Yale University Press, 1998. 147–69.

Grenier, Richard. Review of *Thelma & Louise*. *Commentary* 92 (September 1991): 50–52.

Healey, Jim. " '*All This for Us': The Songs in Thelma & Louise*." *Journal of Popular Culture* 29.3 (Winter 1995): 103–19.

Johnson, Albert. "Bacchantes at Large." *Film Quarterly* 45.2 (Winter 1991–92): 22–23.

Kamins, Toni, Cynthia Lucia, Pat Dowell, Elayne Rapping, Alice Cross, Sarah Schulman, and Roy Grundmann. "Should We Go Along for the Ride? A Critical Symposium on *Thelma & Louise.*" *Cineaste* 18.4 (1991): 28–36.

Khouri, Callie. Thelma & Louise—*Something to Talk About.* New York: Grove/Atlantic: 1996. Screenplay.

Lipton, James. Interview with Susan Sarandon. *Inside Actors' Studio.* 1998. Television interview.

MacEnulty, Pat. "*Thelma & Louise*: A Feminist Fable." *Mid-American Review* 13.2 (1992): 102–7.

MariAnna, Cara J. "The Seven Mythic Cycles of Thelma and Louise." *Trivia* 21 (1993): 82–99.

Maslin, Janet. Reviews of *Thelma & Louise. New York Times* (May 24, 1991; June 16, 1991).

Melville, Herman. "Billy Budd, Sailor." 1924. Reprint. Chicago: University of Chicago Press, 1962.

Robinson, Lillian S. "Out of the Mine and into the Canyon: Working-Class Feminism, Yesterday and Today." In *The Hidden Foundation: Cinema and the Question of Class,* edited by David E. James and Rick Berg. Minneapolis: University of Minnesota Press, 1996. 172–92.

Schickel, Richard. "Gender Bender." *Time* 137 (June 24, 1991): 55–56.

Schwartz, Richard A. "The Tragic Vision of *Thelma & Louise.*" *Journal of Evolutionary Psychology* 17.1 (March 1996): 101–107.

Shakespeare, William. *The Complete Works of Shakespeare.* 3d ed. Edited by David Bevington. Glenview, IL: Scott, Foresman and Company, 1980.

Spelman, Elizabeth V., and Martha Minow. "Outlaw Women: *Thelma & Louise.*" In *Legal Reelism: Movies as Legal Texts,* edited by John Denvir. Urbana, IL: University of Illinois Press, 1996. 261–79.

Sturken, Marita. *Thelma & Louise.* London: British Film Institute, 2000.

Thynne, Lizzie. "The Space Between: *Anne Trister.*" *Immortal, Invisible: Lesbians and the Moving Image,* edited by Tasmin Wilton. New York: Routledge, 1995.

Taubin, Amy. "Ridley Scott's Road Work." *Sight and Sound* 1.3 (July 1991): 19.

Valero Garces, Carmen. "*Thelma & Louise*: Gender Conflict and Genre Debate Interwoven in a Film." *Revista Espanola de Estudios Norteamericanos* 7.11 (1996): 57–66.

When Thelma Met Louise. The Movie Channel, 1991. Television documentary.

Winter, Kari J. "On Being an Outlaw: A Conversation with Callie Khouri." *Hurricane Alice* 8.4 (Spring 1992): 6–8.

OTHER FILMS

Ashley, Robert. Review of *G.I. Jane. Sight & Sound* 7 (November 1997): 42–43.

Canby, Vincent. Review of *Black Rain. New York Times* (September 20, 1989).

———. Review of *The Duellists. New York Times* (January 14, 1978).

———. Review of *1492. New York Times* (October 8, 1992).

———. Review of *Someone to Watch over Me. New York Times* (October 9, 1987).

Clark, Mike. Review of *Hannibal. USA Today* (February 9, 2001).

Conrad, Joseph. *The Duel, A Military Tale.* 1908, Reprint. Garden City, NY: Garden City Publishing Co., 1924. (*The Duellists*)

Corliss, Richard. Review of *Hannibal. Time* (February 4, 2000).

Delaney, Bill. Review of *G.I. Jane.* In *Magill's Cinema Annual.* Detroit: Gale Research Company, 1998. 218–20.

Doll, Susan. Review of *Black Rain.* In *Magill's Cinema Annual.* Detroit: Gale Research Company, 1990. 52–55.

Dowell, Pat. "*Black Rain*: Hollywood Goes Japan Bashing." *Cineaste: America's Leading Magazine on the Art and Politics of the Cinema* 17.3 (1990): 8–10.

Ebert, Roger. Review of *Hannibal. Chicago Sun-Times* (February 9, 2001).

Hofmeister, Timothy P. "Achillean Love and Honor in Ridley Scott's *Black Rain.*" *Classical and Modern Literature: A Quarterly* 13.1 (Fall 1992): 45–51.

Kermode, Mark. Review of *White Squall. Sight & Sound* 6 (May 1996): 64.

Lane, Anthony. Review of *Hannibal. New Yorker* (February 12, 2001): 88–90.

Le Beau, Bryan F. Review of *1492. American Studies* 34 (Spring 1993): 151–57.

Lowry, Brian. "Review of *White Squall.*" In *Ridley Scott,* by Paul M. Sammon. New York: Thunder's Mouth Press, 1999. 147–49.

Maslin, Janet. Review of *1492. New York Times* (October 18, 1992).

———. Review of *G.I. Jane. New York Times* (August 22, 1997).

———. Review of *White Squall. New York Times* (February 2, 1996).

Mitchell, Elvis. Review of *Gladiator. New York Times* (May 5, 2000).

———. Review of *Hannibal. New York Times* (February 9, 2001).

Rodriguez, Rene. "*Gladiator*: A Headbangers' Ball." *Miami Herald* (May 5, 2000): 7G.

———. Review of *Hannibal. Miami Herald* (February 9, 2001).

Rozen, Leah. Review of *Hannibal. People* (February 1, 2001).

Simmons, Allan. "Cinematic Fidelities in *The Rover* and *The Duellists.*" In *Conrad on Film.* edited by Gene M. Moore. New York: Cambridge University Press, 1998.

Strick, Philip. Review of *1492. Sight & Sound* 2 (November 1992): 41–2.

Susman, Gary. Review of *Hannibal. Boston Phoenix* (February, 2001).

Wollen, Peter. "Cinema's Conquistadors." *Sight & Sound* 2 (November 1992): 21–23.

Index

About the Author

RICHARD A. SCHWARTZ is Professor of English, Fellow of the Honors College, and Director of the Film Studies Certificate Program at Florida International University. He is the author of *Cold War Reference Guide*, *Cold War Culture*, *Encyclopedia of the Persian Gulf War*, and *Woody, From Antz to Zelig* (Greenwood, 2000).